EDWARD IV

GLORIOUS SON OF YORK

EDWARD IV
GLORIOUS SON OF YORK

JEFFREY JAMES

AMBERLEY

First Published 2015

Amberley Publishing
The Hill, Stroud
Gloucestershire, GL5 4EP

www.amberley-books.com

ISBN 978 1 4456 4621 3 (hardback)
ISBN 978 1 4456 4622 0 (ebook)

British Library Cataloguing in Publication Data.
A catalogue record for this book is available
from the British Library.

Typesetting and Origination by Amberley
Publishing
Printed in the UK.

CONTENTS

England and Wales, locations and battle sites.

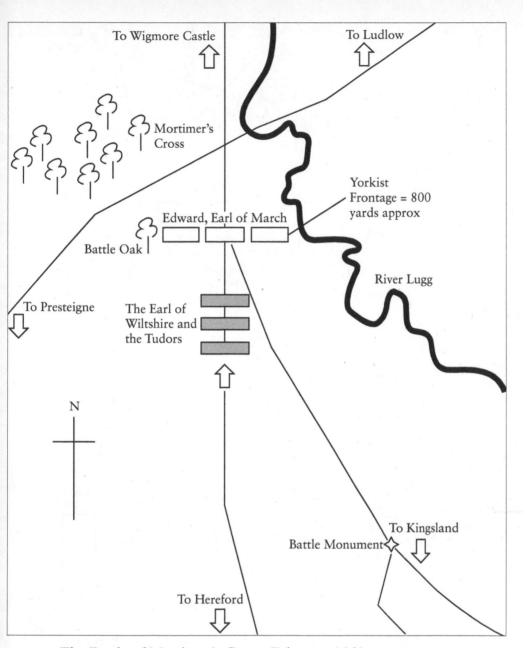

To Wigmore Castle

To Ludlow

Mortimer's Cross

Yorkist Frontage = 800 yards approx

Edward, Earl of March

Battle Oak

River Lugg

To Presteigne

The Earl of Wiltshire and the Tudors

N

To Kingsland

Battle Monument

To Hereford

The Battle of Mortimer's Cross, February 1461.

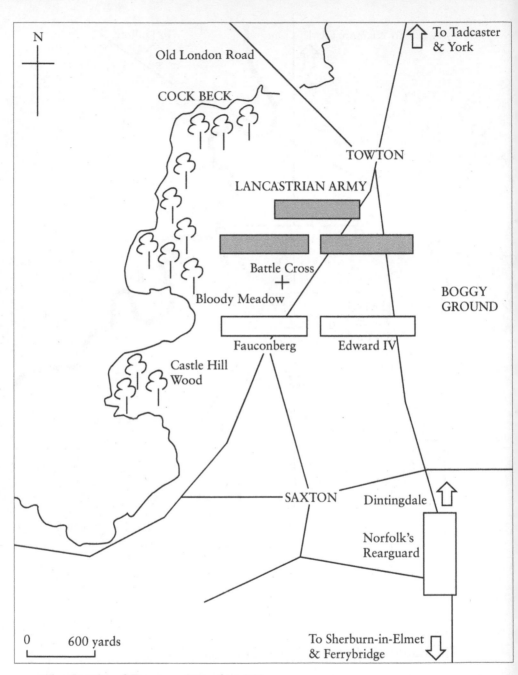

The Battle of Towton, March 1461.

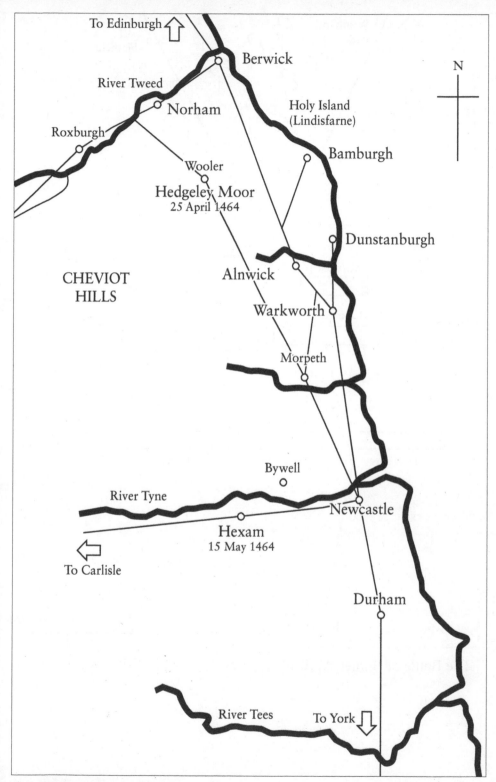

To Edinburgh

Berwick

River Tweed

Norham

Holy Island
(Lindisfarne)

Roxburgh

Bamburgh

Wooler

Hedgeley Moor
25 April 1464

N

Dunstanburgh

CHEVIOT
HILLS

Alnwick

Warkworth

Morpeth

Bywell

River Tyne

Newcastle

Hexam
15 May 1464

To Carlisle

Durham

River Tees

To York

The North East of England, 1464.

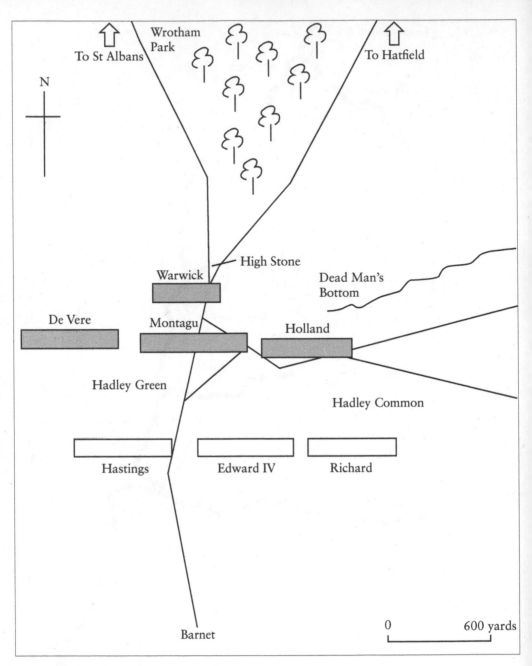

The Battle of Barnet, April 1471.

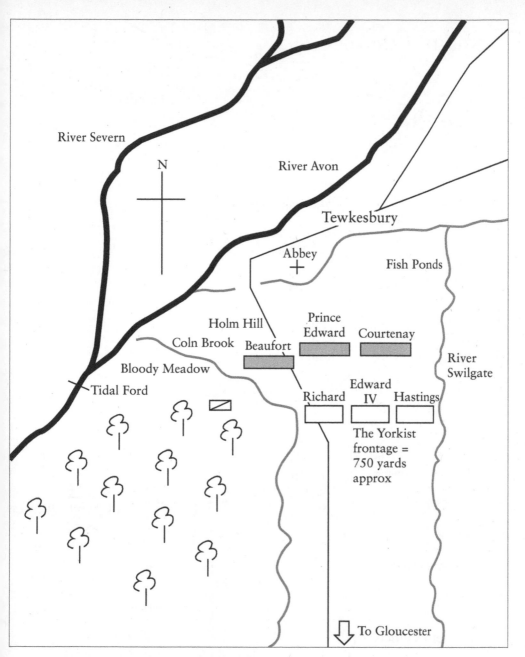

The Battle of Tewkesbury, May 1471.

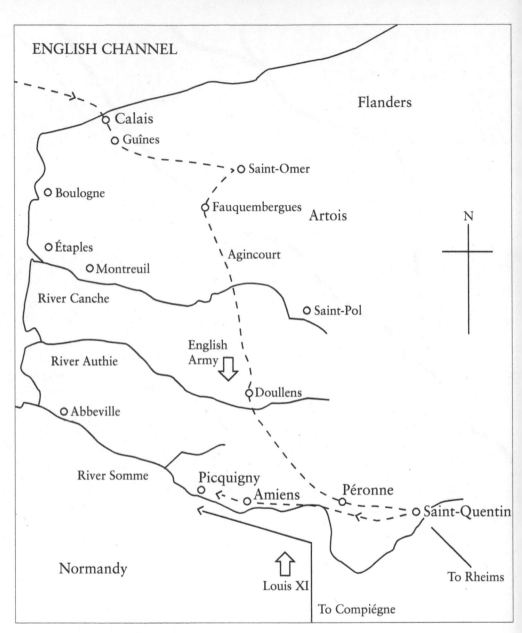

ENGLISH CHANNEL

Flanders

Calais
Guînes

Saint-Omer

Fauquembergues
Artois

Boulogne

Agincourt

Étaples
Montreuil

Saint-Pol

River Canche

English
Army

River Authie

Doullens

Abbeville

River Somme

Picquigny

Amiens

Péronne

Saint-Quentin

N

Normandy

Louis XI

To Rheims

To Compiégne

Northern France, 1475.

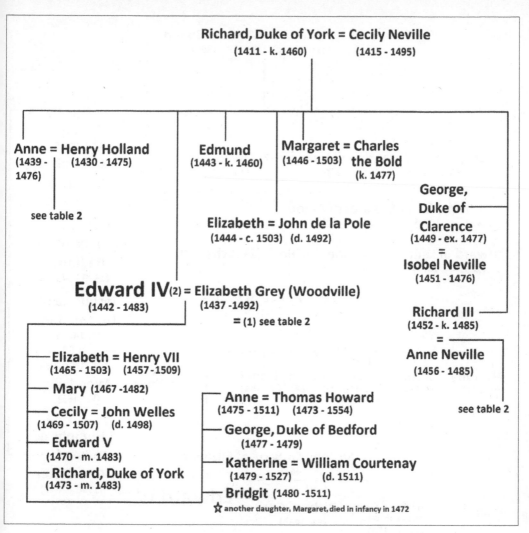

Simplified House of York.

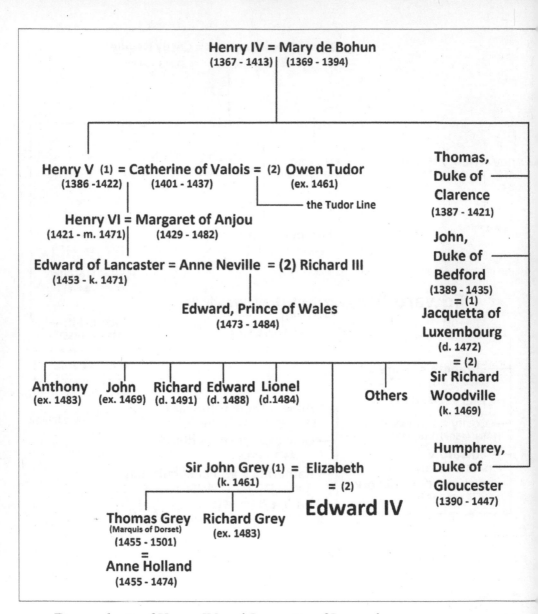

Descendants of Henry IV and Jacquetta of Luxembourg.

PROLOGUE

The depth of winter, hedgerows and hillsides brittle with frost. Across level fields, immobile in the keen dawn, Yorkist forces under the command of young Edward, Earl of March, block the road north. They confront a larger Lancastrian force out of Wales, led by the earls of Wiltshire and Pembroke. To the east, flanking the embattled armies, the once rippling River Lugg lies frozen. High, wooded ground stretches westward to the border, the slopes shielded by Edward's bowmen. A head-on clash between the belligerents has become inevitable. The Lancastrian army comprises an unwieldy mix of nationalities. Many of the men are ill-clad and poorly equipped, in particular the 'rough, rugged-headed Irish kern', javelin-wielding foot soldiers who form the army's vanguard. Wiltshire and Pembroke hope that strength of numbers will prevail against the Yorkist's fewer but better-accoutred men-at-arms and archers.

Suddenly there is a great commotion. Three suns have risen like candles in the pale, clear-shining sky. Men on both sides recoil in fear. Edward is an exception. He sees the spectacle as an omen of destiny, a mark of God's partiality. He kneels in prayer, drawing the sign of the cross. Stooping, he kisses the earth. Only now does battle commence. The plucky Irishmen attack bravely but fall in heaps when struck through by flighted arrows. Bodies litter the battlefield like so many hedgehogs. Wiltshire bravely leads forward his second line but is driven back by another barrage of missiles. The attackers flee down the Roman road toward Hereford; others head south-eastward, skirting the frozen banks of the Lugg, back through leafless woods and hoar-blanched meadows. Edward orders a vigorous pursuit. His mounted men-at-arms make short work of those they overrun. Wiltshire and Pembroke manage to regain their horses and make their escape back westward across the mountains, but the aging Owen Tudor, Pembroke's father, is less fortunate, seized before attendant pages can secure his mount. He and a number of other captured Lancastrian officers are bundled back to Hereford on carts. Unmoved by words of restraint, Edward commands they be executed. Owen's head is lopped off beside the market cross. It is a head once claimed to have graced a queen's lap, but now a mad woman combs out the matted hair and washes blood from the hard-set, rictus face, setting candles beside the body, for Owen Tudor has died in this week of Candlemas.

Few English monarchs fought harder for kingship than King Edward IV, personified by Shakespeare as 'this Sun of York', an allusion to the three suns which are said to have risen prior to the Battle of Mortimer's Cross, fought on 2 or 3 February 1461. Philippe de Commines, a courtier serving the Duke of Burgundy, recalled Edward as 'the handsomest prince my eyes ever beheld'. Tudor historian Sir Thomas More described him as 'princely to behold, of body mighty'. Like his namesake, Edward I (known as Longshanks), our fourth Edward was very tall. When his skeleton was uncovered at St George's Chapel, Windsor, in 1789, it measured over six feet and three inches in length. He must have been an enormous man by medieval standards. His best-known surviving likeness depicts someone free from the characterisations which in some kingly portraits betray weakness or instability (Henry VI), meanness and cunning (Henry VII) or outright villainy

(Richard III). Edward appears to have had the build and look of Henry VIII. Like Henry, he too would in later life put on a great deal of weight, but would not live long enough to suffer the same physical indignities as his bloated and heavily ulcerated grandson. Naturally charismatic, with abundant charm and bonhomie, de Commines described Edward as a king who approached every man (and woman) 'of high and low degree' with great familiarity. Down to earth, easy-going and with an eye for the ladies, his enjoyment of the trappings of luxury has sometimes been portrayed as a weakness, but might more generously be extolled as a virtue: a necessary display of status and achievement in an age which demanded it. Appearance was important to the governing classes in the fifteenth century; Edward's deportment elevated him in a moral as well as a physical sense. Toward the end of his life, his expanding frame would sport the costliest of clothes, furs and jewels and he would trail a string of mistresses in his wake.

The second half of the fifteenth century was a dangerous time for noblemen and royals. Edward's father, paternal grandfather, three brothers, two close cousins, father-in-law and three brothers-in-law all died violent deaths. The period between June 1469 and May 1471 has been described as one of great instability 'without parallel in English history since 1066'. Governance changed hands three times, the crown twice and several major battles for the throne were fought.[1] Fortunately for Edward, luck almost invariably favoured him on campaign: extreme weather conditions, freezing atmospheric phenomena, blinding snowstorms and sudden fogs, as if conjured by the fates, all worked to his advantage. Though unwarlike in comparison to warrior kings like Richard I or Henry V, Edward had the knack of seizing the initiative and winning battles. From the age of eighteen, in the eleven years between 1460 and 1471, England's first Yorkist king contested seven major clashes of arms, some of which rank among the most important of the medieval period. Mortimer's Cross (sketched above) was but a starter for bigger, more savage fights to come. Contested near York later the same year, the Battle of Towton has been characterised as England's most brutal battle, its outcome described as akin to a national disaster in terms of casualties inflicted. The Battle of Barnet, fought ten years later, gained the dubious accolade of being the fiercest battle fought in Europe for a hundred years.

Everybody of note was almost everyone else's sibling, illegitimate sibling, cousin or in-law during this period. Several generations of dukes, earls and barons with near-identical titles emerged to fill the gaps left by their slaughtered fathers or brothers during the stop-start Wars of the Roses. At Barnet, Edward's forces included the bodyguards and retainers of two brothers, a brother-in-law and his main opponent's brother-in-law. He was challenged by forces commanded by two of his first cousins and another of his brothers-in-law.[2] To add to the complexity, until Henry VI's death ten years into Edward's reign, England had two kings. Edward and Henry are each credited with two official periods when they ruled: Henry regained his crown as a proxy for others, Edward on the other hand won it back for himself, remaining the only English monarch ever to gain and regain his crown through force of arms.

Born on 28 April 1442 at Rouen in Normandy, Edward IV was not the son of a monarch but of a powerful father with kingly pretensions – Richard, Duke of York – and a well-connected noblewoman – Cecily Neville, a young beauty famed as 'the Rose of Raby Castle', the place where she was brought up as a girl. The long war with France known as the Hundred Years War had over ten years to run when Edward was born. Its prosecution had cost Edward's father the medieval equivalent of a fortune in loans to the government, almost none of which would ever be repaid. When Edward was just eight years of age, three of Henry VI's ministers, accused of corruption, were brutally murdered – a dramatic denouement of governance unique in English history. Dissent appeared to be the new norm, the battle cry was reform. Like the Peasants' Revolt of 1381, the rebels in 1450 adopted 'the true commons' as their rallying cry. Historians now view these men as standard-bearers of progressive change. Soon after this, English refugees and soldiers were streaming back across the Channel. The Hundred Years War with France had ended on the fatal field of Castillon, where England's top soldier had fallen in the fighting. When news of the disaster reached Henry VI it sent the English king mad. Not only were England's last few possessions in France lost, the English Crown was by this time bankrupt too. These events formed a tumultuous backdrop to Edward's father's emergence as a dynastic alternative to what was progressively seen as a failed Lancastrian regime.

Westminster elites, corruption, populist agendas, retrenchment from Europe, unpopular foreign wars, regime change – even the Scots were up in arms! Although there appear to be parallels with today, the political and economic landscape of mid-fifteenth-century Western Europe, of course, differed markedly. The impact of the Hundred Years War and more importantly the Black Death of 1348 had created labour shortages in England and on the Continent, helping to undermine old feudal structures. Even after the Hundred Years War was over, Charles VII's France was not a unified state and remained ostensibly claimed in law by the English Crown. Everywhere the French king's domains were hemmed-in and bounded by semi-independent political dukedoms which created a hotbed of instability. The city of Paris, with an excess of 100,000 souls, housed a much greater population than London, yet even with the English expelled Charles VII controlled only a patchwork of modern-day France, specifically Normandy, the Isle de France and Champagne, plus half a dozen provinces in the centre and the south, including Gascony and Languedoc.[3] Charles's vassals maintained a fierce rivalry against him. The dukes of Burgundy and Brittany – 'princes of the blood', therefore rulers in their own right – were said to have conceded homage to him through courtesy, not necessity. For better security the Bretons routinely allied themselves with the English, but not so the great dukedom of Burgundy, which was a political and geographic unit powerful and extensive enough to stand alone on the European stage, a quasi-imperial state rivalling England and France militarily and economically. Historian Anne Curry has viewed the three protagonists, the English, French and the Burgundians, as 'an eternal triangle', fostering intrigue and jealousies. Burgundy's duke, Charles the Bold, son of Philip the Good, was described in an address to the English Parliament as 'one of the mightiest princes of the world that bears no crown'. His dukedom encompassed the present French province of Burgundy, plus Picardy and almost the whole of what we might now consider the Benelux region: Belgium, the Netherlands and Luxembourg. Burgundy was England's main trading partner, but terms of trade were often weighted in favour of the former, a source of aggravation to many Englishmen.

Much that occurred during the first, eventful thirteen years of Edward's rule remains opaque: marriages carried out in secret, accusations of witchcraft, shady alliances, unexplained deaths, broken oaths, malicious slanders, blood feuds, treacherous siblings, proxy wars and rival kings. These years have been described as among the darkest of our annals, and not just for their lack of primary source material. Motivations and rivalries that existed within a closely intermarried nobility were of paramount importance in shaping what occurred. For this reason, any biography of Edward IV must be as much about the king's family and contemporaries as about himself: they include Edward's short, stocky father, Richard Plantagenet, Duke of York, described as England's most illustrious failure of the Middle Ages; the period's great facilitator of political change, Richard Neville, Earl of Warwick, known to history as the Kingmaker; the pious and ill-starred Henry VI, son of the equally pious but more warlike Henry V; Henry VI's steadfastly loyal queen, Margaret of Anjou, a woman much maligned by Shakespeare as the 'she-wolf of France', but who bravely defended her husband's and her son's rights with all the means she could muster; Edward's elusively seductive wife, Elizabeth Woodville, an allegedly pious and upwardly mobile commoner who the king married in secret, putting love above the interests of the State; and Edward's ambitious brothers, George, Duke of Clarence, and Richard, Duke of Gloucester, the latter England's most enduring bogeyman.

The story of Edward's longer and more eventful reign is often told as a précised curtain-raiser for his youngest brother's shorter one, and is therefore seen retrospectively through the distorting lens of Richard's infamy. Richard brutally usurped the throne once, yet Edward did it twice, with equal brutality. Close blood was no barrier to ambition. Brother George might have toppled Edward had he not played his hand too soon. Brother Richard more sensibly waited until Edward – a dangerous man to cross – was dead before making his move. No wonder one foreign observer at the time called the Yorks a family of 'bloody butchers'.[4]

I

BITTER RIVALRIES

Six hundred years ago in the summer of 1415, Edward's grandfather Richard, Earl of Cambridge, was summarily tried for treason, stripped of his lands and titles and executed at Southampton on the eve of King Henry V's departure from England at the start of the momentous Agincourt campaign. He was accused of attempting to promote his brother-in-law Edmund Mortimer's claim to the throne by planning the king's assassination. Edmund had, arguably, a better claim to the throne than Henry V, being descended from the second son of Edward III, Lionel, Duke of Clarence, not the third son, John of Gaunt. Though the focus of the conspiracy, it appears Edmund had been a reluctant participant. It was he who alerted Henry to the plot. Pardoned of any involvement, he accompanied the king to France and served at the Siege of Harfleur before being invalided home. He lived for a further ten years before dying of the plague in Ireland.[1]

The Earl of Cambridge's four-year-old son, also named Richard, was in the meantime placed by Henry V into secure custody, where he remained virtually a prisoner for the best part of seven years. Only when the political climate in England had stabilised did the king waive the Act of Attainder (dispossession) placed on Cambridge's family, enabling Richard to reclaim his father's confiscated lands. Additionally, as a mark of renewed favour, Henry awarded the boy the vacant title Duke of York. The king then had Richard's wardship sold on to Ralph Neville, Earl of Westmorland. Neville paid a high price for it, but it proved well worthwhile. When Edmund Mortimer died childless in 1425, Richard became heir to vast estates in Ireland and the Welsh Marches. Even before this, he had inherited land in Yorkshire, the East Midlands, Essex, Suffolk, Berkshire, Hampshire, Wiltshire and Somerset. Richard's network of castles included a number of substantial fortresses, such as Sandal in Yorkshire, Fotheringhay in Northamptonshire and Ludlow in Shropshire. Married by this time to Ralph Neville's attractive daughter Cecily Neville, by his mid-teens Richard had emerged as the greatest landowner in the kingdom. Aged just nine when she was wed, Cecily was the twenty-second child born to her father. All her siblings were married into the nobility, which meant that her own children would later be linked in a familial sense to the households of nearly every great magnate in the kingdom.

In 1436, aged just twenty-five, Richard, Duke of York (known in the narrative from now on as simply York) succeeded the recently deceased Duke of Bedford to the lieutenancy of France. Henry V had died fourteen years earlier while campaigning in France, aged just thirty-six. Underlining York's pedigree, a Royal Commission dated 8 May 1436 asserted the new king's desire to see France ruled by 'some great prince of our blood'. The king in question was now Henry VI, who succeeded his father when he was just a baby.

By strict accounting, the Hundred Years War was in its ninety-ninth year, but would drag on for another seventeen. Memories of Crecy (1346), Poitiers (1356) and Agincourt (1415) had faded. English forces now more often suffered setbacks and defeat than victory, the most important of these reverses being the raising of the Siege of Orleans by forces inspired and led by Joan of Arc in

1429. At one time the boy-king Henry VI had gloried in the title King of England and France, and not just in a nominal sense – loyal Parisian troops were willing to fight for him, but no more! The Treaty of Arras in 1435, which saw the defection of England's main ally, Duke Philip the Good of Burgundy, to the diplomatically astute French rival King Charles VII was the catalyst. The English were by now fighting a rearguard action to maintain a presence on the Continent. The cost of maintaining the war had become crippling. The important twenty-square-mile English enclave of Calais, home to in excess of 10,000 souls, soaked up half the country's annual income, requiring over 1,000 soldiers to man, who invariably mutinied when they were not paid on time.[2]

York's own military record in France was mixed. In the summer of 1436, just a month or two into his appointment to the lieutenancy, Paris fell to the French king and the duke was unfairly blamed. Better was to come. Assisted by his field marshal Lord Talbot, England's pre-eminent soldier, further French advances were stemmed, the fall of Rouen was avoided and Dieppe was recaptured. In 1441, on his second tour of operations in France, York and Talbot led an army 3,000 strong to the relief of Pontoise, an important English garrison town on the banks of the Seine to the west of Paris. A complicated game of cat and mouse between York (the cat) and the French King Charles VII (the mouse) ensued. The French crossed and re-crossed rivers to escape fighting a decisive action. They were Fabian tactics which worked to their advantage. It was a far cry from a quarter of a century before when the French chivalric code had demanded that their knights charge the English virtually on sight. York and Talbot together did at least raise the siege momentarily, but found themselves so desperately short of supplies that their army was forced to retreat to Rouen. The garrison at Pontoise held out for a further month or two before capitulating on 19 September, although not before 500 of its defenders had been killed resisting the final French assault.

After a series of further reverses suffered by the English, the need to cement a truce between the warring parties became paramount. A royal marriage between Henry VI and the darkly attractive teenage Margaret of Anjou, niece of Charles VII, was soon on the cards, and the match was eventually sealed in the spring of 1445. The arrangement, backed by the Treaty of Tours, came at heavy financial cost and loss of territory for the English. The whole province of Maine – a precariously settled buffer zone located between English Normandy and French Anjou – was ceded back to France. A wave of rejoicing is said to have overwhelmed the French inhabitants of towns along the Anglo-French border, whose lives had been made miserable by the English occupation for the best part of a generation. Henry saw the price of peace as worth it to end such a long-running conflict and to secure the longer-term retention of Normandy and Gascony, still in English hands. Despite this, Henry's council at Rouen (English-held Normandy's capital) feared the likelihood of being abandoned – 'like a ship tossed on the sea by many winds, very close upon total ruin'. Meanwhile, stripped of their lands and livelihoods in France, English settlers from Maine arrived back in England homeless and demanding compensation. When, sure enough, further losses of territory, including Normandy, were suffered after a renewal of hostilities, a petition drawn up in 1452 accused the king of abandoning his faithful subjects and placing them under the authority of the French, 'your said adversaries'. Many former expatriates claimed they had been 'reduced to beggary'.[3]

Margaret of Anjou, in her mid-teens when the treaty of 1445 was signed, was just 'a game-piece' to seal the accord. She is unlikely to have later encouraged her husband to give up land to secure peace with her former countrymen, although this is how it may have appeared at the time. Perhaps the expectations in England of her being able to moderate the demands of her uncle, the French king, were set too high.[4] It was hardly Margaret's fault that in August 1449 three French armies invaded Normandy and rapidly overran the province, nor that innumerable fortresses and strongholds were 'surrendered to them', 'surprised', 'taken by subtlety', 'taken by assault', 'delivered up' or 'abandoned' in quick succession.[5] Worse would follow: a major English defeat at Formigny on 15 April 1450, where heralds counted 3,774 English dead – payback, it was said, for French prisoners slaughtered by order of Henry V at Agincourt thirty-five years earlier. Caen was surrendered on 1 July and Cherbourg fell on 12 August. The English even feared the French might follow up their success by making landings on the Isle of Wight. Carisbrooke Castle, near Newport, described as in 'jeopardy and peril', received hurried stockpiles of military supplies. A mandate for the purchase of munitions for the defence of the Isle of Wight, raised on 27 August 1450, listed the urgent need for 'habiliments of war' – 'fowlers, serpentines, culverins, pipes of gunpowder, longbows and sheaves of arrows, crossbows, long spears, and body and head protection'.[6]

York's position with respect to Henry's peace initiative of 1445 is unknown, but most likely he remained broadly in accord with the government's strategy. In the summer of 1449 he withdrew with his family to Dublin in Ireland, itself ever a simmering war zone. In medieval times it was normal for an heir to the throne, other than a king's sibling, to be sent overseas. In part this was to counter any sudden threat the claimant might pose to the Crown. In this respect, York was waiting in the wings, indentured in a state of diplomatic exile, positioned dynastically, in his mind at least, as heir presumptive. Openly, York never condemned what increasingly became seen to have been a badly bungled sell-out to the French in Maine and an untoward military collapse in Normandy. Only at the end of the summer of 1450 – a summer which saw pent-up anger at the English government's policies erupt into violent protest – did he first voice criticism of Henry's regime, but even then not of Henry directly.

Domestic problems in England began that year with the murder of one of Henry VI's chief ministers, Adam Moleyns, Bishop of Chichester, killed by riotous, unpaid soldiers on the beach at

Portsmouth. Anger was running so high in England at the time that the government's leader, William de la Pole, Earl of Suffolk, himself the target of much of the finger-pointing, acknowledged that criticism of his regime 'ran in every commoner's mouth'. With parallels to many governments from our own time, military disasters abroad and charges of corruption at home had fatally weakened Henry VI's administration. The rioters' cry of 'the sea is lost, France is lost', encapsulated the gloomy mood of the day, but economic problems also lay at its heart, namely a troubling decline in trade, remedies for which lay outside the capabilities of medieval governments. The years between 1430 and 1480 are now known as the period of 'the great slump', half a century of decline marked by a collapse in overseas trade, in part the result of the long-running war and political instability in Europe.

Then, as now, commerce was England's lifeblood, with London, a burgeoning city, being wholly dependent on the free flow of goods up and down the Thames. However, the English Crown had no navy it could call its own. Henry V's warships, the remains of a once strong fleet, lay rotting at their berths along the Solent. His son, Henry VI, was reduced to issuing licenses to powerful ship owners to patrol the seas on his behalf, leading inevitably to an upsurge of piracy and disputes with powerful mercantile neighbours like the North European league of Hanseatic Ports, centred on Lubeck.

William de la Pole may have privately opposed Henry's peace policies but nevertheless got the blame for them. A veteran of the Hundred Years War and at one time a prisoner of the French, since being ransomed he had administered Henry's faltering regime to the best of his abilities. It was he who had arranged the king's marriage to Margaret of Anjou, a girl to whom he became devoted, yet his fall could not long be prevented. He faced trumped-up treason charges plus a string of minor offences. He pleaded his case in person to the king, but public opinion weighed against him and he was removed to the Tower to await trial.

Henry needed a scapegoat, but putting loyalty above politics the king instead dismissed all charges of treason and only reluctantly accepted de la Pole's guilt on lesser charges of corruption. The king further declared the sole penalty his servant should face to be five years' banishment, judged best for the earl's own safety, to begin on 1 May 1450. Passions had been stirred up to such an extent, however, that when de la Pole set sail for the Continent to begin his exile, his ship was overtaken by a vessel chartered by his enemies, called the *Nicholas of the Tower*. Dragged from his berth, the terrified first minister endured the indignity of a mock trial, followed by a brutally inept execution. Dumped on the beach at Dover, his corpse was later formally buried at Wingfield in Suffolk, the family home.[7]

William de la Pole's killing marked the beginning of a summer of populist direct action led by a shadowy insurgent known as Jack Cade, a man whose true identity has never been fully established with any degree of certainty. Cade used a string of aliases, sometimes the surname Mortimer – an indirect appeal to York to join the protest perhaps, since Mortimer was York's family name on his mother's side. Cade's manifesto implicated York in the riots more directly, claiming Henry should be advised by 'men of his true blood from his royal realm … now exiled from our sovereign lord's person [an allusion to York in Ireland]'. With Henry and Margaret still childless, and with the earlier death of Humphrey, Duke of Gloucester, Henry's last surviving uncle, the question of the succession had become moot. Although not yet openly declared, York considered himself to be positioned next in line to the throne. To stir up trouble and appeal to York to return to England, Cade's men spread the lie that de la Pole had sought to elevate his own son as a contender and that others might do the same. The thorny question of the succession – not just the economy and foreign policy – was now fast becoming a vexed one.

At the end of May or in early June, Cade's mainly Kentish rebels, now several thousand strong, dug in on Blackheath, beside

Greenwich, to the east of London. William Gregory's Chronicle described how 'there they made a field, dyked and staked well about, as it had been in the land of war'.[8] Despite the king having at his disposal the might of three dukes, four earls, a viscount and a large number of barons, the sheer scale of protest militated against him addressing the rioters in person. Churchmen were sent instead, but to no avail. Henry was eventually forced to resort to arms, but by the time his vanguard arrived at Blackheath the rebels had already up and left. The king's mounted men-at-arms set off in pursuit, only to be roughly handled by Cade's makeshift rearguard. Two royalist noblemen fell in the fighting. Cade's men were not a mere rabble. Gregory's Chronicle confirms 'they kept order among them' at all times; they had mustered in the same way as militia might and had elected their leaders from men with experience of fighting on the Continent.

This small victory hardened rebel resolve. News of the success brought in newcomers. Rumours of random acts of terror inflicted on Kentish villagers by the king's ravaging forces inflamed passions. Some retainers of the king became sufficiently emboldened to make demands of their own, calling for the arrest and punishment of other supposed traitors within the government. On 29 June, the insurgents returned to the heath, joined there by men from Surrey and Sussex. On the same day, another of Henry's ministers, William Ayscough, Bishop of Salisbury, the last of the so-called 'gang of three' – Moleyns, de la Pole and Ayscough – was murdered at Edington, in Wiltshire. His death completed the most ruthless cull of any governing clique in English history, setting the tone for much that would follow.[9]

Henry VI had by this time distanced himself from the riots by travelling north to Kenilworth, near Coventry. Giving in to the pressure, he sanctioned the sacrifice of some of the men named by the rebels as traitors. These unfortunates were duly executed at Cheapside. Among them was James Fiennes, Lord Saye, described by a contemporary as a 'dastard of renown'. Saye was charged with treason and extortion. Once beheaded, his head was placed on a staff and positioned on London Bridge so as to kiss the severed head of his earlier-executed son-in-law William Crowmer, the hated Sheriff of Kent. Cade is then said to have triumphantly rode about the city with Saye's battered and bloodied torso trailing behind him. Concessions made on the king's part should have quelled the riots, but there were by now far too many rioters for even Jack Cade to handle. Events span out of control. Unrestrained looting broke out and alarmed Londoners took matters into their own hands. They armed themselves and fought a pitched battle with the insurgents throughout the night of 4/5 July, eventually driving the rioters back across London Bridge to the south bank of the Thames. Gregory's Chronicle related how 'from that time until the morrow eight of bell they were ever fighting on London Bridge, and many a man was slain and cast in [the] Thames, harness, body and all'. The battle marked the climax of the insurrection. Defeated, Cade made a run for it, but was tracked down and killed in Sussex. His body was brought back to London and ritually dismembered there; his severed head was placed on a spike on London Bridge and other body parts were sent to Blackheath, Norwich, Salisbury and Gloucester – gory displays proving that the leader of the revolt had been brought to book. It appeared to the authorities that the demands the rioters espoused had been suppressed, yet just over a decade later the newly crowned Edward IV would play back many of the grievances aired by Cade's insurgents to justify his ousting of Henry VI. The implication was that he was merely completing the job started by others in 1450, championing reform in the name of the common good.

York had remained in Ireland throughout the period of rioting in Southern England. He only returned to England once events settled down, albeit without the king's specific leave to do so. If he had actively encouraged Cade's revolt as part of a staged assault on the monarchy he must have done so circumspectly. No evidence has ever come to light indicating this to have been the case, but in the fevered atmosphere gripping Southern England in the summer of 1450 anything might have seemed possible.

Prior to his return to Westminster, York specifically attacked Henry's cousin, the forty-four-year-old Edmund Beaufort, Duke of Somerset, a nephew of the late Cardinal Henry Beaufort, Henry's great-uncle and one-time first minister.[10] This was not merely a personal quarrel – York had good reason to be critical of Beaufort. The latter had held extensive land rights in Maine and had demanded compensation before he would voluntarily cede them back to the French king as part of the peace arrangements following the marriage of Henry to Margaret of Anjou. A more engaged or less patient monarch than Henry VI might have forced the issue. Instead bargaining between the parties went on for over a year until Beaufort gained what he wanted. Not until 1449, four years after the transfer of territory had first been agreed, was Maine handed over, much to the annoyance of both York and the French. The money needed to compensate Beaufort came from taxation. It was money the English government could ill-afford, payments made all the more unforgivable in York's eyes because he himself was still owed enormous sums and had as a result fallen into debt. He saw it as self-seeking of Beaufort to accept monies from a government which had none to spare, and was not backward in saying so. In York's view, the loss of Normandy was largely due to Beaufort's mishandling of the situation there. In English hands since 1419, Rouen, Edward's birthplace, had been surrendered by Beaufort on 4 November 1449. He handed over the keys in person to secure his own safety and that of his family. He had even agreed to pay the French a large ransom and had given up a number of hostages, including England's great champion, Lord Talbot. Officially still the Captain of Rouen, York was outraged by his rival's self-interested conduct, especially since York's own officers had been at their posts when the town was lost.

York's unheralded return from Ireland at the head of an army in September 1450, much to the alarm of Henry's government, coincided with Edmund Beaufort's return from France. A later indictment dated from 1459 claimed that York 'came out of Ireland with great bounce [ostentation] ... with a great multitude of people harnessed and arrayed in the manner of war'. Henry's government had attempted to forestall him by occupying Beaumaris in Anglesey with troops, but York landed his forces elsewhere in Wales. Circumstantially York's and Beaufort's returns were linked: York planned to bring on a confrontation. When pressed to explain himself, he claimed he had merely come to declare his loyalty to Henry at a time of mounting crisis. There was a clause in his indentures which gave him leave to return from Ireland in the event of an emergency. Relying on this as a loophole, he offered to actively champion justice, saying, 'I offer and will endeavour to execute your [Henry's] commandments against such offenders in redress of their misrule to the utmost of my power.'[11]

Meanwhile, Parliament drew up a list of charges against Edmund Beaufort, among them his supposed pocketing of wages due to the army and his stripping fortresses of cannon and supplies for pecuniary advantage. Beaufort might have faced disgrace and ruin. Instead the penalties he received were modest. After a short time Henry welcomed his favoured cousin back into government and promoted him to Lord High Constable of England, the most prestigious military appointment in the realm. Whether intentionally or not, Henry appeared to be backing Beaufort over York. Tensions between opposing camps escalated. Corfe Castle in Dorset, one of Beaufort's strongholds, was broken into and ransacked by York's tenants. Beaufort personally suffered rough handling when he came under attack from a London mob over a thousand strong – probably incited by York's supporters. As a consequence, the bruised and dishevelled duke was hurriedly removed to the Tower for his own safety.

York, taking centre stage, portrayed himself in the role of a reformer. He sought to utilise the political capital gained from

Cade's revolt to enforce change and gain for himself a greater say in government. Henry, however, was distrustful of York's motives. At the end of the year, the king reasserted himself, secured Edmund Beaufort's release from the Tower and despatched York from London into Kent and Sussex to mop up after the recent rebellion. He then presented Beaufort, in April 1451, with the lucrative and commanding captaincy of Calais, the garrison of which represented the nearest thing the English had to a standing army. To add insult to injury, York was stripped of his Irish lieutenancy. Henry's cards were now on the table for all to see.

In February 1452, in what became known as the Dartford incident, York allowed his frustrations to boil over. At the head of an army drawn up in a strong defensive posture on Brent Heath behind the River Darent, with 'much great stuff and ordnance', he publicly accused Edmund Beaufort of seeking to undermine him through envy, malice and untruth, claiming his rival sought to disinherit him and his family from the line of succession. This was the first occasion York had directly threatened the use of force, or specifically raised the subject of the succession as a concern. The threat failed. Henry called his bluff by leading an army against him, encamping at Blackheath a few miles to the west. Few backed York. Richard Neville, Earl of Salisbury, and his son Richard, Earl of Warwick, York's relatives and later close allies, chose to remain loyal to Henry. Marginalised politically and outnumbered militarily, York capitulated. Under guard, he was made to walk in solemn procession through the city to St Paul's to swear a humiliating oath of loyalty. His opponent, Edmund Beaufort, walked freely, side by side with Henry. York might have faced further humiliation, even imprisonment, but for a panic in London caused by the rumour of the approach of an 11,000-strong force led by his son Edward, Earl of March, who was not yet ten years old, enabling him to sidestep rough justice and safely fall back to his base at Ludlow.

The aftermath of the Dartford incident is one of very few episodes from Edward's youth we know about, albeit the story may well be apocryphal. It is, however, noteworthy for two reasons: first, that a fifteenth- or sixteenth-century audience would consider it not unreasonable that a child should lead such a large armed force; second, because it indicates York's son to have been considered self-assured and politically aware from an early age. Insecurity provoked by his father's arrest and censure may have served to hasten Edward's maturity. If all of this is true, the young earl was lucky his threat of force did not backfire on him. Even though speaking against the king was not yet a treasonable offence, raising an army against him was. A more ruthless monarch, someone like Henry V, might have seized father and son and had the former beheaded and the latter placed in secure custody. With hindsight, Henry VI should have done so. The fifteenth century would prove that 'might [alone] made kings' – a truth that too often escaped Henry, but would rarely, if ever, escape Edward. In the end, Henry proved keener to secure a reconciliation than to press his advantage. What the episode probably did do was to engender a sense of political isolation for York and his family, resulting in a closing of ranks, a siege mentality.

Much of Edward's childhood had probably been spent overseas in Normandy or Ireland, but by 1452 he and his younger brother Edmund were living at least some part of the time at Ludlow Castle, Shropshire – a prestigious marcher stronghold overlooking a loop in the River Teme, protected by steep cliffs down to the river to the south and west. Their father was the Lord of Ludlow, one of a number of powerful lordships which – like the northern marcher fiefdoms toward Scotland which were bestowed on families like the Stanleys, Percys and Nevilles – granted a degree of semi-independence to the holders. Just one of a series of fortresses along the Welsh borders, Ludlow Castle lay strategically located midway between Hereford and Shrewsbury. First acquired by Edward's ancestor Richard Mortimer in 1301, it originally boasted a deep, dry moat, quarried out from the natural rock to defend the castle's southern and eastern flanks. By Edward's time, however, an extensive defensive wall (outer bailey) encompassed it, as well as a prosperous 'planted' market town – what we today might call a new town, with suburbs extending outside the walls and across the river. Ludlow was then and remains now a bustling hive of activity. The castle, its grounds, the town and the surrounding countryside provided a secure home for young Edward and Edmund. The boys would have been familiar with Ludlow's broad marketplace, its churches, its wide main streets and its network of narrow back lanes.

There was an age difference of just thirteen months between York's two elder sons. Both had been born at Rouen. They might almost have been twins. Letters written jointly by them have survived from these times, thanking their father for gifts of clothes and promising him they would be diligent in their studies. The boys, both earls, formally signed themselves E. March and E. Rutland. If Edward and his brother's upbringing was anything like Henry V's, the two young earls would have been provided with a military tutor from the age of seven or thereabouts. They would have been coached in knightly skills, like riding, jousting, archery and swordsmanship, and provided with a sound education to prepare them for their high-ranking positions. A set of ordinances dated September 1473, for Edward's own son, the ill-fated Edward V, would lay down a strict regime for the boy: early rising, matins, breakfast, followed by instruction, including 'such noble stories as behoves a prince to understanding and knowledge'. After lunch there was to be time set aside for physical activities, including the carriage of arms, followed by an evening of prayer (vespers), then supper and bed. Serving the future Edward V at table were to be men of good character, all dressed in the royal livery. At night, while the prince slept, a trustee was detailed to watch over him at all times. It is very probable that Edward and his brother Edmund's upbringings would have been organised in much the same way.

After York's retirement to Ludlow, matters stabilised for a time.

This was helped by news from abroad that Lord Talbot had won Bordeaux back from the French in October 1452. The following year, however, violence suddenly erupted between members of two rival marcher families, the Nevilles and the Percys. These two northern clans were not merely large landowners, they were major power brokers in their own right, wardens of the marches of the North, capable of raising sizeable armies. Tudor estimates rated the Percys as able to muster around 11,000 men from their Northumberland, Cumberland and Yorkshire estates in the event of war. The current Percy earl, Henry, was the son of the famous first Earl of Northumberland, Harry Hotspur, who fell in battle at Shrewsbury in 1403 after rebelling against Henry IV. Hotspur's mother was Elizabeth Mortimer, eldest daughter of the same Edmund Mortimer, Earl of March, who had avoided censure during the Southampton plot in 1415. The Percys had lost lands as a result of their defeat at Shrewsbury. The Nevilles, on the other hand, having picked the right side to fight on, had seen their fortunes improve. Only after the accession of Henry V were the Percy clan rehabilitated. Henry had then needed a strong, loyal Percy presence in the North of England to bolster the Nevilles in warding off the threat of Scottish invasion while he campaigned abroad. The two families got on well enough at first. Intermarriage helped, a case in point being Ralph Neville's wedding to Henry Percy's widowed sister in 1426. Not until the border wars with the Scots of 1448/9 was renewed tension triggered. The cause is obscure, but the fighting that broke out between the two families on Heworth Moor on 24 August 1453 was likely its culmination, when young Thomas Percy laid a trap on the moors east of York for a Neville bridal party. Both sides arrived mob-handed and a brawl broke out. Nobody died and the wounds incurred were slight. The affair hardly warranted the label battle, yet at least one contemporary commentator, William of Worcester, saw the fight – coinciding as it did with Lord Talbot's defeat at the Battle of Castillon – as 'the beginning of all the great sorrows of England'.[12]

It resulted in Henry VI's government passing a Bill that year for a new tax to raise 13,000 archers for homeland security.

Henry VI's reign had commenced on 1 September 1422 when he was just a nine-month-old baby. His accession passed without incident, underlining the strength of the royal Lancastrian line and conflicting with later Tudor claims that a deep-seated dynastic schism between Lancastrians and Yorkists had wracked the royal family since the deposition and killing of Richard II in 1399. The accession of a baby created problems of guardianship rather than legitimacy. Henry succeeded not only to the English throne but also, by the Treaty of Troyes in 1420, to the throne of France. It was virtually an imperial mandate. The responsibility of ruling had to be carried on the broad shoulders of his uncles – the surviving younger brothers of Henry V – and required a separation of duties. John, Duke of Bedford, acted as viceroy in France, while Humphrey, Duke of Gloucester – described by a contemporary as a man given over more to pleasure and letters than to arms and 'who valued his life more than his honour' – oversaw domestic rule, sharing the king's charge with the astutely ardent Cardinal Henry Beaufort, Henry VI's great-uncle.

Throughout Henry's childhood, nothing pointed to him being anything other than an ordinary child with a firm grasp on reality, kept well abreast of current affairs. On one occasion, at twelve years of age, the boy-king had intervened in council to beg his two powerful uncles to make up after falling out over the conduct of the war in France. On another, when Duke Philip the Good of Burgundy broke his alliance with the English, the thirteen-year-old Henry wept when he heard the news and later complained to Burgundian envoys, saying the duke had abandoned him in his boyhood, in spite of all his oaths. In part it had been the Duke of Bedford's death on 14 September 1435 at Rouen which occasioned the volte-face on the part of the Burgundians – that and the need for Duke Philip to defend himself from attack from the Holy

Roman Emperor, who, alarmed at the rising power and territorial reach of Philip's duchy, had declared war on Burgundy just weeks before. The defection occurred at a critical moment, just a week or so after English peace talks with the French had broken down. An accord was struck between France and Burgundy immediately afterwards, whereby the Burgundians gained the province of Picardy and control of a number of important frontier towns along the Somme. The following year the English were expelled from Paris.

Possibly the most traumatic memory of Henry's childhood, however, was of his mother, Catherine of Valois, distancing herself from him when Henry was aged just seven, the queen having commenced a scandalous relationship with Edmund Beaufort, Duke of Somerset – later the great rival of Edward's father, Richard, Duke of York. Catherine did not attend her son's coronation in 1429, nor did she accompany him to Notre Dame Cathedral in Paris the following year, when Henry was crowned there. She was by this time too wrapped up in her own complicated private life. That a queen should give in so openly to carnal lust deeply shocked contemporaries, and when her dalliance with Edmund Beaufort led to another affair with a relatively obscure Welshman named Owen Tudor, who she secretly married and by whom she bore several children, she was hurriedly removed from the king's side and moved to a new household.[13]

As an adolescent, Henry had become increasingly dominated by his close male relations – Cardinal Henry Beaufort and Humphrey, Duke of Gloucester in particular – an experience which may have created an anxious dependence in him. Some historians have taken the extreme view that Henry ended up with no independent will of his own. However, his single-mindedness in driving for a peace accord with the French in the second half of the 1440s, against the advice of his then first minister, William de la Pole, belies this assertion. As an adult, Henry took many decisions of State on his own head. Rather than a complete fool, he was merely a mild-mannered, somewhat vague young man.[14] He had a number of kingly qualities – piety, self-restraint, fairness and a good grasp of ceremony being the most obvious examples – but he lacked a warrior mentality: his ambitions were constructive rather than destructive. King's College Chapel at Cambridge, incomplete at the time of his death but completed later to specifications drawn up by him, is considered his masterwork. Henry was basically a good man, even if, in the final analysis, he was a bad king; a man more interested in dealing with matters concerning morals and religious observance than with affairs of State. Yet in negotiating a peace with France, Henry acted with cogency, risking the wrath of his increasingly sidelined uncle Humphrey of Gloucester, who remained a staunch supporter of maintaining England's foreign interests and the continuation of the war. When Humphrey made his opposition to peace known and acted aggressively toward the government, Henry, with William de la Pole's backing, ordered his one-time protector's arrest and imprisonment. A trial might have resulted had the duke not expediently suffered a stroke and died on 23 February 1447. His death caused a minor crisis. Much loved by the commons, rumours that Humphrey had been murdered forced an inspection of the body. When no marks of violence were discovered, doubters spread rumours that the duke had been smothered, or worse. The unlikely thrusting of a hot poker into the bowels remained the popularly supposed fate of murdered royalty.

Only later, when pressure of events became too much for him, did Henry buckle, suffering a mental breakdown in Wiltshire in the summer of 1453. If shocking news caused it, none could have been more alarming than the first reports of Talbot's defeat and death at the Battle of Castillon beside the Dordogne River on 17 July that year. A national hero, Talbot died after his horse fell on top of him, trapping him and rendering him helpless. A French soldier finished him off with an axe. The fall of Bordeaux resulted. The war was lost. A month after the news of Talbot's death, Henry became, to all intents and purposes, insane. Likely brought on by stress, although almost certainly a hereditary complaint, his condition left him comatose; according to the chroniclers, he had 'his wit and reason withdrawn'. Coping with kingship had suddenly become too much for a man who had been badly cowed as an adolescent and may have had problems asserting himself ever since.

Today, the king's breakdown is explained as inherited schizophrenia. Henry's maternal grandfather, the French King Charles VI, had in later life been known as Charles the Mad. In August 1392 he had suddenly gone berserk, striking down four of his knights and attacking and almost killing his brother. His delusions included the feeling he was made of glass and might at any moment shatter. The psychosis may have been inherited directly from Charles's mother, Joanna de Bourbon, and therefore been carried down the female line. Henry VI may have inherited the same disorder from his own mother, Catherine of Valois, Charles the Mad's daughter.

Henry's breakdown changed everything. Nobody could be confident of his recovery. His madness lasted for a full eighteen months without remission. The affliction appeared to contemporaries as an act of God or the agency of malign sorcery. The fact that the king's French grandfather had also suffered lifelong bouts of insanity raised fears in England that Henry would end up the same. Seven months pregnant, Margaret of Anjou called for the application of holy water and invoked the power of relics, hoping for a miracle. She too was at her wit's end. On 13 October 1453, with the king plunged in depression, she gave birth to a baby boy whom she named Edward, after the pre-conquest Edward the Confessor. When she presented the babe to her husband, the king made no sign of acknowledgement or recognition, a circumstance that was said to have severely shocked the queen and attendant courtiers.

Supported now by his Neville in-laws, York quickly took advantage of the situation as it unravelled. Through a surrogate, he called for Edmund Beaufort's impeachment on charges of treachery. The charges were delivered at a Great Council meeting held in November 1453. Fearing open conflict, the lords caved in to York's demands. Beaufort was arrested and marched off to the Tower. Understandably feeling vulnerable so soon after the birth of her son, with the king stricken and Beaufort incarcerated, the queen in desperation put herself forward as regent to rule in her husband's place. Had the country not still been at war, wracked by internal dissension and with a long minority now a distinct possibility, her proposal might have been taken up, but in a male-dominated, militaristic age, the lords of England were never likely to have favoured a woman over a man, unless as a last resort.[15] The highest ranking nobleman at large in England was the Duke of York, so the choice naturally fell on him to take over the reins of governance. Named defender and protector of the realm on 27 March 1454, York set about the necessary task of restoring order and initiating long-overdue reform. He made sure to involve his eldest son and Edward was reported as riding out at his father's side when travelling to London that spring, the twelve-year-old Earl of March described as heading a troop of smartly turned-out fighting men.

The establishment of York's protectorate and Beaufort's removal to the Tower defused tensions for a time, but Edward's father remained frustrated, unable at first to gain a quorum at council. His powers were restricted to maintaining order and the defence of the realm. Many lords feigned sickness or other pressing business to avoid attendance at council, leading to Parliament dissolving itself before any of his reforms could be debated. Other than York's hard-core supporters, few men wanted to be seen to have in any way profited or taken advantage of the king's illness, but there were, of course, exceptions; among them was Edward's twenty-four-year-old brother-in-law, Henry Holland, Duke of Exeter, who was married to York's eldest daughter, Anne. In an act of open rebellion just two months after York's appointment, Holland laid claim to the duchy of Lancaster, and with a small armed force led what amounted to a limited Lancastrian uprising. York rode north, quelled the revolt without any blood being spilt and incarcerated his son-in-law in Pontefract Castle – the grim northern fortress where Henry VI's grandfather had allegedly starved Richard II to death after usurping the throne in 1399.[16]

Holland's reckless behaviour may have been the result of financial worries rather than anything more sinister. He craved a ducal lifestyle but did not have the wherewithal to fund it. Being among Henry IV's nearest adult male relatives (Holland's grandmother had been Henry IV's sister), he may also have expected to have been more involved in the running of the country, or even to have been made Lord Protector instead of his father-in-law. It would appear York went out of his way to be fair when in power, but naturally rewarded those he found to be most loyal and compliant. Foremost was York's brother-in-law, the fifty-four-year-old Richard Neville, Earl of Salisbury, who gained the position of Lord Chancellor of England; York's nephew, the twenty-five-year-old Earl of Warwick, (Salisbury's eldest son, also named Richard, after his father), also benefitted, gaining rapid resolution of a disputed inheritance.

The Neville's support for York could hardly have been foreseen. Until then, Salisbury and Warwick had remained firmly in the government camp. Salisbury had campaigned in France and had witnessed first-hand the trial of Joan of Arc in 1431. He had also attended Henry VI's coronation in Paris in December of the same year. Warwick too had military experience, being a veteran of the Scottish wars of 1448/9. Both men had up until then been firm supporters of King Henry, with close familial Lancastrian connections. For them to have thrown their considerable weight behind York meant a major realignment of loyalties. Antipathy towards the Percys after Heworth Moor must have been a factor influencing their decision. Warwick in particular proved to be a highly ambitious and remorselessly vindictive man. There would never have been any love lost between him and the Percys. Feuding worsened when forces under the command of two of Salisbury's sons intercepted Thomas Percy, Lord Egremont, and his strong bodyguard at Stamford Bridge on the road to York on 31 October 1454. Almost 100 men were killed in the severest fighting yet between the rival families. Condemned for being the instigators of the affray, Lord Egremont and his brother were ordered to pay the Nevilles £11,200 compensation and were incarcerated for a time in Newgate prison. At Ludlow, fearing perhaps a Percy-led backlash, Edward took it upon himself to muster a substantial army. York publicly admonished his twelve-year-old son for acting precipitately, although in all probability it had been he who had initiated the call to arms.

Following a trend which had begun during the troubled reign of Richard II, noblemen raised private armies as a matter of course during this period. The fact that Thomas Courtenay, Earl of Devon, one of Henry VI's more unruly subjects, could employ 800 mounted troops and 4,000 foot soldiers when feuding in the West Country underlines the fact that some of them were substantial forces. Courtenay was later the instigator of violence so severe that his actions predisposed many of the lords of England to side with York against Henry, arguing for firmer governance. The Hundred Years War had been a highly profitable enterprise for the English nobility, leading to the emergence of heavily armed, factionalised entourages. Men maintained as retainers wore the badge of the lord they served, a practice known as 'maintenance and livery', or 'bastard feudalism'.

When, after ten months or so, Henry eventually recovered his senses, York, lacking the support he needed to hold onto power, found himself once again sidelined. One of Henry's first acts was to order the release of Edmund Beaufort from the Tower. Beaufort's official release date was set as 4 February 1455, but it is likely he had already been covertly removed from the Tower by this time to avoid any confrontation with the Yorkists. Now also numbered among York's foremost enemies, Henry Holland gained his release from Pontefract in March. In a show of defiance at the way the political wind was blowing, York and the Nevilles, accompanied by armed retinues, left court without royal permission to do so. Following this, Henry summoned a Great Council meeting at Leicester. Its objective was ostensibly to build bridges between the rival groups, but the subtext may have been to hold York and his supporters to account for alleged abuses of power. True or not, fearing the worst, York mustered his forces and called for the help of his Neville allies. Word that the Yorkists were arming filtered back to the king. Unsure of support in London, Henry set off for the Midlands on 21 May with the troops he had to hand, mainly the household retinues of his core supporters. An account of the campaign found in the Archives de la Cote d'Or at Dijon claimed that up to 3,500 persons issued out of London at the king's side. Henry had also written to the authorities at Coventry on 18 May requesting they muster as many armed men as possible to join up with him on route. The city fathers raised 100 archers, led by an experienced captain, but not in time to influence fast-moving events. Just four days after the letter was sent, the Yorkists assailed the king at St. Albans.

First St Albans

Prior to coming under attack, Henry's commanders took up a defensive posture within the town of St Albans itself. They utilised a ditch which flanked the town's eastern perimeter and erected barricades across streets leading to the town centre. St Albans' defences had been built at the time of Henry III, during the Second Barons' War. The town had then been known as 'little London' for the strength of its walls, but these had long since fallen into disrepair, despite attempts made to strengthen them during the first tenure of Abbot Whethamstede (which lasted from about 1420 to 1440), an eyewitness of the battle.[17] The unwarlike Henry, in the process of putting on his armour, is said to have bravely planted his standard in St Peter's Street, but then sought to parley. Last-ditch negotiations to avert bloodshed were spun out over several hours. The aging Humphrey Stafford, Duke of Buckingham, spoke for the king. Thomas Courtenay, Earl of Devon, acted as intermediary for York, even though the earl had arrived with the king's party. York aggressively demanded Henry hand over certain named traitors, in particular Edmund Beaufort and Thomas Percy, Lord Clifford. When the king refused, equally aggressively exclaiming he 'would like to know what traitor dare be so bold and that he would destroy them, every mother's son', York ordered an attack.

Abbot Whethamstede later recounted how 'men ran to their posts, while the bells of the Abbey Church and St Peter's peeled out a loud alarm'. Frontal attempts on the Lancastrian position at first failed. Only when Warwick's men, numbering around 600, managed to break through into the narrow streets of the town from the rear did the Lancastrian position crumble. The cry, 'A Warwick! A Warwick!' announced their coming. Surrounded, the king's army was defeated after less than an hour's fighting. The fiercest clash occurred in St Peter's Street, around the clock tower, Queen Eleanor's Cross and the marketplace. Whethamstede recalled, 'Here you saw one fall with his brains dashed out, there another with a broken arm, a third with a cut throat, and a fourth with a pierced chest, and the whole street was full of dead corpses.'

Four royal bodyguards are said to have died at the outset, shot through with arrows. Henry was slightly wounded in the shoulder. Stafford and Courtenay were wounded too. Warwick's attack had been so sudden and unexpected that neither the king nor the accompanying lords had had time to don their helmets and neck armour, being described as 'out of array' when the onslaught came. Warwick's use of surprise as a tactic might have been frowned upon in more chivalrous times, but the desperate fighting during the latter stages of the Hundred Years War had bred a more bellicose style of warfare than hitherto.

Edmund Beaufort died where he fought, in the doorway of an inn, after killing four of his assailants. The Nevilles made sure other private scores were settled too. The sixty-one-year-old Henry Percy, Earl of Northumberland, and Lord Clifford were among those killed. Blood feuds were underwritten for years to come. It was reported that in the land from then on there was 'evermore a grouch and wrath'. Accompanied by James Butler, Earl of Wiltshire, and by the badly wounded Humphrey Stafford, Henry was dragged to the abbey for safety. Prior to this he had been taken to the house of a tanner to have his wound dressed. From there he had gamely reiterated his threat to brook no quarter should the rebels not desist from their attacks. James Butler – the king's unpopular Lord Treasurer and the man who had replaced York as Lieutenant of Ireland – might have suffered the same fate as others that day, but cleverly managed to escape from the abbey dressed as a nun. Stafford remained at the king's side. The exhausted duke was in no fit state to make a run for it, having been shot in the face by an arrow. Lower-ranking wounded were dragged away in carts. Altogether, the royalist army suffered around 120 casualties, with forty-eight notables, including Edmund Beaufort, Henry Percy and Lord Clifford accounted for and buried in the abbey at the abbot's insistence. Common soldiers were heaped into graves in St Peter's Churchyard. The Dijon account claimed that altogether 200 men may have died; also that the battle may have been more protracted than is now generally assumed, lasting from around ten o'clock in the morning until half past two in the afternoon.[18]

York is said to have entered the abbey precincts after the fight and begged the stricken king's pardon on bended knee but still with sword in hand. It is not known whether or not Edward was with him. The Earl of March was only fourteen when the battle was fought, but at least one chronicler mentions him accompanying his father to Leicester, placing him at his father's side prior to the fighting. Given the earlier instances of the young earl's military involvement, raising troops and supporting his father, this could well have been true. Henry V had acted as co-commander in his father's army at a similar age during the wars against Owen Glendower's Welsh rebels in 1400. To say Edward was too young to have participated would be to make unwarranted assumptions. Even so, most historians doubt Edward's participation at St Albans, claiming that his exposure to 'grim visag'd war' did not come until four years later.

2

CAPTIVE THRONE

After the battle at St Albans, Thomas Courtenay, Earl of Devon, accompanied York and the king back to London, but while there fell out with the Earl of Warwick over the rights and wrongs of a private feud in the West Country. Taking matters into his own hands, he rode west and resorted to violence. At Exeter, the earl, 'with many riotous persons', is alleged to have looted the church and bombarded Powderham Castle. At Clyst Bridge, east of Exeter, on 15 December 1455, his forces openly clashed with their Neville-backed opponents. Casualties were slight, but Courtenay was arrested and threatened with trial. Only Henry VI's later intervention saved him from execution. Tensions for a time subsided. In large part this was down to Henry's genuine willingness to seek peaceful outcomes, encouraged by, among others, the convalescent Humphrey Stafford and the chastened Thomas Courtenay.

Right up until the eve of St Albans, Stafford, a moderate, had been trying to effect a compromise between Edmund Beaufort and York. York and Stafford had much in common. They were both wealthy magnates, made wards of court as boys; both, too, had emerged heavily out of pocket at the end of the French Wars – but whereas Stafford remained solidly, if not uncritically, behind the king, being described as 'anxious to protect an increasingly vulnerable monarch and maintain the status quo', York, though expressing loyalty, acted otherwise, sparking the worse violence to come.[1]

Had York been more ruthless he might have made more of his victory at St Albans, and it is tempting to speculate to what lengths Edward, or his younger brother Richard for that matter, would have gone to in similar circumstances. York was cast in a more cautious mould. All he gained in the end was a second, brief protectorate, granted by an intimidated parliament on the premise the country was teetering toward anarchy. It seems the fight at Clyst Bridge had persuaded many lords to back York in imposing order. York's biographer John Watts has since posed the question as to whether or not the duke was merely an opportunist, willing to take advantage of the Lancastrian regime's difficulties, but without a clear plan of how to proceed.[2] There would appear to be truth in this: as soon as parliamentary pressure for a resumption of normalcy grew too strong, York had to stand down. It seems very few of the lords of the land had formally consented to his second protectorate and Edward's father had failed to make a compelling case against Henry's fitness to rule. York's protectorate was terminated on 25 February 1456. From its wreckage he did at least regain the lieutenancy of Ireland. Moreover, in one of Henry VI's bigger misjudgements, the re-empowered king, looking to build bridges, formally confirmed Richard Neville, Earl of Warwick, in the crucial post of Captain of Calais. From then on, Dublin and Calais became a loaded, twin-barrelled shotgun aimed at the heart of the Lancastrian regime.

After the abandonment of his second protectorate, York and the Nevilles agreed to pay compensation to the sons of the noblemen killed at St Albans. Warwick's settlement on the children of the late Lord Clifford came to £666. The new Earl of Northumberland (the third of that title, and another Henry) and the Percy, Lord Egremont, were allotted between them the hefty sum of £8,000. Egremont had not long before escaped from Newgate prison, after spending two years behind bars for his part in the fighting at Stamford Bridge. At a series of meetings convened in London to forge a reconciliation, probably at the urging of the increasingly concerned Queen Margaret, those who gathered came armed to the teeth. Some, like Salisbury and Warwick, attended only under duress. York rode to London accompanied by 400 troops, including 140 men-at-arms. Salisbury had between 400 or 500 men, including eighty men-at-arms. Nineteen-year-old Henry Beaufort, now titled 2nd Duke of Somerset following the death of his father, and Henry Holland, Duke of Exeter, brought around 800 fighting men between them, their contingent being described as 'a great fellowship'. However, the Percys were by far the largest contingent, boasting 1,500 men. These were the retainers of Henry Percy, the new Lord Clifford, Lord Egremont and Sir Ralph Percy. Warwick's men were the last to arrive at London, numbering 600 strong. All his soldiers were well turned out, dressed in red and sporting Warwick's livery badge, the white ragged staff.

Rival groups were separated by the London militia. Companies of archers provided by the city's mayor and aldermen patrolled the streets. It was as well they did: a plan was soon hatched by the Percy's to ambush York and Salisbury on their way to Westminster, but because of tight security the plot failed to materialise. Interminable rounds of council meetings ensued, ending on 25 March 1458 with the king and queen's so-called 'Love Day' – a hoped-for reconciliation of all the noble families – held in the grounds of St Paul's. Promises to compensate the families of victims at St Albans had already been made by this time. They had, however, been agreements entered into under protest, with fingers tightly crossed.

The 'Love Day' event may have first been proposed by the

queen. In a chivalrous age, such an intercession would have been in accord with the time-honoured role of queens as moderators. A king using his queen in such a way did not compromise his manly status. Moreover, a wife's 'gentler touch' might avoid settling differences later on the battlefield. In the event, neither the Percys nor Lord Clifford were at St Paul's for the 'Love Day's' climax. They had by this time returned north to avoid confronting the Yorkists face-to-face. Because of this failure to shake hands on the deal, the queen's initiative has ever since been labelled a sham, described by various commentators as 'theatrical', 'hollow' and 'shabby'. What is more, despite walking hand in hand in procession with York at St Paul's, if Margaret thought she could persuade him through charm and flattery to accept a more circumscribed role in government she would soon be rudely disabused.

The 'Love Day' was not the first time that Margaret and York had met. York had escorted the Angevin princess through Normandy in 1445 when on her way to the coast to meet her husband Henry for the first time. She and York's wife, Duchess Cecily, had become good friends. Even after St Albans the two women remained close enough for Cecily to confide in Margaret her concern that her husband might overreach himself. Margaret, like Cecily, lived in fear of renewed violence – especially so, since she had become a mother. Although of a determined and resolute disposition, after the murder of William de la Pole (a man Margaret may have treated and loved as a surrogate father), she had dreaded another rising of the commons. She had also come to fear York's posturing and bluster and Warwick's conniving.

After gaining the captaincy of Calais during York's second protectorate, Warwick had made his primary base across the Channel from where he brazenly raided foreign shipping. Even before the battle at St Albans, the earl had been branded as a dangerous troublemaker by the queen and her allies. Warwick had the common touch. His buccaneering exploits endeared him to locals in the south-eastern shires and with the London merchant class. Wool and woollen cloth were the staple trade goods from England to Flanders, much of which was traded through the cartel of middle-men at Calais. It was commerce that Warwick had championed in the past. He played on this as well as rallying support in Kent through open-handedness, dynamism and popular appeal. When Henry's exasperated government attempted to blockade him at Calais, Kentishmen smuggled supplies across to him from Sandwich. A French raid on Sandwich in the spring of 1457, a year before the 'Love Day' at St Paul's, had appeared to some contemporaries as an attack on Warwick personally, inspired by Margaret in league with her countrymen. The French on that occasion had landed in three parties and had reached the town centre, which they had largely destroyed, killing, among others, Sandwich's mayor. Rather than applaud the raid, however, the severity of the French attack helped focus minds in England (the queen's included) to the dangers posed by foreign enemies, and may have been a trigger for the later reconciliation attempts held in London.

The 'Love Day' settlements at first appeared to hold, but it soon became clear that Warwick was flouting royal authority when it suited him. In May 1458, the earl plundered a Castilian fleet. A few weeks later, in violation of a longstanding truce, he did the same to a Hanseatic mercantile convoy navigating the Straits of Dover. The Germans of the Hanseatic towns were unpopular with Londoners and the Calais-based wool merchants, mainly because special licenses granted by the Crown allowed them to operate outside of the monopoly that then existed. The earl's actions therefore gained applause in London, Kent and Calais, even if not at the royal court. Warwick was also alleged to have held unsanctioned meetings with agents of foreign powers.

Summoned back to England in the late autumn of 1458, Warwick was forced to account for his actions. At Westminster a brawl broke out between a number of his retainers and some of the king's men, allegedly egged on by Henry Beaufort, Duke of Somerset. The following year, fearing for his life after an armed confrontation at Coleshill in Warwickshire, Warwick fled north to join his father. Soon after this he returned to Calais to rally the garrison there for an attack on England. The royal court took evasive action, relocating from London to the Midlands, where armed support could better be mobilised. An order for 3,000 bow staves and 3,000 sheaves of arrows, raised on 7 May 1459, read, 'We considering then enemies on every side approaching upon us, as well as upon the sea as on land, willing and intending to resist them to their great rebuke with the grace of Jesus, for that [purpose] thereto [require] ... habiliments of war, as bows, arrows and other stuff.'[3]

By now, if not before, the queen had become a major player in government, wholly allying herself to York's enemies, including the sons of the men killed at St Albans. The king may have been suffering recurring bouts of mental illness. Also allied to her were Humphrey Stafford, Henry Holland and Henry VI's half-brothers, Jasper and Edmund Tudor, the illegitimate sons of Owen Tudor and Catherine of Valois. Other notable Lancastrians included John Talbot, Earl of Shrewsbury, the son of the great Lord Talbot killed at Castillon; and James Butler, Earl of Wiltshire. In a letter contained among the Paston Papers, Margaret of Anjou's portrayal as 'a great and strong laboured woman' provides a suggestive contemporary depiction of her at this time as loyal and well intentioned, but has been used subsequently in a negative sense to portray her as becoming overly powerful and aggressive. It was not a coincidence that the royal policy of appeasement after St Albans coincided with the influential Talbot's period as Lord Treasurer, since Margaret and Talbot worked tirelessly together to keep the peace, all the while undermined by Warwick's unlawful escapades and by Edward's father's baleful belligerence.[4]

Blore Heath and Ludford Bridge

The next milestone toward all-out war was the Yorkist lords' exclusion from a Great Council meeting at Coventry. Like other medieval kings, Henry often travelled outside the capital with his ministers to hold sessions of parliament. This was partly to ease the burden on those travelling from the far reaches of the realm, but he also needed to be seen by a broader set of subjects than just Londoners. Parliaments took place during kingly progresses around the country at places such as Bury St Edmunds, Coventry, Leicester, Reading and Winchester. Again fearing censure, York called for his supporters to concentrate their forces. In response, Salisbury gathered his retainers and set out to join his brother-in-law, then at Worcester. On 23 September 1459, a Lancastrian army commanded by Lord Audley intercepted him in Staffordshire, setting up what might best be described as a medieval roadblock across the road between Newcastle-under-Lyme and Market Drayton, on Blore Heath.

The Yorkists had as many as 5,000 men, the Lancastrians one or two thousand more. The Lancastrian position may have extended for upwards of three-quarters of a mile – a sufficiently large frontage to block the only routes south and south-west and force the Yorkists to either withdraw or give battle. Rather than attempting to break through however, Salisbury's men defended an entrenched wagon laager, a style of fighting typical of the Hundred Years War. In a protracted encounter lasting a full afternoon, which saw the Lancastrians launch a series of desperate uphill attacks on the Yorkist position, Salisbury's commanders emerged triumphant, killing the enemy commander as well as over 1,000 of his men. A monument to Lord Audley now stands in a field just to the south of the Newcastle Road, beside the Hemphill Brook, described as 'a square pedestal, seemingly of great age, with a rude cross standing upon it, now much battered and injured'. Just down the forward slope of the Yorkist position, it marks the spot where Audley fell, probably the culminating point of the Lancastrian attack.[5]

Heading south, weakened somewhat, the victors combined at Worcester with the other Yorkists, including York and his elder sons, Edward and Edmund. Warwick was there too. The earl had returned from Calais with reinforcements comprising approximately 500 men under the command of Andrew Trollope, Calais's garrison commander and the foremost soldier of his day. In Worcester Cathedral those assembled vowed loyalty to each other; all were determined to rid the king of his so-called 'evil ministers'. While there, however, word reached them of a much larger army than their own bearing down upon them. They retreated back first to Tewkesbury, then to a previously prepared defensive position beside Ludford Bridge, spanning the broadly tumbling River Teme, which separated the fortified town of Ludlow from the more ancient hamlet of Ludford on the south bank. The Lancastrian forces approached late the following day, 12 October, through high, wooded ground via Leominster and Richard's Castle, their movements hindered, according to the later Act of Attainder, by 'the impediment of the ways and straightness, and by let [abundance] of water'. The Act also mentioned the Yorkists laying ambushes and sending out skirmishers to disrupt the royal army's advance. Although these allegations indicate York organised an active defence, the charges may simply have been 'legal flummery' common to all such legal documents.[6] On the other hand, supporting the notion that the Yorkists had prepared well, William Gregory's Chronicle described York's position as 'a great deep dyke … fortified with guns, carts and stakes' set before their battles.

It soon became clear the Yorkists had seriously overstepped themselves. They were confronted by a royal army more than twice their size, with Henry VI at its head. The retinues of just six Yorkist peers of the realm faced the forces of twenty loyalist peers. York may have hoped to catch the King's forces in disorder before they had time to deploy, but failed to do so, despite the enemy taking all afternoon to embattle. Caution, a characteristic of York's that was unfortunate in a rebel, got the better of him. Without opposition, he allowed the more numerous Lancastrian forces to take up an equally strong position as his own, probably on rising ground to the south-east of the town. Once it became clear they faced the king in person and that they were heavily outnumbered, many men, Andrew Trollope and his contingent among them, deserted to the Lancastrians. The Burgundian chronicler Jean de Waurin later said that the Earl of Warwick trusted Andrew Trollope in a fight more than any other man. Having him and his veteran soldiery on hand should have given the Yorkists an edge, but when they deserted – Waurin later claimed Calais's commander had received a written appeal from Henry Beaufort, promising him a full pardon should he jump ship – it became clear the game was up. A desultory and ineffectual overnight cannonade commenced, but there was to be no fighting. Even so, the bloodless Battle of Ludford Bridge dramatically illustrated Clausewitz's premise that 'possible engagements are to be regarded as real ones because of their [sometimes decisive] consequences'. Had the two sides come to blows, the outcome of the Wars of the Roses would have been markedly different.[7]

After spreading the rumour that Henry VI had suddenly died, the Yorkist leaders hightailed it back into the town to the castle and then westward into Wales, destroying bridges along the way to hamper pursuit. In doing so, they abandoned their foot soldiers to the king's mercy. The Act of Attainder passed by the parliament which met on 20 November 1459 at Coventry – the so-called 'Parliament of Devils' – stripped those attainted of their lands and titles and accused the Yorkist leaders (York, Edward, Edmund, Salisbury and Warwick, among others) of acting like cowards and of dishonourably stealing away from the battlefield by using the excuse that they wished to refresh themselves in Ludlow and would soon return to their battlements.[8] By any yardstick, being named and shamed in this way after the flight from Ludford Bridge was a decidedly inauspicious and somewhat chastening start to the future king's public career – a stain on his honour that only a continuation of the war might erase. Among those left behind at nearby Wigmore Castle was Edward's mother, Cecily, and his younger siblings. The conflict had yet to reach the pitch where women or children were butchered. George, aged ten, and Richard, aged seven, remained unharmed when the Lancastrians burst in on them. The duchess and her children were quickly secured and taken into custody. They would later be sent to reside at the home of Edward's aunt, the Duchess of Buckingham. The inhabitants of Ludlow were less fortunate, being left, in words from Gregory's Chronicle, to the 'misrule of the king's gallants ... wet-shod with wine'. The town was sacked, women were raped and the castle looted.

York and Edmund took ship to pro-Yorkist Ireland, where York remained genuinely popular because of his support for Irish home rule. Accompanied by the Earl of Salisbury and his son Warwick, Edward made the longer journey to Calais. By separating his two elder sons, York sensibly mitigated the risks involved should one or other party be apprehended. Crucially, Salisbury's brother, William, Lord Fauconberg, managed to keep control of Calais and its garrison. The Yorkist earls arrived there in time to reinforce the fortress and prevent its capture by the king's forces. Had any of the fugitives been taken before reaching safety, their lives would have been forfeit. Along the way, the runaways were helped by Joan Dynham, who hid them at her home at Nutwell, near Exmouth, and procured a ship to take them to the Continent. Later, when crowned king, Edward would reward her for her 'true service' to him and his compatriots. He would also seek to make amends to the townsfolk of Ludlow. One of his first acts on becoming king would be to formally incorporate Ludlow as a borough 'for laudable and gratuitous services'.

Even before the earl's flight to Calais, Henry VI had appointed his twenty-one-year-old namesake, Henry Beaufort, to the captaincy there. The young duke had fought by the side of his father, Edmund, at St Albans and had been among the wounded dragged off in carts. Afterwards, he had been kept under lock and key by Warwick and had not been released until York's second protectorate imploded. He had then taken his dead father's place as one of York's (and later Edward's) most implacable and militarily talented Lancastrian opponents; de Waurin even came to believe that Henry Beaufort's adult life became dominated by a desire to avenge his father. His animosity to York first manifested itself at a Great Council meeting summoned at Coventry in the autumn of 1456, where he had to be restrained from launching a physical assault on the duke. A month later, he assaulted Warwick and Warwick's younger brother John Neville. There was no reparation for this from the Lancastrian authorities. Rather than suffer censure, Henry Beaufort was appointed Constable of Carisbrooke Castle and gained the lieutenancy of the Isle of Wight, a military posting which reflected the government's faith in his ability to confront any full-scale French invasion of the south coast; something seen as an imminent risk after the savage French raid made earlier on Sandwich.

The Yorkists did well to hang on to Calais in the face of Henry Beaufort's mounting challenge. The Lancastrian commander raised an army 1,000 strong in November 1459, but Calais's defenders fought him off. After establishing his forces in the surrounding area, ably assisted by the turncoat Andrew Trollope, Beaufort launched a number of further raids. They were attacks described as 'full manly made assaults', but which nevertheless failed to make headway. At around the turn of the year the Yorkists hit back; men from Warwick's fleet supported by loyal Kentishmen fell on Beaufort's provisioning squadron at Sandwich, dispersing, destroying or capturing most of his ships and taking a number of high value prisoners. Then, once the weather had set fair, Warwick sailed to Waterford in the south of Ireland to liaise with York. In his absence, another attempt on the fortress at Calais was made by Henry Beaufort, now basing himself at the nearby stronghold of Guines. Guines was one of two outlying fortresses ostensibly sited to protect Calais; the other was at nearby Hammes. Only with difficulty did the ill-provisioned duke manage to scrape a force together to confront the Yorkists, and when he did, still outnumbered, his army was crushed by Lord Fauconberg at the Battle of Newnham Bridge, fought in the Pas de Calais on 23 April 1460. Whether Edward fought there is not known, but he may well have done.

When Warwick returned he did so bearing news that York had not only decided to renew his assault on his enemies in England, but also to claim title to the throne. Edward would later recall this as representing a decisive moment in his life. Plans to invade England were soon afoot. At the end of June, the Yorkist earls, like many invaders from the Continent of Europe before them, left Calais on a favourable wind before disembarking safely at the harbour at Sandwich. The beachhead had been secured in advance of their landing by Lord Fauconberg and Warwick's close associate Sir John Wenlock, a man who had earlier fought on the king's side at St Albans and had been wounded there. He had then declared for the Yorkists at Ludford Bridge and had fled to Calais with them and had, like them, suffered attainder.

Heading westward, gathering willing recruits along the way, the Yorkists arrived at London on 2 July and entered the city after some initial half-hearted resistance on the part of the local authorities. Ill feeling toward the Lancastrian government in the countryside remained unresolved. After Jack Cade's rebellion, men who had participated in the rising had been indiscriminately hanged and property had been confiscated. Hardened Lancastrians like James Butler, Humphrey Stafford and Lord Scales had acted for the Crown. Butler and Scales became widely berated as two of Henry's most hated oppressors, and their behaviour after Cade's rebellion has since been described as akin to 'judicial terrorism'.[9] Although the city leaders may not have wished to come down firmly in support of any particular faction, Warwick's strong Kentish following and memories of Cade's march on Blackheath persuaded them to avoid a confrontation.

At St Paul's the Yorkist earls swore solemn oaths on holy relics, proclaiming they remained loyal subjects of the king, while at the same time demanding radical changes in government. Warwick secured a loan of £1,000 from city merchants with whom he was on intimate terms. It was to be used, he said, 'for the sake of peace and of prosperity for the king and kingdom'. The earls also promised 'to preserve the Queen and the honour of [her infant son] Prince Edward'. All these protestations were made in the teeth of rumours being spread accusing the seven-year-old prince of being 'a false heir', a bastard 'gotten in adultery'. Reports later reaching Italy spoke of the Nevilles seeking to raise the teenage Edward, Earl of March, ahead of the queen's son in the succession because the latter was not the king's legitimate son. Known in the narrative henceforth as Edward of Lancaster, or simply Lancaster, Prince Edward's paternity from then on became a persisting issue. Although headline tales of 'licentious and incestuous queens' are an age-old stereotype, accusations of the twenty-three-year-old Margaret of Anjou's infidelity, readily accepted by some among a credulous medieval audience, are still touted by historians today.

The Yorkist's next objective was to secure the king from the grasp of his so-called 'wicked advisors' in the Midlands. Without Henry being physically in Yorkist hands there was no way, legally, of carrying through the reforms York had promised. The task of capturing the king was delegated to Lord Fauconberg, the largely unsung lynchpin of Yorkist military success to come.

Described in a contemporary poem as 'a knight of great reverence', Fauconberg had in the past fought alongside men of the calibre of the great Lord Talbot. At St Albans in 1455 he had remained loyally at the king's side, and was one of very few knights in Henry's immediate vicinity to emerge from the fray uninjured. He may also have been with the wounded but defiant king when York knelt at Henry's feet to do penance in the Abbey. It was probably not until three years later, sometime after York's second protectorate had run its course, that he switched sides to the Yorkists – probably for the sake of family loyalty.

Northampton

On the outskirts of London, Fauconberg divided the Yorkist army into three battles or divisions. He personally took command of the vanguard, Warwick was assigned the main body and Edward the rearguard. Seven bishops accompanied the rebel army, strengthening its legitimacy. Salisbury and Wenlock remained behind with a sizeable force to blockade the Tower. The fortress's garrison and its throng of holed-up Lancastrian supporters within would have posed a direct threat to the Yorkist rear unless blockaded.

The opposing royal army, with King Henry in attendance, occupied a readily defensible position at Northampton, south of the River Nene. Not knowing exactly where the Yorkists would strike along the coast, or whether or not York and the rebel earls might attack simultaneously, Henry's commanders had chosen a central position to concentrate the royal army, buying them time, forcing the rebels to operate on what military men might call 'exterior lines'. The king's forces were arrayed facing south, described in the John Silvester Davies' Chronicle as embattled in 'a strong and mighty field, in the meadows beside the nunnery [Delapre Abbey], armed and arrayed with guns, having the river at his back'.[10] Only the size of King Henry's vanguard, assessed by de Waurin as upwards of 1,300 men, is reliably recorded. If accurate it would imply a Lancastrian total of approximately 4,000. The royalist strength in artillery came courtesy of the king's commanders stripping the Tower of London of much of its heavy ordnance. Further securing the king's position, a trench had been dug to channel water from the river, forming a moat around the encampment. However, exceptionally heavy rainfall overnight and throughout the following day had drenched the royal cannons, leaving them partly submerged in deep water, thus rendering them in large part impotent, negating Henry's main advantage.[11] Although waterlogged roads and trackways had also served to hinder the Yorkist approach, this deluge of rain became the first of several severe-weather assists Edward would enjoy during his military career, enabling his troops to launch their assault free from heavy enemy artillery fire.

Edward chose to fight in the front rank of the army on foot, side by side with the men of his bodyguard. He later told a contemporary this was always his practice, and there is no reason to think this to be an idle boast. Being taller and better armoured than most, he did not hesitate to put his life on the line with his men. Nevertheless, the idea that Edward was a natural-born war leader needs to be swallowed with a large measure of caution. He was only eighteen when he fought at Northampton. Although by all accounts tall, brave and resolute, he had not campaigned abroad, unless he had fought at Newnham Bridge, nor had he fought in any battle at home. At Ludford Bridge the year before he had been forced to flee for his life. He was unseasoned as a warrior and relied heavily on more experienced colleagues: his cousin Warwick and his uncle Fauconberg in particular. Moreover, prior to the commencement of fighting, Warwick, not Edward, took the lead in the preliminary negotiations which followed:

Then the Earl of Warwick sent a herald of arms to the king, beseeching that he might have hostages of safe going and coming ... and he would come naked [unarmed] to his [the king's] presence, but he might not be heard. And the third time he sent to the king and said that at two hours after noon, he would speak with him, or else die in the field. [When his request to be admitted to the king's presence was again denied] Warwick let cry through the field, that no man should lay hand upon the king nor on the common people, but only on the lords, knights and squires.[12]

According to Abbot Whethamstede, the three divisions of the Yorkist army attacked simultaneously. The fighting might have become protracted had not Edmund, Lord Grey of Ruthin, commanding the royal vanguard, 'turned his coat'. In a premeditated act of treachery, he ordered his men to throw down their weapons, helping Edward's followers scale the barricades into the fortified camp. Davies' Chronicle stated matter-of-factly that 'the Lord Grey, who was the king's vanguard, broke from the field and came to the earl's party'.[13] Grey's motives remain obscure, but his plan to defect may well have been known to the Yorkists prior to the battle's commencement. Whethamstede stated that Grey's 'heart was not with the king', and later the Tudor historian John Leland asserted that Grey openly 'practised (colluded) with King Edward'. Supporting this claim, the Yorkist commanders are said to have told their men not to harm any men wearing Grey's livery badge, *le ravestoc noue*: the black ragged staff.

With their defences unexpectedly breached, the remaining Lancastrians, assailed in front and flank by Warwick's and Fauconberg's men, soon gave way. Cut off from the bridge, many runaways drowned attempting to cross the rain-swollen River Nene. An exception was Henry Holland, who, by divesting himself of his armour, managed to escape. Elsewhere, Warwick's cry to 'spare the commons, but slay the lords', kept the overall death toll low. Taking noblemen prisoner for ransom – a common practice between the English and the French during the Hundred Years War – was unnecessary in England, where the winning side could more readily confiscate the other's lands and wealth by passing Acts of Attainder. This and the intemperate nature of the conflict served to increase the level of butchery meted out between noblemen to unprecedented levels. While common soldiers were rounded up for later release, the clutch of remaining Lancastrian leaders surrounding the terrified king were slaughtered out of hand. It was a brutal cull, reminiscent of St Albans. Targets singled out included Humphrey Stafford, who had threatened Warwick with death if he approached Henry. The duke fell near to the king's tent, hacked to death by a group of Kentishmen: former followers of Cade who were angered by Stafford's repressive policies in 1450. One of the Yorkist's three named 'mortal and extreme enemies', John Talbot, another alleged oppressor of the commons, fell to the same Kentish death squad. Also killed from this 'list of three' was Viscount Beaumont, a man described by his biographer as 'of somewhat extreme, though conventional, piety ... a typical member of the late Lancastrian nobility'.[14] Lord Egremont survived the fighting only to be beheaded later on Warwick's orders. He had been among those who benefited from Edward's father's attainder after Ludford Bridge, having been granted the constableship of Conisbrough Castle, in South Yorkshire, the birthplace of Edward's paternal grandfather, Richard, Earl of Cambridge. The dead were buried in Delapre Abbey or in the churchyard to the east.

After the battle, a thoroughly traumatised King Henry was taken into custody and later brought back to London and installed in the Bishop's palace: not Westminster as might have been expected. Warwick was making a point; anticipating York's return, he was preparing the government for the king's possible deposition. When Henry appeared in public he wore no crown, this again on the earl's orders. Nevertheless, the Yorkists continued to make it clear they wished the king no harm, stating that their quarrel was solely with Henry's corrupt advisors. In parallel, Yorkist propagandists renewed attempts to undermine the legitimacy of Edward of Lancaster's birth. Embellishing earlier claims made regarding the prince's bastardy, they circulated stories claiming King Henry had always had a morbid fear of sex, the implication being that his mental breakdown had been the result of the shock on learning of the queen's pregnancy – in other words, the realisation that he had been cuckolded. Even today, religious mania and a morbid fear of sex is sometimes cited as a reason for King Henry's breakdown. When reports of these slurs reached an infuriated Margaret of Anjou, she responded by sending an open letter to the authorities in London in the name of her seven-year-old son, stating that he had been 'rightfully and lineally born by descent of the blood royal to inherit the pre-eminence of this realm'.

Henry may have avoided sex before marriage – the result perhaps of a heightened awareness of the tensions that sexual indiscretion might cause in the royal household – but that does not mean he failed to enjoy normal marital relations with his young, attractive wife once they were married. The usurped King Richard II may have been a chaste king, but Henry VI was not. Displaying a healthy sense of fun, he had pretended to be a royal messenger to tease his anxious teenage bride on their first meeting at Titchfield Abbey in Hampshire, just after her arrival in England. Such behaviour was typical of courtly love rituals of the late-medieval period, and has been described by one modern author as a 'highly witty, complex, stylised game'.[15] It was a game that Henry happily indulged in, showing an avid interest in reports of his bride-to-be's looks and demeanour, a prenuptial impatience described as heavily staged, as was the fashion of the times. Henry VIII would later do much the same, travelling to Rochester 'incognito' to meet his most recent betrothed, Anne of Cleves.

Henry VI's interest in girls as a young man therefore appears to have been normal; neither is it evident that anyone prior to the birth of Edward of Lancaster thought the queen's pregnancy and the king's sexuality to have been incompatible, nor that his breakdown was in any way linked to the birth. Some observers may have later spoken cagily of it, but that was probably because of defamatory rumours spread by Yorkists. That it took several years for the queen to conceive is, again, not in itself enough to indicate an unconsummated or sexually unsatisfactory marriage. York's own first child, Edward's elder sister, Anne, was not born to the Duchess Cecily until ten years into their marriage. Cecily went on to have a further eleven children, five of whom died in infancy. Wise heads counselled against young girls undergoing the rigours of childbirth. Having once been a child bride herself, the duchess had wasted little time in wishing Margaret of Anjou well when learning of her pregnancy. She had also expressed the genuine hope there would be further offspring for Margaret, 'for the great trust and most comfortable surety and wealth of this realm'. The sense of relief Cecily expressed on hearing the news of the royal birth is palpable and unsurprising. She had probably hoped the birth of a son to the king would end dangerous speculation about the succession and bring her rebellious husband back into line.

Now under close house arrest, Henry retreated back into himself, although this was well short of the severe catatonic state he had suffered in the past. Papal agents informed Pope Pius II – avidly following the drama unfolding in England from Rome – that Henry appeared now 'more timorous than a woman, utterly devoid of wit or spirit', in other words, frightened and severely depressed. Bishop George Neville, Warwick's younger brother, dismissively described Henry as a 'puppet of a king' – his brother, the puppetmaster. Henry may not even have had the consolation of knowing that his queen and young son were safe from harm, since the Yorkist earls would have been quick to sow doubts in Henry's mind regarding the whereabouts of the royal family.

The precise movements of Margaret and her son after Northampton remain unclear to this day, but most likely they fled westwards from Coventry into Wales on receiving the news of the disaster at Northampton. They were probably accompanied by other escapees, including the elusive Henry Holland, Duke of Exeter. At some point along the way, the royal party are reputed to have been robbed of many of their possessions, a story possibly made up or embellished to highlight the desperate state they were in. Toward the end of the year, the fugitives are thought to have sailed from Harlech Castle up along the west coast to Scotland. The once well-known Welsh folk song 'Farewell to Peggy Ban' was likely composed and sung to mark their leaving Wales. In Scotland, queen and prince were welcomed and given refuge by Mary of Gueldres, the Scottish regent. The politically savvy Mary, though sympathising with Margaret, would later seek full recompense for her countrymen's assistance, including the promise of Lancaster's marriage into the Scottish royal family and the ceding to the Scots of the border fortress town of Berwick-upon-Tweed. She would also at a future date ask for Carlisle too. The English-held bastions of Berwick and Carlisle controlled the East and West Marches toward Scotland respectively, so Margaret's acquiescence in agreeing to cede these places could only serve to further blacken her name with the English. On a more personal level, it is likely Mary empathised with Margaret. She too had been on the receiving end of accusations of adultery, regardless of the fact she had presented her late husband, King James II of Scotland, with four sons and two daughters. Mary was officially mourning James's death when the two queens met. The Scottish king had been killed when a metal fragment from an exploding cannon barrel shattered his thigh. He had left behind an eight-year-old heir, a distraught queen and a politically divided Scottish council. The aggressive monarch had only himself to blame for his mortal wound. At the time of his injury he was making the most of English weakness by launching raids across the border. The cannon which killed him had been sited to fire on Roxburgh Castle, which had been in English hands since 1436. It was said that a red birthmark which disfigured James II's face betrayed his fiery nature.

Meanwhile, the Yorkists in London attempted to lure Queen Margaret and her son back south by sending missives purporting to come from Henry. Sensibly, the royal couple had when they last met agreed for the queen to ignore any message which did not come accompanied by a special token from the king: one known only to her.[16] In parallel, Thomas, Lord Scales, the hated Lancastrian defender of the Tower of London, attempted to escape down the Thames. Recognised by locals, he fell into the hands of boatmen who killed him and then stripped him naked, leaving his body at the water's edge for several hours until it was removed. Edward later ensured Scales received an honourable burial. On a strictly personal level, the future king may have been saddened by the nobleman's death. Scales and York had at one time fought together in France and had been close associates, perhaps close friends too. Scales had stood as godfather at Edward's baptism in Rouen Cathedral, but once back in England had formed a close attachment to the queen; an attachment which later placed him in reluctant opposition to the Yorkists. Afforded safe passage out of London, Lord Hungerford and other notables holed up in the Tower fared better than Scales. On another sad note, however, the common officers of the Tower garrison were executed as traitors, apparently on Warwick's orders: a cruel extravaganza choreographed at Tyburn to delight a large crowd, for whom ritual dismemberment afforded a welcome distraction to otherwise humdrum lives. While fighting had raged at Northampton, the Tower guard had cast wildfire into the city from the battlements, killing or injuring a number of women and children. The executions may have been carried out in response to this.

In Ireland, York's time had not been idly spent. At the Drogheda parliament of 8 February 1460, in return for agreeing to what amounted to virtual Irish independence, Edward's father had secured a sizeable force of archers to bolster his armed forces, preparatory to an invasion of England. The details for this invasion had been planned with Warwick when the two men met at Waterford. In the event, the Yorkist earls' attack from Calais predated York's return by four months. His landing near Chester did not occur until the second week of September, by which time the Battle of Northampton had been won and the king had been abducted and brought back to London. The earls' speedy success allowed York time to puff himself up, distance himself from the violence and prepare for a grand re-entrance onto the political stage. A month after returning to England – probably via Anglesey – he marched on London, making what has been described as a kingly progress. His retinue were dressed in liveries of white and blue, sporting York's heraldic device, the fetterlock. According to de Waurin, York was borne along his route by a wave of popular sentiment – the commoners of England noisily urging him to continue on to Westminster and seize the crown.

Duchess Cecily had joined her husband at Hereford, either to share his moment of triumph or in an attempt to dissuade him from acting too precipitately. Warwick had already rendezvoused with the duke's party at Shrewsbury. Ever the dutiful son, Edward had remained in London to care for his younger brothers, George and Richard, and his sister Margaret, housed in chambers at the Temple. On 10 October 1460, York strode into parliament flanked by armed bodyguards. His intent, he said, was to challenge Henry for the crown of England. He openly claimed he had the better lineal right to rule. He even had the gall to place his hand on the Chair of State, as if testing it for firmness: a provocative act which brought shocked silence instead of cheers. Warwick was as surprised and angered by this as anyone else present, but cannot have been altogether ignorant of what the duke had meant to do. The earl's exasperation was at York's ham-fistedness rather than his intent. A less swaggering, more self-effacing stance on the part of Edward's father would doubtless have resonated better with the lords of England, who, stunned and embarrassed, retired to Blackfriars to consider what might best be done. According to de Waurin, Edward's brother Edmund, who had accompanied his father from Ireland, approached Warwick and said, 'Dear cousin, do not be angry, for you know that it [the crown] belongs to my father, and he shall have it.' Warwick was too angry to reply. Edward said on Warwick's behalf, 'Brother, offend nobody, for all shall be well.' The tension of the moment is palpable. Warwick turned on his heel and angrily left the brothers to confer.

Edward became the go-between in the prolonged negotiations which followed. The details of the eventual offer took two weeks to be drafted. Throughout, Parliament must have gambled that York and his Neville allies would hold back from physically deposing the king. The threat that the Yorkists might resort to force, ride roughshod over Parliament and trump up an excuse to kill or imprison anyone who stood against them, acted to focus minds. In closed session, York may have attempted to bully Henry into abdicating and there is evidence to suggest Henry feared for his life for a time. York was said to have kept Henry prisoner 'by force and strength', and it was later said that the distracted monarch repeatedly made visits to Westminster Abbey to stand beside the plot laid aside for his burial. However, it is unlikely York would have ever contemplated regicide. Henry's outright deposition or death would have created a backlash against the perpetuators, attracting overwhelming support for Margaret and the seven-year-old Edward of Lancaster at home and abroad.

Parliament's eventual proposal was to leave Henry in place as king, but to amend the royal succession and settle it on York and his sons. Edward was tasked to persuade his father to accept these terms. Doubt as to Edward of Lancaster's paternity, up until then just a malicious rumour spread by the Yorkists, had by now been raised as an established fact. By their proposed ruling, the lords disbarred Henry's son and heir from the succession. The parallel of Charles the Mad disowning his son, the Dauphin, as part of the Treaty of Troyes in 1420 may have been considered as a precedent. In the case of the Dauphin, however, not only did the mad French king disinherit his son and heir in favour of Henry V, his queen also accepted the likelihood of her son's illegitimacy. This was something the less tractable Margaret of Anjou was never likely to do.

York retired with his two elder sons to keep up an all-night vigil and mull over what had been proposed. He was doubtless disappointed not to have been offered the crown outright. Nevertheless, next day (Friday 31 October) he formally accepted the compromise and swore on his solemn oath that nothing would be done at his instigation to shorten the king's life. Henry also agreed to Parliament's ruling, thereby disinheriting his son. All this was done on oath. As York was ten years older than Henry, the likelihood was that Edward or another of York's sons would succeed as king, rather than York himself. Though probably frustrated by the outcome, York determined to abide by it. There existed a degree of subtlety in the proposed arrangement, which was not lost on the Yorkists. Outright war between York's faction and the Lancastrians could now no longer be avoided. Queen Margaret and her many supporters were never going to accept the prince's exclusion from the succession without putting up a fight. York could expect a savage response from the Lancastrians. Time-honoured right of might would prevail, something for which only God, and not Parliament, could be held accountable. The attainders passed against the Yorkists at Coventry, the year before were repealed and new awards were made, including York's gaining the honour of the duchy of Cornwall and the revenues of the duchy of Lancaster. With the king now effectively a captive held in check, the next move lay with Henry's dark queen.

3

SUN OF YORK

In the late autumn of 1460, Henry Beaufort and Andrew Trollope arrived back to Dorset from Dieppe in ships provided by the French king, Charles VII. They wasted little time in asserting the queen's authority in areas remaining loyal to King Henry. As late as November, Beaufort was recruiting at Exeter. Messengers alerted Edward's father to this growing threat. York concluded, wrongly, that an attempt might soon be made by his enemies in the West Country to link up with Lancastrian allies in the Severn Valley; either that, or they may move directly on London to recover King Henry. Alerts were sent to places like Bath and Gloucester for the duke's supporters to be on their guard. At the same time, Margaret of Anjou, with Edward of Lancaster at her side, convened a great meeting of loyal Lancastrian lords at Hull, gaining their backing to commence hostilities by ravaging Yorkist territory in the North of England. Her protégée, the young Lord Clifford, a man keen to avenge the death of his kinfolk, took the lead, recruiting men by 'most dread proclamations'. Now faced as well by this Lancastrian concentration in Yorkshire, York was suckered into dividing his forces. Part went with him into the North, another part went with

Edward to Shrewsbury to recruit there and to guard the routes out of Wales into the English Midlands. The remainder stayed in London with Warwick to guard the king.

York's plan may have been to overwinter in Yorkshire, then to deal with the insurrection there when the weather moderated. He hurried north from London, setting up his base at Sandal Castle, a York family stronghold built on a grassy knoll, comprising a lofty donjon with flanking round towers and a steep descent to the north-east. Moated and impregnable by direct assault, the castle lay just two miles to the south of Wakefield and less than a mile from the bridging point to the town across the Calder River. To the west lay heavily forested tracts of countryside toward Woolley Edge. More woods and a lake lay to the south. Only to the east, toward Pontefract – where, unknown to Edward's father, the enemy was massing – was the land more open.

York had with him his teenage son, Edmund, as well as the Earl of Salisbury and Salisbury's son Thomas Neville, plus two elder relatives, Sir John and Sir Hugh Mortimer, the bastard brothers of the late Edmund Mortimer, Earl of March, who had died of the plague at Trim Castle in County Meath thirty-five years earlier. They had probably accompanied York back from Ireland.[1] On the road north, York attempted to recruit additional support, but it being very late in the year he was probably unsuccessful. Now the lawful heir apparent to the crown, he is said to have boasted that none would dare stand against him. He was being arrogant and naïve. In a catastrophic misjudgement with far-reaching consequences, he neglected to fully take into account either the queen's resolve in opposing him or the determination of the brothers and sons of the men slaughtered at St Albans to see their dead relatives avenged. He failed, too, to take account of the impatience of his opponents. Massed a few miles to the east, notwithstanding the prevailing harsh weather conditions, they and their northern retainers were even now preparing to offer battle.

In the West Country, meanwhile, Henry Beaufort, Andrew

Trollope and young Thomas Courtenay, son of the Earl of Devon who had fought at St Albans and who had by this time died of natural causes, reacted quickly on learning of York's northerly march. Riding at the head of a hand-picked mounted force up the Fosse Way to Coventry, their cavalry vanguard clashed with York's outriders at Worksop on 21 December. They then continued north to link up with the Percys at Pontefract. Had the more militarily-astute Fauconberg been in command, the trap being sprung by York's enemies might have been avoided. Instead, caught unprepared in the open against overwhelming numbers, his army was crushed on the banks of the River Calder.

Wakefield

A near contemporary described the fight at Wakefield as 'a sore battle', fought in the south fields between Sandal Castle and Wakefield Bridge. Described as coming against the Yorkists 'suddenly', reconstructions suggest Lord Clifford with the Lancastrian vanguard approached along the Pontefract Road from the east, screening the main body of troops under Beaufort and Trollope, catching one of York's mounted foraging parties by surprise. Possibly Clifford had broken the terms of a previously agreed truce, or perhaps York had been betrayed. The brother of the Earl of Westmorland, part of the Neville clan which remained loyal to Henry VI, was claimed to have fought there 'under false colours'.

Reacting to the plight of his foragers, but underestimating the enemy strength, York probably led his bodyguard out from the castle precincts. He was then himself surprised and set upon. According to Abbot Whethamstede, who was not an eyewitness, the Yorkists were crushed by sheer weight of numbers. Those of York's followers not killed at the onset fled. Tradition has it that York was unhorsed and slaughtered just 400 yards from the castle walls toward the river, beside the old road from Barnsley to Wakefield, where a small, hedged-around space enclosing a stone cross once lay and where a very ancient willow was rooted. Tudor historian Edward Hall described the spot as in 'the plain ground between his castle and the town'. Unearthed skeletons place the greatest slaughter as occurring beside the river. The implication is that the Yorkists, cut off from the castle, broke back toward the bridge over the meandering Calder in the hope of making it to safety on the north bank.

Edward's younger brother Edmund, Earl of Rutland, was probably killed during this flight phase of the battle. According to the contemporary chronicler William of Worcester, he was slain by Lord Clifford on Wakefield Bridge as the earl fled the battle. Clifford is said to have taken grim satisfaction settling scores for the brutal cull of his father and other relatives at St Albans. John Leland, writing in the 1540s, claimed Clifford later gained the nickname 'the butcher' for his conduct at the battle. Edmund, overwhelmed, is alleged to have pleaded for mercy, Clifford all the while dealing out death blows, exclaiming, 'By God's blood, thy father slew mine, and so will I do thee and all thy kind' – high drama, but not factual. Edmund was a tall, strapping man-at-arms like his brother Edward, and more plausibly gave a good account of himself in battle.[2] Edmund's great-uncles, Sir John and Sir Hugh Mortimer, also died with sword in hand, as did Salisbury's son, Sir Thomas Neville. Salisbury was initially spared, but at Pontefract the locals, with whom the earl must have been unpopular, prised him away from his guard and butchered him. The heads of York, Edmund and Salisbury were then removed to the City of York and impaled on Micklegate Bar for public display. The Lancastrians mockingly adorned Edward's father's head with a paper crown; 'Let York look on York!' was the cry.

Upon receipt of the shocking news from the North, terrified southerners prophesised the likelihood of greater devastation 'than witnessed for the last thousand years'. When York's anxious duchess was told of her husband and son's deaths, she immediately put in place plans for her two younger boys, George and Richard, to be shipped to Utrecht for safety. In the meantime, she placed them into hiding outside the capital. She herself chose to remain in London, determined to weather the storm. In London with her, Warwick redoubled efforts to bolster his forces. On the Welsh Marches, a stunned Edward did the same.

York's motives in first seeking to topple Henry VI remain intriguingly obscure and are argued over to this day. Some see him as an overly cautious bungler, the tool of the Nevilles; others as a well-meaning harbinger of reform and a victim of circumstance; or, at the other extreme, an ambitious and frustrated dynast. Though claiming he was acting for the common good, in reality it appears York wanted power, but could not decide how far to go until the last minute, 'whereupon – fatally – he went too far'.[3]

The mantle of York's unfulfilled destiny passed now to his eldest son, Edward, Earl of March, and a younger, more dangerous generation of Yorkists was given its head. Warwick in particular was empowered. Already one of the richest men in the kingdom, his father's murder left him richer still. The Wakefield campaign demonstrated, too, a new, aggressive style of leadership and resolve among the Lancastrians. They had mimicked Warwick's unconventional tactics at St Albans by relying on surprise and guile as much as brute force to gain the victory. Ideals of chivalry were long past their apogee. The three leading Lancastrian noblemen at the battle – Henry Beaufort, Henry Percy and Lord Clifford – were all sons of men killed by York's forces at St Albans. They all had burning scores to settle. Moreover, Trollope had turned his coat and now had a price on his head; a marked man, he had nothing to lose by acting ruthlessly.[4]

Neither Margaret nor her son, Edward of Lancaster, witnessed the fight at Wakefield. Both were probably in Scotland at the time of the battle. News of the victory and York's death must have filled

Margaret with renewed hope. She quickly set plans in motion to march south. Like Margaret's movements, Edward's up until this point are not known with any certainty. Most likely he was at Shrewsbury when he received the appalling news from Yorkshire. Conflicting accounts place him there or at Gloucester at the turn of the year. Being the main companion of his youth, news of his brother Edmund's death must have been an immensely heavy blow for the future king to bear – perhaps more so than his father's death.

Of those with Edward, Lord Fauconberg was the by far the most experienced of the Yorkist commanders.[5] Another strong-arm man was William Hastings, a close ally of Edward's father; later to be made a baron, he would become Edward's lifelong friend and ally. With Edward too was Sir William Herbert, a relatively obscure Welsh country-squire who would later be ennobled, becoming, it was said, Edward's 'master-lock in Wales'. Like Fauconberg, Herbert too was a veteran soldier, therefore much valued by Edward at this time of crisis. Also with Edward was Herbert's younger brother Richard and Sir John Wenlock.

Well-supported and now styling himself Duke of York, Edward might have struck north immediately rather than remain in the Marches or venture into Wales, but a pressing threat soon materialised – an unruly band of foreign mercenaries led by James Butler, Earl of Wiltshire, and a company of Welsh spearmen led by Henry VI's half-brother Jasper Tudor, Earl of Pembroke, and Jasper's father, Owen. The foreign mercenaries hailed from Brittany and Ireland. Butler, who had made his getaway from St Albans dressed as a nun, had since been active across the Irish Sea (where he had previously held the lieutenancy) and on the Continent, raising forces.

Given the Tudor's importance as the progenitors of a later dynasty, it is worth briefly sketching their background up until now. As mentioned, Owen Tudor had had a number of children by Queen Catherine of Valois. Although they were half-brothers and sisters of Henry VI, none of them had any legally recognised lineal claim to the English throne. The two eldest, Edmund and Jasper, had at first shied away from throwing their weight into the bear pit of English politics, but to encourage them to do so and to enhance their status Henry had created them earls of Richmond and Pembroke respectively in the winter of 1452, an elevation which also formally acknowledged them as his true half-brothers. What is more, the following spring he granted the wardship of his ten-year-old cousin, Margaret Beaufort, to Edmund and sanctioned a marriage between the two. A direct descendent of Edward III, Margaret had great inherited wealth and it is feasible that Henry – at the time childless – planned for the first male offspring of the marriage to become his heir.[6] Within a year or two, Edmund and Margaret were wed, the latter losing her maidenhead when aged just twelve or thirteen. Even in medieval times this was viewed as a serious breach of decency. Being very slight, the resulting pregnancy and childbirth nearly killed her. Her son, Henry Tudor (later to become Henry VII of England), would be her only child. The lusty and impatient Edmund died of plague before his son was born, leaving his brother Jasper to support the widowed Margaret and her child.[7]

Jasper had been among the men who benefited most from the late Duke of York's attainder and the confiscation of Yorkist estates in 1459, so had become York's implacable enemy. Even before that, as early as the spring of 1457, he had replaced Edward's father as constable at a number of castles in Wales, including Aberystwyth and Carmarthen. It is not certain if he was at Ludford Bridge with Henry in the autumn of that year, but he is known to have attended the 'Parliament of Devils' at Coventry in the late autumn, arriving in the Midlands accompanied by 'a good fellowship'. Early the following year, with York exiled in Ireland, Jasper had taken further advantage of York's fall from grace by subduing the duke's castle at Denbigh. Having raised an army to reinforce Henry Beaufort in the north, his aim now was to crush any immediate opposition and break out into the West Midlands; either that, or to simply seek out and destroy Edward and his army and take control of the important Yorkist base at Ludlow. All this may have been part of a Lancastrian master plan earlier orchestrated with Beaufort, Clifford and Trollope on the queen's behalf.

Being on home turf, so to speak, local scouts would have kept Edward abreast of enemy movements, enabling him to dictate the course of the short campaign that followed. Marching south from Shrewsbury, he concentrated his army at and around the Mortimer family stronghold of Wigmore Castle, near Leominster in Herefordshire. An extensive marcher outpost, the castle dominated routes north and into the English Midlands from Hereford to the south and from across the Welsh hills to the west and was built on a steep, narrow ridge, strengthened further by a series of deep ditches and strong walls. A fortified site here had first been established in 1067 by William FitzOsbern, just a year after the Conquest. The medieval castle boasted a large outer baily which housed stables, storage sheds, cattle pens and granaries, as well as an inner baily encompassing the main living quarters and a heavily defended shell keep. The latter had very thick walls and was set upon a huge, conical mound of earth known in Norman terminology as a motte. For almost three centuries Wigmore had been the stronghold of Edward's forebears, suffering a protracted siege in the mid-twelfth century and then temporary abandonment early in the fifteenth. By 1461, the castle keep, inner and outer bailies and outbuildings, as well as the nearby abbey must have been sufficiently well maintained and serviceable to shelter and provision Edward's forces. How substantial these forces were is not known: estimates range from the tens of thousands down to just a few thousand, and it is more likely that the lower estimates are true. That the castle remained habitable is borne out by the fact that Edward's mother and younger siblings had been staying there when Edward, his father and brother had fled the country after the debacle at Ludford Bridge. Edward and his brother Edmund had spent a considerable amount of time at the castle during their childhood and teenage years. As heir to the lordship of Ludlow, recruiting on his family's behalf would have been brisk. Being familiar with the locale since childhood, Edward – in consultation with Sir Richard Croft, a loyal retainer of Edward's late father whose lands lay nearby – would probably have himself been instrumental in making the key decision to deploy his forces a few miles further to the south of the castle at the strategic, centrally located crossroads known as Mortimer's Cross.

Mortimer's Cross

An ancient waymarker still extant shows the crossroads at Mortimer's Cross to be six miles from Leominster to the east, eight from Presteigne on the Welsh border, ten from Ludlow to the north and nineteen from Hereford to the south. Local place names still echo of the famous fight: Battle Oak, Battle Acre Cottage and Bluemantle Cottage, the latter named after a Yorkist herald. The Yorkist army deployed here astride the Roman road from Hereford to Shrewsbury across the enemy line of advance on the morning of 2 or 3 February 1461. Edward anchored his left flank on the icy banks of the meandering River Lugg and set his right flank on rising ground to the west. He and his commanders would probably have arrayed the Yorkist army in much the same way as English commanders had done in France during the latter stages of the Hundred Years War, with protection to its front (stakes, carts, etc.), behind which would have been entrenched the central body of dismounted men-at-arms, billmen and archers, perhaps with more bowmen echeloned on the hillslopes to the right and beside or across the river on the left – the latter maybe positioned at an acute angle so as to threaten an advancing enemy's right flank.

The opposing Lancastrian host most probably approached

the battlefield from the south, along the road from Brecon and Hay-on-Wye, from the direction of Hereford. Reconstructions which suggest a two pronged approach, with one division arriving from the south and another from the west across high ground from the direction of Presteigne, underestimate the difficulties inherent in coordinating such a strategy in mid-winter. Another consideration weighing against this possibility would have been the likelihood that Edward's army, centrally positioned, would have defeated one division before the other could come up. The approaching Lancastrian army was a mix of types and nationalities. There were companies of Welsh spearmen as well as units of native Irish (often referred to by their Gaelic name, *kern*) armed with javelins and long knives. Accompanying them may have been groups of Hebridean gallowglass – forbidding, well-armoured, axe-wielding mercenaries from the Western Isles. As well as the plate-armoured men-at-arms accompanying the Tudors, there was also a contingent of Bretons and Frenchmen. Disadvantageously for them, however, the numerous languages spoken in the Lancastrian ranks may have hampered effective command and control.[8]

The Battle of Mortimer's Cross is best known for a supposed supernatural heavenly display which occurred either on the day of battle, or the day before.[9] It was the week of Candlemas, one of the most important Christian festivals of the year, associated with three events: the birth of Jesus, Jesus' first entry into the Temple at Jerusalem and the celebration of the purity of the Virgin Mary. This trinity was represented just after dawn by the remarkable sight of three suns rising in splendour before closing together. Coming on the eve of the Feast of the Purification, the religious anniversary of Candlemas marked the fortieth day after Jesus' birth – the baby Jesus in the Temple being described as 'a light for the Gentiles' – a good early Christian fit to an old Pagan rite celebrating the end of the dark days of winter. Chapels across the land would have been ablaze with candles. Now, before the battle, it seemed the morning sky was too.

Coming so soon after the death of his father, brother and uncle, Edward perceived the three suns to be a sure sign of God's support for his cause. After witnessing the inspiring spectacle, he is said to have immediately knelt down in prayer, thanking God. We can imagine him later addressing his army, proclaiming the justness of his cause, explaining the wondrous sight as a harbinger of success. Once again before a major battle, Edward must have supposed himself to have been favoured from the heavens. At Northampton a torrential downpour had quenched the King's guns. Now, on a freezing dawn at Mortimer's Cross, a myriad of super-cooled ice crystals refracting the sun's image created the illusion of three suns rising like candles on the horizon: an omen of destiny. It would later become the motif of Edward's favourite royal livery badge, the golden sun in splendour. Only now was battle joined.

> When they [the armies] came in sight of each other the archers dismounted uttering a loud and horrible cry, dreadful to hear, and then began to march at a good pace in good order against each other, and the archers to draw [their bows] so fast and thick that it seemed to the beholders like a thick cloud, for the sun lost its brightness so thick were the arrows ... after the arrows were exhausted they put their hands to swords and axes.

The quoted extract is from a description of the commencement of another battle of the period, penned by the contemporary Burgundian chronicler Jean de Waurin. Its immediacy conjures the terror of medieval combat. A poem from the Elizabethan period, specifically in respect to Mortimer's Cross, recounted how the Lancastrian vanguard of Irishmen, with James Butler at their head, assailed the Yorkist bowmen 'with darts and skains [daggers]' and how it amazed the men of the March to behold men so ill-armed throw themselves forward so boldly.[10] The poem tells how many of the attackers fell in droves when Edward's archers loosed their arrows upon them, but how the brave *kern* made good the gaps in their ranks. At some point, however, a complete collapse occurred along the Lancastrian line. A great slaughter followed. Although Mortimer's Cross was a relatively small battle – only a handful of England's great magnates were present – according to Gregory's Chronicle 3,000 Lancastrians were slain. Davies' Chronicle claimed 4,000. It seems that with so many foreigners involved, the death toll at Mortimer's Cross was much higher in comparison to Northampton, where the Yorkists had spared the common English soldiers.

Those Lancastrians that broke in flight fled variously back south down the road toward Hereford or westward across the mountains, toward the Welsh border. Many may have come to grief along the Lugg's frozen banks. A lone relic of the battle, the remains of a barbute-style helmet, has been uncovered downstream in modern times, which might indicate this to have been the case. Jasper Tudor and James Butler contrived to escape on horseback, the latter's critics claiming he had done so even before battle was joined and at odds with poetic evidence to the contrary. The sixty-year-old Owen Tudor, with eight other Lancastrian captains, failed to regain his mount and was captured in the battle's aftermath, later to be executed in the marketplace at Hereford, presumably on Edward's orders. Not yet out of his teens, Edward cannot yet have become disposed towards pity; throughout his life he would be more inclined to mercy. On this basis the likelihood must be that Owen Tudor's execution was an act of reprisal for the earlier killings at Wakefield rather than simple military expediency. His common-law wife, described in Gregory's Chronicle as 'a mad woman', is said to have washed her husband's decapitated head then set it upon the highest point of the market cross. At first Tudor is said to have refused to believe that he was about to be killed. Only when he saw the block and axe and had the collar of his red, velvet doublet ripped off in preparation for execution did he realise the full gravity of his fate. He then lamented how 'this head that shall lie on the stock was once wont to lie on Queen

Catherine's lap'; he had once tripped while dancing at court and had landed with his head in the queen's lap. Realising his end to be near, the Welshman then gave himself up into God's hands, 'full meekly' facing death. Driven to distraction by grief, combing out her late husband's blood-matted hair and washing the gore from his face, his wife is said to have set a hundred candles about him, invoking the salving spirit of Candlemas.

Mortimer's Cross was a resounding victory for Edward, bolstering his self-confidence, laying the foundation for future success. Not until Henry Tudor's challenge in the 1480s would an army again emerge from Wales to seriously threaten the Yorkists. Edward remained for several days engaged in mopping-up operations and recruitment. Jasper Tudor and James Butler were on the run and there may have been other men too that Edward wished to apprehend. Jasper fled west to Tenby, a place previously fortified by him. He later resurfaced in Scotland. In a letter dated 25 February 1461, the earl expressed the bitterness he felt at his father's death, as well as for his own sorry plight. He would spend the best part of the next quarter of a century as a fugitive. The energetic but much derided James Butler headed north, eventually rejoining the main Lancastrian army.

Critics have since suggested that rather than set off on a chase for elusive runaways, Edward would have been better advised to immediately march east in support of his cousin Warwick, who was by this time busily and imaginatively preparing for the imminent arrival of the queen's army from Yorkshire. Conspiracy theorists have speculated that Edward may have been content to see Warwick, his future enemy, come to grief, but such claims rely on foresight which was lacking at the time. Whether Warwick specifically counted on Edward's support is not clear. He had prepared well militarily and may have considered his army strong enough to oppose the queen without requiring substantial reinforcement. Commissions of array had been sent out by him in the name of King Henry to raise additional troops. Some Welsh spearmen under Fauconberg's command may also have been despatched eastward by Edward, but whether they arrived in time to reinforce Warwick is not clear.

Henry's captivity, if anything, had strengthened the queen's position. Her earlier failed bid for the regency had now become an accomplishment by default. In Edward of Lancaster's name she enjoyed the support of some of the most powerful men in the land. By 20 January 1461, just over a fortnight after the battle at Wakefield, the queen and prince were at York. Grim, rook-pecked prizes adorning Micklegate Bar welcomed them upon arrival. The royal couple had journeyed from the Scottish borders with a strong retinue, including several companies of Scots who almost immediately turned back northward. The Percys had raised the North at the queen's behest and a royal proclamation had been sent out to the county of York calling for every loyal man able to fight to be ready in his best array to advance upon the traitors at London and rescue King Henry. Several thousand such men had mustered on the outskirts of the city.

Margaret's army marched down Ermine Street via Lincoln, Peterborough and Royston. Being wintertime, providing food and forage for the mass of soldiery and camp followers proved difficult – a problem that became exacerbated when Warwick banned the shipment of supplies to the Lancastrians from towns along their route. Margaret had sought provisions from the Scots, but had left York before their convoy of carts had arrived. Underprovided, chroniclers speak of the royal army despoiling, robbing and destroying all manner of cattle, victuals and riches on the road south. The advancing horde were compared by churchmen to heathen Saracens, not Christian men. It was alleged that the northerners were allowed to treat all land south of the Trent as fair game for plunder, in lieu of wages. The worried prior of Croyland Abbey, near Peterborough, assessed the oncoming host as, 'spreading in vast multitudes over a space of thirty miles in breadth and, covering the whole surface of the earth just like so many locusts'. A thirty-mile frontage implies the Lancastrian outriders fanned out in advance of the main army in search of supplies, but it was probably because they failed to find enough that many of the northerners deserted – wastage only partly offset by the arrival of new levies.

Commentators saw the coming confrontation as a struggle between northern barbarism and the civilised south – a theme Yorkist propagandists played up, but which was only partly true. Although substantially northern in character, with levies from Northumberland, Yorkshire and Lincolnshire (but not Scotland, as is sometimes assumed), the queen's army also contained elements from the southern counties and from the Midlands. The counties of Somerset and Devon had raised troops in the South West for service in the North, some of whom may have seen action at Wakefield. Margaret's main power base lay in the Midlands, so she would have been reinforced from the towns and countryside on route.

Opposing her, Warwick expended part of his great wealth on a rich panoply of military gizmos: caltrops (cavalry traps), barbed cord netting (medieval barbed wire), many hundreds of pavises (wooden shelters for bowmen) and guns – specifically mentioned are 'serpentines', light field guns and imported, handheld firearms. In the past the English had been slower than the French to harness the military potential of field artillery and handguns, but the lesson of Castillon, where Charles VII's massed artillery had cut to pieces Talbot's frontal assault, had hit home. Warwick dug deep to fund mercenaries too. These were men raised over and above a nobleman's standing force of household bodyguards and retainers. Some hailed from Burgundy. Among them were a company of hand-gunners (arquebusiers) and another of petardiers: bombers who hurled bombs containing wildfire into the opposing ranks. There may have been mercenary pikemen, as well as halberdiers, professional soldiers – forerunners of the famed continental landsknechts – whose habit of slashing their clothing seeded the fashions of Tudor times. As well as these troops, substantial local levies were raised by royal commission. Margaret and her supporters might have concentrated a mighty strength in the North, perhaps 20,000 fighting men, but Warwick's army massing in the Home Counties matched and possibly exceeded them in number.

Second St Albans

On 12 February Warwick, with King Henry in attendance, marched out from London at the head of his bodyguard. The dukes of Norfolk and Suffolk; William FitzAlan, Earl of Arundel; Viscount Bourchier; Lord Bonville; and Warwick's brother John Neville joined up with him in Hertfordshire. Warwick is said to have taken up position near a small town called Sandridge, just to the north-east of St Albans, in a place called Nomansland. Protected to its front by ordnance, the Yorkist battlefront lay across open common land, along a ridge of high ground. The army may have been strung out over a three- or four-mile frontage. Why the divisions of the army were separated and spread so thinly is an open question. Possibly Warwick and his commanders remained unsure of the direction of the Lancastrian attack, so were hedging their bets; either that, or they expected an attack on a very broad front.

Reconstructions of the battle suggest the queen's commanders surprised the Yorkists before dawn on the morning of 17 February. Henry Beaufort probably assumed overall operational command of the Lancastrian forces. Instead of attacking frontally, he despatched an advance force westward to Dunstable under the command of Henry Holland, Duke of Exeter, which quickly overwhelmed a small Yorkist covering force placed there. Then, by means of a covert night march, Beaufort's main body fell upon

Warwick's left flank at St Albans, defended by a strong detachment of archers. Brisk fighting erupted at dawn in the narrow streets of the town. The fiercest action is thought to have occurred round the steps of Queen Eleanor's Cross where the attackers were eventually repulsed under heavy bowshot. Failing to break through from the town itself, the Lancastrians pushed around through the northern outskirts of St Albans, driving back a company of unsupported billmen deployed there. They then surprised Warwick's vanguard as it took up a new position across the Sandridge road at Bernard's Heath. Gregory's Chronicle described how Warwick's commanders were surprised while manoeuvring:

> Like unwise men [the Yorkists] broke their array and took another, and before they were set in order to battle, the queen's party was at hand with them in [the] town of St Albans, and then all thing was to seek and out of order, for their prickers [scouts] come not home to bring no tiding how night that the queen was, save one come and said that she was nine mile off.

The Lancastrians had caught the Yorkists at a disadvantage while turning to face their threatened flank. Savage fighting ensued, but this quickly swung in the queen's favour. In particular, Warwick's hand-gunners came unstuck. Several of them were killed when their firearms blew up in their faces. It was at this stage of the fighting too that Andrew Trollope probably fell foul of one of Warwick's caltrops, injuring his leg. An unreliable Italian account of the fighting placed Margaret at the head of her troops in the midst of the affray, but this seems most unlikely. She and her son would have been kept well back from the front line, out of harm's way. Margaret was not a warrior-queen like Boudicca, as she has sometimes been portrayed. Nonetheless, it was *her* core support that appear to have won the day, not the more numerous northerners. Gregory's Chronicle confirmed, 'The substance that got the field were [the Queen's] household men and knights.'

The chronicler reckoned, 'There were not above 5,000 men that fought in the queen's party, for the most part of the northern men fled away.' At odds with this, Abbot Whethamstede's eyewitness account specifically praised the northerner's hardiness in battle. Referencing a Roman military text, he claimed Warwick's southerners, being born nearer to the sun, as a consequence had less blood than northerners and were unfit to fight a savage enemy – a case of medieval ethnic stereotyping which Edward's later victories in the north would invalidate.

Remaining on horseback throughout because of the need to be in several different places at once, Warwick proved unable to redeploy his strung-out divisions. Had he done so, he might yet have prevailed. However, at the crisis of the battle the scant evidence suggests that many of his men proved insubordinate and refused to fight. Discouraged by the alleged defection of a Kentish captain called Lovelace, many deserted and others fled. To make matters worse, the majority of the Yorkist guns were either facing the wrong way or lay some considerable way back from the fighting. They appear to have hardly figured at all in the battle. Davies' Chronicle recounted, 'Ere the gunners and Burgundian hand-gunners could level their guns they were busily fighting and many an engine-of-war was ordained that stood in little avail or nought.' Intermittent snowfall and sleet may also have played its part in negating any advantage Warwick might have amassed in artillery.[11]

Sensing defeat, Warwick fought his way out from the press of disordered troops and fled west with what forces he had to hand; crucially, he fled without the king, who remained under guard a mile or so from the main battle lines under the cover of a broad oak tree. Most of the king's escort had by this stage also fled, leaving Henry free to rejoin his wife and seven-year-old son. Once reunited, the relieved monarch is said to have blessed and knighted Edward of Lancaster on the spot. The prince in turn then knighted thirty men who had distinguished themselves in battle. Among them was Andrew Trollope, credited by his own account of slaying fifteen Yorkists despite carrying a nasty leg wound. The Lancastrian victory seemed complete. Promises made on oath by Henry to disinherit his son, exerted under duress, were immediately set aside.

Had Margaret and Henry immediately advanced on Westminster, the crushing Lancastrian victory at St Albans might also have proved decisive. Instead their advance stalled at the gates of the city. The royal couple may have deliberately thrown away their chance of occupying the capital rather than risk it being sacked, but more likely they were prevented from doing so by the resistance of the Londoners themselves. Fear engendered by tales of the queen's army's looting and ill-discipline – St Albans had been plundered and inhabitants had been molested by the drunken Lancastrian rank and file – had stiffened resistance in the capital. But such resolve was not true of everyone: Warwick's brother Bishop George Neville, recently made Lord Chancellor of England – a man described by Professor Charles Ross as 'smooth-tongued and unprincipled' – hurriedly set off from Westminster for the relative safety of Canterbury.[12] Duchess Cecily was also apprehensive. She had already lost a husband and a son and must now have been concerned for Edward's safety. After Wakefield her two younger sons, George and Richard, had been secreted away, lodged at the home of a local widow named Alice Martyn. Later they would be packed off abroad. Edward would one day reward the widow Martyn with a pension of 100 shillings a year, the grant citing her 'keeping our right entirely beloved brethren, from danger and peril in their troubles'.

Attempts made by three Lancastrian noblewomen – Anne, Duchess of Buckingham; Jacquetta, Dowager Duchess of Bedford, and Lady Scales – to reassure the Londoners that the queen's troops would be kept under tight control were made in vain. Reports of the northerner's looting had been widely disseminated.

Hedging his bets, the Mayor of London nevertheless organised carts containing food to be loaded up for the Lancastrian soldiers outside the gates. When this became more widely known, a group of locals seized the carts and distributed the provisions to London's poor. The Lancastrians further hindered their cause by threatening to bring to justice a number of men in the city who they considered traitors. Earlier, two of Henry's Yorkist guards – Lord Bonville and Sir Thomas Kyriell – had been executed, something that would have become widely known within the city. Allegedly Henry had promised the pair that they would come to no harm if they laid down their arms and submitted to him after the battle. This promise had then been broken, probably on the urging of Thomas Courtenay, the newly made Earl of Devon, whose dead father had been Bonville's sworn enemy. Kyriell, however, was an old soldier who had joined the Yorkists late on, so there is no obvious reason why he should have been targeted, especially as staunch Yorkists like Warwick's brother John Neville and Lord Berners were spared. In John Neville's case this may have been because Henry Beaufort's younger brother Edmund was incarcerated in the Tower, vulnerable to a revenge killing by Warwick. Given the vagaries of the retribution meted out by Lancastrians, it is therefore unsurprising the Londoners were loath to allow their forces entrance into the city.

Running desperately short of supplies, units of the Lancastrian army fell back on Dunstable. Then came the ominous reports of military reverses on the Welsh Borders, the brutal slaying of Owen Tudor and the linking up of Edward's victorious forces with the remnants of Warwick's army at Chipping Norton in the Cotswolds. Word soon spread that the two men were even now marching eastward at the head 'a great company of Welshmen'. News of this broke like a bombshell; all thought of occupying the capital was dismissed and the queen's army, with King Henry now at its head, fell back northward. Yet even in retreat the mood in the Lancastrian camp remained upbeat. Falling back from

London may not have seemed too great a setback for the victors of St Albans. The Lancastrian royal family had no great affinity in London; the great northern capital of York could serve them equally well. Though baulked by the stubborn Londoners, their commanders had every reason to believe the Lancastrian cause might yet prevail. Outside of London, the bulk of English noblemen still recognised Edward of Lancaster, not Edward, Earl of March, as the true heir to the throne – this in the face of remorseless, Warwick-inspired Yorkist propaganda claiming otherwise. When drawn north the previous year, York had been crushed. Now the Yorkists would of necessity be forced to retrace the late Duke of York's steps. Trailing her coat, the queen rode back northward, her troops again despoiling the land.

Although Warwick had been crushed at St Albans, Edward's victory at Mortimer's Cross had in large measure offset the earl's defeat, and because of this the Yorkist approach on the capital toward the end of February was triumphant. Warwick may have lost one king, but he could soon make another. Upon arrival he manipulated the authorities at Westminster, arguing that Henry had gone back on his word by reinstating his son as heir and that he had as a result forfeited his right to rule. He presented Edward to them – tall, healthy and brave – the antithesis of Henry. Warwick stressed that Edward had been conceived in wedlock and was of the royal blood, contrasting the Earl of March's pedigree with Edward of Lancaster's alleged bastardy. He also reminded the gathered lords that they had legally elected Edward's dead father and male heirs as Henry's successors. Now that the Lancastrian king had reneged on his solemn word, it was right that Edward should be proclaimed king. The daunting figure of Lord Fauconberg at the head of a growing and revitalised Yorkist army backed him up. Little wonder that when asked whether Henry was worthy to continue to reign as king, the common people are said to have cried out, 'Nay, Nay!' When asked if Edward, Earl of

March, should be made king, they cried out with one voice, 'Yea, Yea!'[13]

On Sunday 1 March 1461 the articles of Edward's title to kingship were read out by Warwick's brother Bishop George Neville at a great gathering at St George's Fields. Two days later a carefully stage-managed council meeting was convened at Baynard's Castle, the London residence of the dukes of York – a grand building erected in Venetian style close to where the River Fleet emptied into the Thames. The meeting's objective was to formally agree Edward's crowning. At Edward's side were the Earl of Warwick; John Mowbray, Duke of Norfolk; Bishop George Neville; and the Bishop of Salisbury, as well as other lesser men of firm Yorkist allegiance. Although a relatively small gathering, the investiture gained legal status. On 4 March 1461 Edward was proclaimed king and entered Westminster to begin his reign.

Even taking account of Edward's victory at Mortimer's Cross, the newly made king owed his crown in large measure to Warwick's machinations. Some even saw Edward as Warwick's creation – like Henry before him, a mere puppet of the earl's. The Governor of Abbeville wrote to the French King to jibe that the English now had two rulers: 'Warwick and another whose name I have forgotten.' The papal legate Francesco Coppini wrote to the Pope in April 1461 saying, 'Warwick has made a new king of the son of the Duke of York.' The word 'made' is the crucial one, bestowing on Warwick ever since the accolade 'Kingmaker'. Most probably Coppini was in the best position to understand the dynamics within the Yorkist camp. He had joined up with the earls at Calais and had acted as Warwick's unofficial intermediary ever since. However, those who knew Edward well would have been under few allusions as to the new king's resolve. Though young and inexperienced he was confident and self-assured, quick to learn and held a strong sense of his own destiny. The Milanese ambassador, Prospero di Camulio, was among those who recognised the likelihood of Edward proving to be a successful monarch. He stated,

The chances in favour of Edward are great, both on account of the great lordship which he has in the island and in Ireland, and owing to the cruel wrongs done to him by the Queen's side, as well as through Warwick and London which is entirely inclined to side with the new king ... [London] is very rich and the most wealthy city of Christendom, this enormously increases the chances of the side that it favours.[14]

The Yorkist takeover might plausibly be seen as an extreme method of securing otherwise attainted lands and titles. Should the Lancastrians have regained unfettered power, Edward stood to lose the great duchy of York; Warwick too would have faced ruin. Both were desperate men. Edward needed a mighty subject like Warwick and city financiers to back him, as well as capable associates like Lord Fauconberg to head up his army, but otherwise he needed little encouragement to grab what was offered with both hands. The other option was to continue as a rebel and face possible exile. There being 'no virtue like necessity', even before arriving in London he was calling himself 'by the grace of God, of England, France and Ireland [the] very true and just heir'.[15] There were now two kings in England: one newly enthroned at Westminster and another at York. Edward's was a kingship forged in war, claimed through necessity and hastily underwritten in law; Henry's remained sanctified by time-honoured succession of birth. Some contemporaries saw Edward's enthronement as a new dawn. An old poem declared,

> The time is come to void your distress,
> Edward IV the old wrongs to amend,
> Is well disposed in will, and to defend
> His land and people in deed with kin and might;
> Good life and long I pray him send;
> And that St George [be] with him in his right.[16]

Edward now stood determined to contest his claim by 'right of might'. Having received a rousing accolade in London, it was clear he had the makings of support, but the Yorkist situation remained perilous elsewhere around the country. In Henry Beaufort and Andrew Trollope, the Lancastrians had generals who had proved their prowess: men willing to engage in unconventional, offensive operations, rather than rely on more traditional defensive strategies. Warwick's propaganda campaign, including the besmirching of the legitimacy of Henry's son, had for a time served its purpose, but now with Henry at large Yorkist claims of Edward of Lancaster's bastardy could be refuted more readily. Probably for this reason Warwick changed tack, renewing his propaganda offensive by sowing rumours that Margaret had had her husband poisoned and that she and Henry Beaufort were now united in more ways than one. The Lancastrians attempted some half-hearted disinformation in return, including scare stories that Edward's army intended to ravage the North in revenge for the queen's army's earlier depredations in the South Midlands. In an attempt to drum up support, Henry VI wrote to one of his followers, saying, 'the late Earl of March has made great assemblies of riotous and mischievously disposed people ... come to us in all haste possible [to] resist the malicious intent and purpose of our said traitor.'

Meanwhile, in a foretaste of what became a characteristic feature of his leadership, Edward wasted no time organising the coming campaign. He deferred any formal coronation until later. 'The new king would not rest easy until he has annihilated the other king', wrote the papal legate Coppini. The *Croyland Chronicle* claimed that Edward desired immediate consummation of his claim to the throne by test of battle, saying, 'Like unto Gideon or another of the judges, acting faithfully in the Lord, [he] girded himself with the sword of battle.' In parallel, the young king published a broadly targeted general pardon welcoming former Lancastrians into his service to bolster support. Excluded from this, among others, was the traitor Andrew Trollope, who had a price of £100 put on his head. Funding was secured from pro-Yorkist city financiers to pay the wages of the soldiers.

By the end of the first week of March all was in readiness. Led by Fauconberg, the Yorkist vanguard set off northward on 11 March. Warwick had left the capital even earlier 'with a great puissance of people', to scour the West Midlands and drum up support there. Edward followed on 13 March with the main body, travelling north via Cambridge (18 March), Nottingham (22 March) and Pontefract (Friday 27 March). The young king's royal harbingers rode ahead to prepare suitable accommodation each evening. The professional soldier John Howard and his East Anglian contingent, which comprised the Yorkist rearguard, joined the army on route, bringing with them a welcome £100 donation from the Abbess of Bury St Edmunds. Having fought with Talbot at Castillon – likened there to a wild bullock – the thirty-something Howard was already an experienced campaigner. He may have taken over operational command of the Yorkist rearguard from the outset, since its nominal commander John Mowbray, Duke of Norfolk, had been intermittently indisposed through illness. (He would die six months later of whatever it was that ailed him.)

On route, the City of Coventry presented the Yorkists with £80 to pay the wages of 100 archers, money accounted for as made available 'for the repressing of our adversaries and rebels'. There were also Welsh levies with Edward, veterans of Mortimer's Cross. There may have been some Irishmen and Bretons too: men who had changed sides rather than risk being slain when cornered on the banks of the River Lugg. Thanks to Warwick's diplomacy an armed contingent had arrived from France, sent by France's new king, Louis XI. A Burgundian party may also have arrived by then. In a very short time, Edward had raised a strong following. A contemporary poem, 'The Rose of Rouen', confirms this: among those marching with the king were said to be

Edward IV

Men from the garrison of Calais,
From London, Essex and Kent,
Along with all the south of England,
Unto the waters of the Trent.

4

CONSOLIDATION

The first clash of arms occurred on Saturday 28 March at Ferrybridge, a strategic crossing point on the River Aire, just north of Pontefract in Yorkshire. The bridge had been partially destroyed by the Lancastrians and an advance party sent by Fauconberg crossed here to create a bridgehead and make repairs.[1] After bivouacking on the north bank of the river, these men came under surprise attack from the Lancastrians at dawn the next day. Arrows hissing overhead and hooves thundering in the distance caused immediate panic in the makeshift Yorkist camp. Lord FitzWalter, a veteran of Mortimer's Cross, was killed outright when emerging half naked from his tent. One of Warwick's illegitimate brothers was also struck down in the fighting. On the north bank, Warwick was fortunate to get back across the damaged bridge with nothing more than a leg wound. He was said to have become so hyped up by his lucky escape that on rejoining the main body of the army he slit his horse's neck open with his sword and declared, 'Let him fly that will, I will tarry with him that will tarry with me!' The story is doubtless made up, but serves to underline the premise that ordinary foot soldiers distrusted their officers not to spur their horses to flight when the going got tough.

At some point that morning Edward personally led a detachment forward to confront the enemy in an attempt to force the river crossing by 'a narrow way', dismounting to do so; however, with Lancastrian resistance holding firm, he and his men were forced to fall back to regroup. The next ploy was for mounted detachments under the command of Sir William Blount and the Kentish captain Robert Horne – subordinates of Fauconberg's – to be detailed to ride to Castleford, three miles upstream, and turn the enemy flank. Once across the river at Castleford they fell like a thunderclap on the Lancastrians, who fled back toward the main body of their army formed up to the north between the villages of Saxton and Towton. During this encounter the young Lord Clifford was slain, struck in the throat by a headless arrow when removing his gorget (neck armour) 'either for heat or pain'. Notched up by Edward toward squaring accounts for the brutal killing of his brother Edmund, the lord's body was unceremoniously cast into a common burial pit. Also killed was a certain John Neville, an obscure nobleman from the branch of the Neville family which had remained loyal to Henry.

The rest of the Yorkist vanguard and probably the whole of the main body of the army were able to cross the river in the wake of this success; some part marched to Castleford, the rest crossed the Aire at Ferrybridge. Both of these bodies then advanced toward the main enemy position on the higher ground to the north, leaving Fauconberg's sappers to rebuild the bridge at Ferrybridge – a necessary chore to facilitate the lagging rearguard's crossing and the passage of the army's heavy guns.

Towton

Overnight the two opposing armies bivouacked no more than a few miles apart. Although described as 'England's most brutal

battle' and 'the most important battle that ever took place in
the civil wars of England', very little is really known about it
other than when and where it was fought – on Palm Sunday in
'a field between the towns of Sherborne-in-Elmet and Tadcaster
in Yorkshire, called Saxton Field and Towton Field [a few miles
to the south-west of York]'.[2] No surviving eyewitness accounts of
the fighting survive. Reconstructions rely on contemporary letters,
lists of participants and later anecdotal accounts. Much of what
follows should therefore be heavily peppered with 'perhaps' and
'maybe', but for the sake of readability is not.

The night before battle was bitterly cold with snow clouds
massing overhead. Innumerable crackling campfires lit up the
plateau. Men huddled close together for warmth, impatiently
awaiting supplies of food being brought up to the front lines.
Scurriers wearily patrolled the forward areas and flanks, alert after
St Albans to sneak attacks. Edward and his commanders found
billets at Sherburn-in-Elmet and at Saxton, just a few miles to the
south. Billets for the Lancastrian officers were found overnight
at Tadcaster and in the hamlet of Towton itself. Assuming the
overall sizes of the opposing armies when fully concentrated were
about even (and it is a big assumption), then overnight and on the
morning of Palm Sunday, 29 March, the Yorkist army was the
more vulnerable of the two. At the time of their bivouacking, not
all of Edward's main body had crossed the Aire. What is more,
the rearguard which made up approximately a third of the army's
strength lay half-a-day's march away. The Duke of Norfolk's illness
and his need to rest had slowed its momentum; inclement wintry
weather may also have been a factor. With only two-thirds of the
army present at first light, Edward's commanders were forced to
conform to the enemy's broader frontage and were of necessity
drawn up less deep than might otherwise have been the case.

The Lancastrian position stretched east to west for less than
a mile, on rising ground to the south of the village of Towton,
occupying approximately 1,200 yards of frontage. Its right flank

was anchored on the narrow, wooded gorge of the Cock Beck, a tributary river which ran in broad meanders into the Aire. Its left flank abutted boggy ground, deterring any turning movement from the east on the part of the Yorkists. Sleet and snow falling throughout the day of battle made already sodden ground here virtually impassable. There is no record of the Lancastrians creating a fortified camp, or that they embattled behind obstacles or relied on artillery, but they may have done – too little is really known of the battle to be sure of anything. Warwick would later claim that the Lancastrians outnumbered the Yorkists, but we only have his word (the word of a master propagandist) for it. Even the command structure of the Lancastrian army is uncertain. Neither King Henry, Queen Margaret nor her son were anywhere near the fighting. Among the leaders known to have been present were Henry Percy, Henry Beaufort, Henry Holland, Thomas Courtenay, Lord Rivers and his son Anthony Woodville, Lord Dacre, Andrew Trollope and Sir Thomas Hammys. Clifford had been killed at Ferrybridge. Percy and Beaufort most likely shared joint command with Hammys, described in Gregory's Chronicle as the 'captain of all the [Lancastrian] foot men'.

To get some idea of how English armies might have deployed for a set-piece battle like Towton we need to look back to the better-documented final stages of the Hundred Years War, to an account written by Frenchman Robert Blondel describing Lord Talbot's array at Castillon on the Dordogne River in 1453, the final battle of the Hundred Years War. He recorded how the battle lines of the English were drawn up in three ranks 'handsomely ... like the solid wall of a city' and how the main body of the army was supported by three units of archers, each composed of 700 men. Two of these, standing 'like firm towers', were placed on the flanks, the other in the centre. The main body of the army consisted of a front line of plate-protected men-at-arms: fighting men who rode to the battle but dismounted to fight. The second line was composed of billmen, a type of foot soldier armed with a spiked, scythe-like pole weapon known variously, depending on design, as a billhook, glaive, goedendag, halberd, guisarme or pike. The third line comprised yet more archers. Leading knights made up the officer corps of the army. The numbers quoted by Blondel indicate an army strength in the region of 5,000 men, excluding non-combatants. The armies at Towton are thought to have been larger, but how much larger is impossible to quantify. 10,000 men aside would have been a tight fit for units drawn up on a battlefield boasting a frontage of approximately 1,200 yards, but hefty reserves may have been piled up behind the front lines. Richard II's army of 1385, a feudal host numbering 14,000 men, had been the biggest army ever at large in England up until that time, but the armies which faced each other at Second St Albans and at Towton in 1461 may possibly have been larger still.[3]

The English tactical doctrine in the second half of the fifteenth century was for archers to shoot off their arrows in an attempt to disrupt the enemy and provoke an attack. Trained to do so from an early age, archers wielding longbows could engage at extreme range in excess of 300 yards and might let loose up to seventeen arrows a minute. A popular phrase on the Continent was to say something was 'as thick as arrows in an English battle'. The impact of a hail of arrows on densely packed ranks of soldiery would have been fearsome. Only quality plate armour worn by the men-at-arms was fully proof against it and even plate was not completely resistant to the impact of a crossbow bolt. An Italian commentator, Dominic Mancini, considered an Englishman's bow and arrow to be thicker than other nations and that the English archer was of a stronger build, 'for they seem to have hands and arms of iron'. Not all English counties could necessarily supply the numbers of archers required for large-scale campaigning. Henry V relied heavily on drafts of archers from Lancashire, Cheshire and South Wales for his 1415 campaign in France. According to historian Anne Curry, 80 per cent of the English army which invaded France were archers, but whereas bowmen were raised en masse for service overseas, whether this was true during the Wars of the Roses is less certain. A herald's description of Henry VII's army at the Battle of Stoke in 1487 states there to have been a billman at every bowman's back, implying that almost 50 per cent of the royal army that day comprised billmen. Leaving aside the less numerous men-at-arms, the balance of the armies which fought at Towton may therefore have been an almost equal split between archers and billmen. Because the opposing archers may have largely cancelled each other out during Edward IV's wars (with a few notable exceptions), decision in battle probably only came when opposing billmen and men-at-arms clashed in hand-to-hand combat.

Handguns and field guns were also becoming more important than hitherto. As we have seen, both sides had been quick to learn the lessons of this new style of warfare. The future Richard III, too young to have fought at Towton, later wrote to King Louis XI thanking him for the gift of a bombard, saying he had always taken great pleasure in artillery and considered the gift 'a special treasure'. The era boasted a growing number of super-heavy bombards. Ottoman Sultan Mehmed's gun at the Siege of Constantinople in 1453 was so big and powerful it could fire a ball weighing half a ton. King James II of Scotland's famous Mons Meg was capable of firing stone balls weighing 440 pounds (200 kilograms). Edward IV's French contemporary, King Louis XI, is known to have established a great artillery park near Orleans, described by the Milanese ambassador as 'a stupendous thing'. Edward too would later take a keen interest in modernising and upgrading the royal artillery train.

The bulk of the common foot soldiers in English armies would have worn stud-reinforced jackets known as brigandines, made from canvas and steel plates, sometimes with shoulder and breast armour attached. There were various types of infantrymen's protective headgear, including the conical bascinet and the squat kettle helmet. Anecdotally archers routinely discarded head protection as it interfered with the process of pulling a bowstring back as far as the ear. A rich nobleman's plate-armour protection may by this time have been shaped in the new Gothic style, elegantly designed, yet fashioned to maximise protection. Grooves and channels in the tempered steel deflected lance thrusts and the strike of swords and arrows; spiked features on some suits of armour sought to lessen the deadly effect of the dominant melee weapon of the age, the pollaxe, a lethal bludgeoning and stabbing tool combining the offensive features of a hatchet, pike and serrated hammer. Once the preserve of common foot soldiers, the pollaxe had become the weapon of choice for most men-at-arms who discarded shields and dismounted from their horses to wield it two-handed. The most common helmets worn by knights and men-at-arms were the salade, or sallet – a helmet kept in position by a chin strap, permitting freedom of movement and unrestricted circulation of air, both things being major drawbacks of a man-at arm's earlier protective headgear – and the Barbute – a helmet with a pointed top, rounded cheek-pieces and a small opening for the face in the style of the Greek helmets of antiquity.

Secondary accounts of the Battle of Towton assert that the Lancastrians employed two mounted cavalry wings. In no other battles of the Wars of the Roses is this known to have been the case, but Towton may have been an exception. When fighting mounted and hand-to-hand, cavalrymen fought with lances, swords, battleaxes, maces and flails, the latter being spiked balls of iron attached to a pole by a chain. Contemporary colour illustrations of battles like Barnet and Tewkesbury, fought ten years later, depict Edward and his knights fighting on horseback wearing black-leaded armour and wielding lances. For these battles the images owe more to artistic licence than fact, since the knights and men-at-arms at Barnet and Tewkesbury (Edward included) are thought to have fought on foot. The risk to unarmoured or partly armoured horses from arrows militated against mounted cavalrymen charging a steady enemy. For this reason expensive warhorses would usually have been kept well to the rear with the baggage, cared for by pages; however, at Towton things may have been different.

On the morning of the battle dawn broke darkly overcast with snow flurries coating the hillsides. Had the day dawned brisk and bright, knowledge that the Yorkist rearguard had still to arrive might have encouraged an immediate and arguably decisive Lancastrian attack. Reconnaissance, however, proved problematic: the opposing forces remained of uncertain strength, restraining the Lancastrian commanders to caution. Bowmen on both sides opened hostilities by firing off arrows into the swirling murk. Fauconberg's archers inflicted the greater damage, assisted by a developing, blizzard-like wind from the south, bringing the Lancastrians to the north within effective range more quickly. Abbot Whethamstede later claimed God made the wind blow strongly in the faces of the Lancastrians, impeding their bowmen.

Around noon, with the blizzard abating, Norfolk's approaching rearguard at last became visible. Seeing that Edward would soon be reinforced, the Lancastrian commanders launched an immediate assault. According to de Waurin's account, Henry Beaufort, Henry Holland and Lord Rivers opened their attack with a successful cavalry charge against the Yorkist left flank. Broken Yorkist troops fled back down the road toward Ferrybridge for eleven miles. The chronicler claimed Henry Percy failed to support the attack from the other flank and was scapegoated as a consequence.

Edward was busy encouraging his troops when the first alarm went up. When he saw Henry VI's banner being hoisted, he placed himself beside his own great banner. Throughout he is said to have fought like 'a new Hector, another Achilles'. Standing head-and-shoulders taller than most men around him, bedecked in shining Gothic armour, he proved an inspiring sight to his followers and an intimidating one to his opponents. Rather than sycophantic embellishment, this description of the young king in battle bears critical scrutiny. The Bishop of Salisbury later remarked that the day might have been lost had not 'the prince [King Edward] single-handed put himself forward as nobly as he did, with the utmost of human courage'. However, it was not Edward's courage alone, nor Fauconberg's archers, nor Henry Percy's negligence, nor even the protracted and bloody hand-to-hand fighting that caused the Lancastrian collapse; it was the belated arrival of Norfolk's rearguard, spearheaded by Howard's East Anglians, described in Hearne's Fragment as 'a fresh band of good men' who, somehow navigating across the unyieldingly boggy ground north of Scarthingwell, pushed in against the Lancastrian left flank and turned the day. Even then the Lancastrians only gave ground grudgingly; assailed in front and flank, the exhausted Lancastrians soldiers, many trapped beside the gorge of the Cock Beck, were in the end subjected to a bloody slaughter. The imaginative *Croyland Chronicler* claimed 'the blood of the slain, intermingled with the snow, ran in horrible wise down the furrows and ditches'.

Other defeated Lancastrians fled north, but the bridge at Tadcaster was down, destroyed on Henry Beaufort's orders to prevent the Yorkists marching on York. Desperate to escape the carnage, heavily armoured men-at-arms and footmen – some wearing thick padded jackets which soaked up water and became incredibly heavy – drowned trying to swim across. Others were killed in the town itself. Unlike at Northampton, common soldiers might not have been spared. Because of regional antipathy and the northern army's ill-discipline on the road to St Albans, the killing may for a time have become indiscriminate. Even plate-armoured men-at-arms when stumbling around on foot were vulnerable to the swarms of pursuing foot soldiers armed with knives and axes. After a later battle an anonymous combatant recalled,

We had a great number of stragglers [foot soldiers/auxiliaries?] following us which flocked about the men-at-arms overthrown and slew most of them. For the greatest part of the said stragglers had hatchets in their hands, wherewith they used to cut wood to make our lodgings, with the which hatchets they brake the vizards of their headpieces and then clave their heads; for otherwise they would hardly have been slain, they were so surely armed, so that there were ever three or four [stragglers] about one of them.

From an early report of the battle, Bishop George Neville in London claimed the dead at Towton lay unburied 'over a space nearly six miles in length and three or four furlongs broad'. Heavily inflated casualty estimates alleged upwards of 20,000 dead: Neville quoted 28,000 'on one side and the other'. They were numbers described by Richard Beauchamp, Bishop of Salisbury, as 'unheard of in our realm for almost a thousand years'. Polydore Vergil's account speaks of 20,000 casualties inclusive of prisoners, indicating that the slaughter was not as all-encompassing as has sometimes been claimed – that at some stage quarter must have been given. Another chronicler more plausibly settled on 9,000 dead. Whatever the true figure, it is clear that the scale of loss at Towton was considered at the time to have been unprecedented in living memory. Local communities in Yorkshire and further afield were sorely impacted for years to come.[4] Bishop Neville wrote of the English nobility, 'O miserable and luckless race and powerful people, would you have no spark of pity for our blood, of which we have lost so much of fine quality by the civil war.' The churchman would rather his fellow countrymen had kept their swords unsullied to do battle with the Turks who were then menacing Europe. The last bastion of the Eastern Roman Empire, Constantinople, had been sacked by them eighteen years before. Bloodletting between Christian brothers seemed to the bishop to be an abject and intolerable waste, whereas a similar slaughter of Turks would have been, in Neville's words, 'a great stroke and blow'.

Andrew Trollope was among those who fell in battle, escaping the otherwise inevitable executioner's axe. As well as Clifford, killed at Ferrybridge, Henry Percy died too, along with a number of other notables including Lord Dacre, shot through the neck by an arrow when removing his helmet to get some air, and Lord

Welles, the latter a veteran of Blore Heath and Second St Albans. Famous for his Houdini-like escape exploits at First St Albans and Mortimer's Cross, James Butler may or may not have been present at Towton, but fled north anyway, hoping to get back to Ireland. On this occasion the plucky grandee's luck ran out. He was captured at Cockermouth in Cumbria and later executed at Newcastle. Captured too was the already badly wounded Thomas Courtenay. Unable to get far because of his injuries, he was taken and beheaded at York. Henry Beaufort managed to escape outright. Other notables who got clean away were Henry Holland, Lord Thomas Ros, Sir Humphrey Dacre, Henry Stafford and Sir John Fortescue. In flight they linked up with the Lancastrian royal family. All rode together post-haste for the Scottish borders.

This clutch of escapees to one side, the weight of Lancastrian lords opposing Edward had been lifted. In a letter from London to the Milanese court, dated 14 April 1461, an unknown correspondent wrote, 'Their side [the Lancastrians] is practically destroyed and King Edward has become master and governor of the whole realm'.[5] After the battle, Edward, now by God's grace a 'full king', knighted six men who had distinguished themselves in the fighting. They included stalwarts like Howard and Hastings. In a grossly disproportionate offset, he executed forty-two captured Lancastrian knights. Little wonder that the Milanese ambassador Prospero di Camulio saw the bloodletting in England as a vicious power struggle, pure and simple, without any redeeming features. After riding in triumph that Palm Sunday through corpse-strewn fields to the City of York, Edward had the mouldering, tar-blackened heads of his father, uncle and brother removed from Micklegate Bar, replacing them with gruesome trophies of his own.[6]

The Lancastrians may have been down, but they were not out. Although Henry's reign seemed as good as over, there remained hope the queen might yet attract sufficient support at home and abroad to confront the new Yorkist regime. As mentioned previously, the Scottish regent's price for granting the exiled royal family refuge at Edinburgh was to press for the marriage of Henry's son, Edward of Lancaster, into the Scottish royal family, as well as the transfer to Scottish control of the fortress towns of Berwick-upon-Tweed and Carlisle. In Italy, reports circulated warnings of fresh outbreaks of violence in England should Henry, the queen and the prince not soon be captured by King Edward. Writing to the pope on 1 June 1461, Francesco Coppini considered Edward IV had 'not yet made himself supreme over the whole kingdom or reduced it to peace'. It was probably for this reason that the as yet uncrowned king lingered in Yorkshire, where he kept Easter, before progressing westward into Lancashire and Cheshire, counties with a strong Lancastrian affinity he hoped to win over. By 26 June, however, he was at Sheen Palace on the final leg of his journey to London. Along the way he was welcomed by the city's mayor, accompanied by a bodyguard of men decked out in scarlet attire, plus 400 common soldiers, well horsed and clad in green. Upon receiving the breaking news of a Scottish attack on Carlisle, Edward hurriedly brought forward the date of his coronation – unnecessarily as it turned out. Although Berwick had been lost on 25 April, the Siege of Carlisle was quickly broken up by Edward's capable cousin John Neville.

Edward's coronation eventually took place at Westminster on 28 June 'with great triumph and honour'. The Archbishop of Canterbury presided. Since the fourteenth-century a king's coronation oath confirmed his observance and upholding of the laws and liberties of England and the maintenance of peace, justice and mercy in the land. Vowing to do this, Edward created thirty-two new knights of the Bath to mark the occasion. Close family members and those who had served him faithfully up until now gained new titles. His twelve-year-old brother, George, became the Duke of Clarence and was made Lieutenant of Ireland – probably the normal practice for those next in line to the succession. Edward's nine-year-old brother, Richard, gained the title Duke of Gloucester. The boys had only recently arrived back from Utrecht. Edward's Lord Treasurer, Lord Bourchier, was created Earl of Essex; the doughty Lord Fauconberg became Earl of Kent. John Neville (Warwick's brother) was made Lord Montagu. Sir William Hastings, knighted after the Battle of Towton, also gained a peerage, henceforth to be known as Lord Hastings. Sir John Howard, the unsung hero of Towton, was elevated too: the upwardly mobile, newly made knight became a baron – under Richard III he would be raised to a dukedom. Sir William Herbert, who would become Edward's lynchpin in Wales, was also made a baron. Edward's father was remembered too. The king found time to order the construction at St Paul's of an elaborate memorial honouring the dead duke. The final construct was adorned with silver roses and golden suns, the main Yorkist emblems, illuminated by candles and guarded by 420 gilded angels.

The Earl of Warwick's rewards were the most spectacular of all. Edward showered great honours on him: Lord Chamberlain, Master of the King's Mews, Warden of the Cinque Ports, Constable of Dover Castle, Captain of Calais, Lord High Admiral of England and Warden of the West March toward Scotland. Lesser honours were also bestowed on him: stewardships, lordships and the like. Many of these were from confiscated Percy estates. Not only did Warwick gain enormously from being on the winning Yorkist side, he also inherited his dead father's landholdings, making him by far the wealthiest magnate in the land. His marriage to Anne de Beauchamp in 1449 had already made him a powerful and well-connected nobleman. Now, like Edward's dead father, Warwick had become an overmighty subject and, as it would turn out, a remarkably greedy one too.

At Edward's first session of parliament on 4 November 1461, the king gained acclaim from the speaker Sir John Strangeways for his 'personal beauty' and for 'his redemption and salvation of his subjects'. Edward thanked the commons for their 'true hearts and tender considerations', remembering too 'the horrible murder and cruel deaths' of his father and brother at Wakefield.[7] It was reported by foreign observers that the English loved and adored their new king as if he were a god, and this for a time may have been true. An Act of Attainder was passed on 113 adversaries, yielding an amassment of landed revenue probably unmatched in medieval times, most of which was settled on men trusted by Edward to establish or tighten provincial control. The young king also remained open to the rehabilitation of former Lancastrians.

Anecdotal evidence indicates Edward to have been a relatively carefree young man, well attuned to taking advantage of new friendships and opportunities, always keen to win men over by his charm. Maintaining such a stance had clear advantages, since there was otherwise the danger that he would become over-reliant on the Nevilles for his core support, a family described by Professor Lander as 'a narrow clique'. Edward's attempts at reintegration – some of which succeeded, but not all – helped to widen the network of men he might call on in the future and also helped kick-start the country back toward normalcy, an important consideration for any leader after a period of upheaval. By 1470, just over eight years into his reign, twenty attainders against former Lancastrians had been reversed.

Not all agreed with the king's approach, however, and some were openly critical. In East Anglia the following year, it was said that the common people grudged the way the king received men who had in the past been his and their enemies. Two men the critics had in mind were Sir Thomas Tuddenham and John Heydon, both pardoned by Edward at around this time. Once members of William de la Pole's court clique, they were men close to Queen Margaret. Tuddenham soon proved disloyal. Caught up in a plot hatched by John de Vere, Earl of Oxford, and Oxford's son Aubrey de Vere, he was arrested with them on 12 February 1462 and executed on Tower Hill a fortnight later.

John de Vere's career is characteristic of these times. A cautious man, the earl had avoided fighting at the First St Albans, being, he alleged, always a day's march behind the king. Keeping his head down, he remained uncommitted to either side until as late as 1459. Then, like most others, he rallied to the royalist camp on the eve of Ludford Bridge. For his belated loyalty he was tasked with raising forces to subdue pro-Yorkist unrest in Essex. After the Yorkist victory at Northampton, fearful of the reception he would receive in London, he retired to his estates, apparently too ill to engage further in public life. Not viewed as dangerous, he was pardoned 'in consideration of his infirmities' by Warwick's incoming Yorkist administration; not so his son Aubrey, a member of the queen's inner circle, who remained at large and fought on the Lancastrian side at Second St Albans and possibly at Towton too. It was Oxford's son's continued intransigence that proved to be the earl's downfall. As mentioned, father and son were among those rounded up with Tuddenham by a commission set up by Edward to root out treasonable activities – an effort which ranged over twenty-five counties and eight cities and which almost immediately netted the de Vere's and their fellow co-conspirators. The condemned men were tried by Edward's new Lord High Constable of England, John Tiptoft, Earl of Worcester.

Edward could ill afford to be squeamish and had by this time become hardened to the spilling of blood. The Lancastrian regime had some fight left in it, especially with the old king at large and capable of attracting support. Plots arising from time to time had to be ruthlessly put down, but to gain wider acceptance the new king also made sure he was seen by as many of his people as possible. At Bristol he was said by *The Great Chronicle of London* to have been 'royally received, with great solemnity'. At the gates of the city he was welcomed by an actor playing the role of William the Conqueror, flanked by two lords. Over the gates stood a giant holding the keys to the city. At the Temple Cross a re-enactment of St George slaying the dragon was played out – a pageant harking at continuity and nationhood, honouring the new king.[8]

Two men in particular were militarily empowered by Edward at around this time: the newly made peers Lord William Herbert and Lord Ferrers. Like Herbert, Ferrers (formally Sir Walter Devereux) had fought with Edward at Mortimer's Cross. He had led a substantial force of retainers from estates in Wales on the day of the battle. Ferrers and Herbert had been allied to the Yorkist cause from the very start. Together they had brought a 2,000-strong army into West Wales in August 1456 to enforce Edward's father's authority there. Their most notable success at that time had been the seizure of Carmarthen Castle from Edmund Tudor. Edmund had been imprisoned by them until it was ordered he be released by command of King Henry, but had, as mentioned before, died of plague shortly afterwards. Herbert and Ferrers had then moved on to capture Aberystwyth, another of York's castle's taken by the Tudors. Both men had then been placed under arrest by Henry VI and had for a time been confined in the Tower, but by the following autumn they were set free. Herbert then broke his parole when he again ravaged Tudor estates, attracting a bounty of 500 marks. He was pardoned as part of the more general series of amnesties following the 'Love Day' at St Paul's.

After Towton, Herbert and Ferrers continued their partnership, capturing the Lancastrian stronghold of Pembroke Castle on 30 September 1462 and defeating the resurgent forces of Jasper Tudor and Henry Holland at the Battle of Twt Hill, outside Caernarvon, a month later. Denbigh Castle fell to them at the turn of the year. They followed up this success by capturing the castle at Carreg Cennen in Carmarthenshire in the spring. By then only the men of Harlech Castle held firm for the Lancastrians in Wales, remaining a thorn in the Yorkist side until the summer of 1468, when Herbert's forces finally captured the castle.

Despite his victory at Towton and successes since, Edward remained insecure. The North of England, though cowed, remained hostile to him. Active enemies were at large across the border in Scotland, a nation ever ready to take advantage of English weakness. Given that he was a usurper, even a minor defeat in the field had the potential to threaten his rule. The last usurper English king – Henry of Bolingbroke, who became Henry IV – had successfully brought his enemies to battle at Shrewsbury in 1403, yet afterwards had never really felt secure upon the throne. Elizabeth I would later say that 'more men worship the rising sun than the setting sun', but there would always be exceptions. Rather than continue to put his life in danger, however, Edward determined to engage his enemies diplomatically, concluding this to be a more effective use of his time than chasing rebels back and forth across the Scottish and Welsh borders – something that could be more effectively delegated to others. With foreign assistance, he sought to stem the supplies of mercenaries and arms shipments to his opponents: in particular those emanating from Scotland and France. The Yorkist king remained aware, however, that delegation could only go so far. When later threatened by a full-scale foreign invasion from those countries, he rode north into Yorkshire to take personal charge of the army. Nagging at Edward too was the need to distance himself politically from Warwick. There is anecdotal evidence that he and Warwick did not always get along. Other than the Yorkist cause they espoused, the cousins may have had little else in common. Warwick sought self-aggrandisement, whereas Edward looked to the long-term survival of his dynasty. Several days after the Battle of Towton was fought, the Milanese ambassador, Prospero de Camulio, had with prescience predicted that 'before long grievances and recriminations will break out between King Edward and Warwick'.[9]

Edward probably felt more at ease with friends of his own making: less pushy and controlling men like the lords Hastings and Herbert, as well as a number of other relative newcomers at court. These included Humphrey Stafford, created Lord Stafford in 1461; Viscount Henry Bourchier, Edward's first Lord Treasurer; John Tiptoft, Earl of Worcester, made Lord High Constable of

England and later Deputy Lieutenant General of Ireland; John Tuchet, Baron Audley, an ex-Lancastrian who Edward trusted as an administrator; Sir John Wenlock, who, like Audley, had fought at Edward's side at Mortimer's Cross, a soldier and diplomat created a baron; Sir Walter Blount, Edward's Lord Treasurer from 1464; Sir Walter Devereaux, made Lord Ferrers; and last but not least, Sir John Howard, the soldier who had turned the day at Towton, described by one modern historian as an unusually 'loyal, dependable magnate'.[10] From this list of 'new men' only Lord Wenlock would in the end prove disloyal.

Of the younger Nevilles, Edward may have warmed more to Warwick's brother John Neville, raised to the peerage as Lord Montagu. Aged around thirty in 1461, John Neville (known from now on in the narrative as Montagu) appears to have been a less calculating personage than his brother, more a soldier than a politician. Twice seized by the Lancastrians, he had lived to tell the tale. Captured after the Second St Albans, instead of facing summary execution, which would arguably have been a prudent expediency on the part of the queen's commanders, he had been incarcerated at York and only freed by Edward's troops after the Battle of Towton. Trusted by Edward to spearhead operations against the remaining Lancastrians at large, he had successfully relieved Carlisle in June 1461. Three months later, operating together with his brother Warwick, he had retaken the port of Alnwick on the main road into Scotland, close to the Northumberland coast. Edward continued to reward Montagu well. Other than the peerage he gained, he was awarded the stewardship of all of the duchy of Lancaster lands in East Anglia.

Prior to the fall of Alnwick, Queen Margaret of Anjou's hopes of support from France had suffered a major setback when the French king, Charles VII, died on 22 July 1461. Charles's successor, Louis XI – a medieval workaholic who did 'everything out of his own head', known as 'the universal spider' for the webs of intrigue he wove and his agile temperament – was more cautious in offering his kinswoman support, even though Margaret allegedly offered to cede Calais to him in return for soldiers and arms. She really needed to meet the new king face to face to push her case, but her envoys in France warned her in correspondence, intercepted by Warwick, against making the perilous journey from Scotland across the North Sea because of heavy Yorkist naval patrols. They concluded their letter by restating their heartfelt loyalty, saying, 'Without death take us by the way, which we trust he will not, till we see the King and you possible again in your realm, the which we beseech God soon to see, and to send you [all] that your Highness desires.'

Yorkist build-up of naval strength in the North Sea and orders for warning beacons to be made ready on the south coast reveal genuine fears of an impending multi-pronged invasion of England. The numbers of enemy troops massing against them were estimated to comprise up to 225,000 soldiers from Scotland, France, Burgundy, Spain, Denmark, Sicily and Portugal. The de Vere executions, mentioned earlier, were carried out during the climate of fear engendered by these (probably overstated) foreign threats. Fear of invasion also facilitated Edward's government being able to raise money in the city to rearm. In a letter dated 13 March 1462, the king wrote to a London Alderman saying the Lancastrians were fomenting 'such war, depopulation and robbery and manslaughter as here before has not been used among Christian people ... [they would seek to extinguish] the people, the name, the tongue and the blood English of this our said realm'.[11] Edward cunningly used the possibility of foreign intervention to bolster support for his fledgling Yorkist regime, discouraging Lancastrian sympathy within the kingdom.

Other than the danger from the Continent, another area of concern for Edward was Ireland. After laying low in Cumbria or Strathclyde for a time, the Earl of Wiltshire's brother, John Butler of Ormond, had managed to escape capture after Towton.

He arrived back in Ireland in the winter of 1461/2. He had strong support in Kilkenny and Tipperary, but was opposed by Thomas FitzGerald, Earl of Desmond, the leader of the pro-Yorkist government in Dublin. In the spring of 1462 open warfare broke out between the two factions. In the summer a running fight occurred at Piltdown, near Rogerstown Castle, in County Kilkenny. Butler's army was destroyed, suffering over 1,000 casualties. The battle effectively ended Lancastrian hopes of gaining influence across the Irish Sea and underpinned FitzGerald control for half a century or more.

Meanwhile, Lancastrian diehards were holding out in Northumberland, where a network of strong, inaccessible castles – the main ones being Bamburgh, Alnwick and Dunstanburgh – provided them with a safe refuge capable of supply from the sea. Persistent Lancastrian counter-attacks had seen the enemy regain previously lost strongholds in the area. During the winter of 1461/2 William Tailboys, a veteran of Second St Albans and Towton, recaptured Alnwick for Henry VI, while his colleague Lord Dacre reoccupied the Dacre-family stronghold at Naworth, near Carlisle.

Such periodic regroupings of insurgents in the North proved impossible to prevent and led to full-scale rebellions occurring in the autumn of 1462 and again in the late spring of the following year. On the first occasion, Sir Ralph Percy, reluctantly holding Northumberland for Edward, had been persuaded by Queen Margaret, at the head of a small army of 800 French soldiers and a few Scots, to hand back the Northumberland castles. The queen and her backers were soon driven off, however, by news of Edward's army's approach. Edward rode north at the head of his vanguard, taking personal command of the army. His relieving force encompassed the retinues of seven earls, thirty-one barons and fifty-nine knights. Such an impressive gathering soon set the enemy to flight.[12] Fleeing Lancastrians took ship at Berwick on 13 November 1462, but gales drove some of their vessels ashore at Lindisfarne, where many French soldiers were slaughtered out of hand by the king's coastguard. Margaret and the French commander Pierre de Breze (the Grand Seneschal of Normandy) were more fortunate, managing to reach Scotland in a rowing boat, buffeted but unscathed.

Edward's northern thrust had paid immediate dividends, but after falling ill on arrival at Durham, probably of measles, he played little or no part in the resulting campaign to reduce the rebel-held strongholds in Northumberland. Though now considered a minor disease, even today in countries with poor vaccination programmes measles can be a very serious illness and there is anecdotal evidence that the king's illness may for a time have appeared life-threatening.[13] While he convalesced, Warwick took command of siege operations. Outside rebel-held Alnwick Castle, the earl posted the forces of Lord Fauconberg, now Earl of Kent, and those of the rehabilitated Anthony Woodville, son of Lord Rivers, who had fought with distinction on the Lancastrian side at Towton but had now thrown in his lot with Edward. Outside Bamburgh Castle forces were placed under Montagu's command, including men led by Robert, Lord Ogle, a soldier with strong familial links in the North East. Ogle had brought 600 men from the North to First St Albans. He may or may not have fought at Towton, but soon after had been busy besieging Carham in Northumberland. He had attended Edward's first parliament, being invested at that time with control of several castles in the North East, including Alnwick and Warkworth. He was also appointed for a time Warden of the East March toward Scotland, before being superseded by Montagu. Edward had backed the right man for the job. It was Ogle and his men who captured the stranded Frenchmen washed ashore on Lindisfarne Island. Confronting Dunstanburgh Castle, Warwick deployed Tiptoft's forces, as well as those of the somewhat suspect Sir Ralph Grey, a man later to be outed as a closet Lancastrian. The ailing John Mowbray, Duke of Norfolk, lay resting at Newcastle. His strong contingent of troops were charged with supplying the Yorkist siege parties with food, clothes and weaponry. As at Towton, John Howard acted for him.

No effort was made to storm any of the northern castles. All were strongly walled and garrisoned and any assault made against them would have incurred considerable expense, loss of life and the destruction of important state assets. Instead the plan was to starve the rebels into surrendering: something that was achieved on 27 December 1462 at Bamburgh and Dunstanburgh after the troops within these places had been reduced to eating their horses. The surrender terms offered by Edward's commanders at the king's bidding were generous – a reflection of Edward's wish to rehabilitate rather than to punish. Perhaps surprisingly nonetheless, Jasper Tudor, an avowed enemy of the Yorkists, was among those who accepted the king's promise of safe conduct and was allowed to return to Scotland unmolested. Even in such dangerous times it seems rules of war were studiously maintained. Even more astonishingly for a modern audience, Henry Beaufort, the architect of the Lancastrian victories at Wakefield and Second St Albans, gained a complete pardon and the full reinstatement of his lands and titles.

Elsewhere only the almost simultaneous arrival in Northumberland of a Franco/Lancastrian/Scots army, led by Pierre de Breze and the Scottish Earl of Angus, prevented the fall of Alnwick Castle and prevented a planned, punitive incursion into Scotland by the English in the spring of 1463. By this time the ailing Duke of Norfolk had passed away and Edward's slowly returning health remained a concern. Sickness was stalking the English encampments too. Edward's soldiers had endured a long spell of hardship, having, it was said by the chronicler John Warkworth, 'lain there so long in the field, grieved with cold and rain'.[14] The newly arrived enemy coalition were probably for a time in a stronger position than the Yorkists. Had they boldly attacked they might have sent the king's dispirited soldiery packing, but in the event de Breze and Angus blinked first. Alnwick was abandoned by them and their army withdrew back across the Scottish border. What historian John Gillingham has dubbed 'the normal battle-avoiding pattern of war on the continent', rather than 'the more immediately decisive, battle-seeking pattern of the Wars of the Roses', militated, for reasons unknown, against a confrontation.[15]

The decision made by Edward to restore Henry Beaufort to his former station, like some of his other decisions at this period, remains baffling, especially so since the duke had already broken his solemn oath to the Yorkists on at least one occasion before and was directly implicated in the deaths of Edward's father and brother. After the Battle of Newnham Bridge, fought in the Pas de Calais in July 1460, he had vowed never again to take up arms against the Yorkist earls, yet had almost immediately done so. Whether Beaufort's reprieve represented a genuine desire on the twenty-year-old king's part to draw a line under past quarrels, or something more facile – vanity, rashness, over-confidence or naivety have all been suggested – is impossible to establish now with any degree of confidence. Edward may genuinely have hoped to win over the likeable and militarily talented duke. Described since as being 'hollow optimism' on the king's part, in truth the long-term success of his regime depended on taking risks with erstwhile enemies. To what extent Warwick colluded in the reconciliation is unclear; had the duke been captured immediately after Towton he would presumably have faced a similar end to other men then classed as traitors. Since Towton, Edward had shown no compunction in sanctioning the execution of lesser enemies. An example was Sir Baldwin Fulford, a naval man once tasked with commanding a fleet to intercept and prevent Warwick liaising with York in Ireland. Fulford's decapitated head now adorned the market cross at Exeter.

An easy man to like, Henry Beaufort shared many of the king's winning ways. Edward is said to have feted him, hunted with him and attended tournaments with him. On one occasion the two men even shared a bed together – a circumstance attributable to necessity rather than passion.[16] The reconciliation proved unpopular, however. In the summer of 1463 Edward rode north with Beaufort and 200 of the duke's men, all 'well horsed and well harnessed'. When the royal party reached Northampton the common people rioted. The situation became sufficiently concerning and widespread for Edward's companion to be hurriedly spirited away to far-off Wales for safety. Edward apparently supplied the townsfolk with 'a tun of wine to drink' to deflect attention, allowing the duke to make his getaway. To avoid further disturbances Beaufort's armed retainers were then sent north to help garrison Newcastle – an odd duty of trust for men who had so recently been Edward's enemies. During this brief honeymoon period between king and pardoned subject, the French king, Louis XI, was told by agents that Edward kept Henry Beaufort, Duke of Somerset, close at all times. The Machiavellian/mafia dictum 'keep your friends close but your enemies closer' comes to mind. Feigning loyalty to Edward, Sir Ralph Percy also gained reprieve. Edward reinstated him at Bamburgh and even allowed the knight the discretion to harbour un-attainted Lancastrians within his castle's walls.

Sir Ralph Percy was more than simply a man with latent Lancastrian sympathies, he had fought on the Lancastrian side at First St Albans and at Wakefield. He missed Towton however. This presumably excluded him from the otherwise all-encompassing Act of Attainder meted out after the battle. It appears Edward did not feel strong enough in the North East of England to rule without Percy backing. Even after the aborted Franco-Scottish invasion of the previous year, Northumberland, Durham, Westmorland and Cumberland remained decidedly Lancastrian in sympathy. Relying on men like Sir Ralph Percy to keep the peace in the North was a risk Edward was probably forced to take. Rather than rely completely on Percy's word, however, the king appointed the energetic Montagu to overall command of the East March, replacing Lord Ogle. Montagu's remit incorporated Sir Ralph's territorial holdings and the castles now once again in Percy's care. The role might have suited Lord Fauconberg, but Edward's sixty-two-year-old uncle had by this time fallen ill and died, possibly of the camp fever which had raged throughout the winter. Although a reluctant Yorkist, remaining until the end emotionally attached to Henry VI, Fauconberg had been the main architect of Yorkist military success up until now and would be sorely missed.[17]

By the summer of 1463 the situation in Northumberland had deteriorated to the extent that Warwick and his brother Montagu were again drawn northward at Edward's instigation. Parliamentary reports from this time mention the Scots and the Lancastrian rebels continually molesting the kingdom. Margaret of Anjou had mustered a sizeable force to threaten England, achieved, allegedly, by promising Mary of Guelders seven English counties as the price of Scottish armed support. In early July a Scottish army crossed the border and laid siege to Norham Castle. Present at the siege were Henry VI, Queen Margaret, Mary of Guelders and her son, the boy-king James III of Scotland. Predictably, Sir Ralph Percy immediately changed sides and greeted both queens with open arms, but what at first appeared to be a promising enterprise soon turned into a fiasco when the Neville brothers surprised the besieging forces at Norham and sent them packing across the border. The Nevilles then launched punitive raids into the southern Scottish shires, ravaging these much-fought-over border areas before falling back into Northumberland. Tiptoft – at the time Edward's Lord High Admiral – operated off the Northumberland coast with the fleet. Edward initially remained behind in Northampton but had advanced to York by the end of the year. The likely reason for his lack of urgency was that while travelling north he had successfully concluded an Anglo-French truce (dated to October 1463) scuppering any lingering hopes Margaret of Anjou might have harboured of forming another grand coalition to confront him.

Not long after this, for reasons that remain obscure, Henry

Beaufort chose to reassert his allegiance to the Lancastrian cause. By December 1463, after narrowly avoiding recapture near Durham, the recalcitrant duke was once again ensconced at Bamburgh Castle with Sir Ralph Percy. With them too was Henry VI, once more a pawn for a would-be power broker. Beaufort hoped to play the same game as the Yorkists had done in the past by using the possession of King Henry's person to assert his authority and legislate against Edward. Not all important Lancastrian eggs were in the same Bamburgh Castle basket however. Frustrated by the expensive and half-hearted support she had received from the Scots, who were now in the process of agreeing a lasting truce with Edward's emissaries, Queen Margaret and Edward of Lancaster had by this time set sail for France.

From Bamburgh, Henry Beaufort was soon raiding inland, threatening to raise a widespread rebellion by fomenting insurgencies in Wales, Lancashire, Cheshire and the North East, where Norham Castle was again placed under siege. Excited foreign observers proclaimed him to be seeking to establish an independent principality in the far north of England in opposition to Edward. Beaufort's defection must have proved a bitter reality check for a king who had staked his hopes on an accommodation with his powerful cousin but had seen them dashed.

Hedgeley Moor and Hexham

By mid to late April 1464, peace envoys from Edinburgh, under a close escort provided by Montagu, were on route south to York. Henry Beaufort determined to ambush the delegation and scuttle the talks, but failed to do so when his quarry was tipped off. Montagu avoided the trap being set for him by taking an alternative road. On 25 April, now ready to fight, Edward's cousin confronted the Lancastrians south of the town of Wooler, near to where the Roman road from Hexham to Berwick crosses

Hedgeley Moor. Beaufort is said to have started out with just 'four score spears and bows too', but by the time the fight at Hedgeley Moor took place the same chronicler had inflated Lancastrian numbers to an improbable 5,000 men. Displaying his true colours at last, Sir Ralph Percy led the Lancastrian charge. Tradition has it that his horse suffered a mortal wound at a place called Percy's Leap. The knight drove his dying charger forward for another half a mile before dismounting, but was then struck down in the resulting melee. As he lay dying he was claimed to have cried out that he had 'saved the bird in his bosom', meaning, presumably, that he had at last redeemed his oath of loyalty to Henry VI. A stone column called Percy's Cross, decorated with the Percy badge of shackle bolts and a crescent, stands today on the spot where tradition states Sir Ralph died. His loss caused a dramatic collapse of morale in the Lancastrian ranks. Gregory's Chronicle relates how Beaufort's army was 'discomforted and put to rebuke, and every man avoided and took his way with sorry hearts'. Beaufort escaped, as did his bodyguard of noblemen.

After securing Norham Castle and escorting the Scottish ambassadors safely to Newcastle, Montagu retraced his steps and brought the survivors of Hedgeley Moor to battle south of Hexham on 15 May 1464. This ill-documented action is reputed to have occurred on a hill beside the heavily wooded banks of the Devil's Water, a tributary of the Tyne. Modern research locates the battlefield site at or near Swallowship Hill, south-east of Hexham.[18] Little fighting took place, the sparse accounts of the battle describe a rout rather than a protracted contest. It appears the Lancastrians were heavily outnumbered and soon defeated. A contemporary chronicle told how 'the duke [of Somerset] with the great part of his army, and the whole of his force was broken into pieces'. Henry Beaufort was caught attempting to flee. No formalities were enacted. The intractable nobleman was dragged to the nearest clearing and immediately beheaded. His burial took place at Hexham Abbey. In a gory repeat of Towton's aftermath, further beheadings were enacted soon after. The first batch were dealt with at Newcastle. Lord Thomas Ros, Lord Hungerford, Sir William Tailboys and two others were all executed there. Tailboys had been captured in a coal pit near Newcastle, along with 'much money ... gold and silver that should have gone to King Henry'. Gregory's Chronicle claimed the coins were to pay the wages of soldiers unwilling 'to go one foot with him [King Henry] until they had money'. The second batch of half a dozen or so men were executed at Middleham Castle in Yorkshire on 18 May. The final executions took place at York, where, after a quasi-judicial process overseen by Sir John Tiptoft, fourteen other unfortunates were decapitated in two shifts for the headsman on 25 and 28 May. The scale of retribution, though sizeable, was not comprehensive. Among those who escaped retribution was Henry Beaufort's younger brother Edmund, who fled to France.

Edmund Beaufort had not taken part in any of the early battles of the Wars of the Roses. After spending two years captive in the Tower, he had been released in the summer of 1463 as a favour by Edward to Edmund's elder brother. His being held captive had doubtless prevented Montagu's execution after Second St Albans. Now styling himself the 3rd Duke of Somerset, the twenty-six-year-old determined to avenge his brother's death.

As recompense for his victories at Hedgeley Moor and Hexham, Lord Montagu was made Earl of Northumberland and was later granted control of all the Percy estates in Northumberland, as well as the full honours of the duchy of Lancaster, including ownership of a number of key castles, such as Alnwick, Warkworth, Tickhill, Knaresborough and Pontefract. Lord Ogle may have been put out by this. He had earlier been granted the custody of some of these forfeited Percy estates. To compensate him for his loss Edward granted him the lordship of Redesdale, as well as other lands forfeited after Hexham, including Harbottle Castle in Northumberland.

The campaign to stamp out the last remaining Lancastrian

resistance in England was all but over. Alnwick and Dunstanburgh Castles were surrendered respectively on 23 and 24 June, the latter after a general assault. Bamburgh held on for a further few days. When summoned to surrender, Warwick's herald stressed to the rebel commander Sir Ralph Grey that Edward did not wish to see the walls slighted because of Bamburgh's strategic importance to the kingdom, saying, 'The King, our most dread sovereign lord, specially desires to have this jewel whole and unbroken by artillery, particularly because it marches close to his ancient enemies, the Scots.' Because he had changed sides before, Grey may have been denied the general pardon offered to others and so refused the summons. A destructive artillery bombardment ensued. The huge cannon which had already overawed Alnwick and Dunstanburgh now poured forth fire and destruction on Bamburgh. The highly prized artillery pieces had names like 'Edward', 'Newcastle' and 'London'. Whole blocks of masonry from the castle were blown into the North Sea, facilitating a general assault. This quickly resulted in the castle garrison's capitulation and the badly wounded Grey's capture after being knocked senseless by falling masonry when a smaller brass gun named 'Dijon' engaged the castle precincts. For his services at the siege, Robert, Lord Ogle, was granted the constableship of Bamburgh for life.[19] Tried at Doncaster by Tiptoft in the presence of the king, Grey was stripped of his knighthood and his spurs smitten off at the heel by the king's master cook, probably using a butcher's knife. He was then hung, drawn and quartered. His torso was buried at the local friary. His head was left to be disposed of at Edward's pleasure.[20]

MAY DAY MORN, 1464

Hushed voices and furtive steps on cold tiles. The gathering is small, the time short. Outside, muffled hoofs champ the cinder path. Within the chapel, bride and groom stand side by side at the low alter. Verses chanted by a page echo on flagstones. Words spoken by a priest, sworn to silence, are subdued. Save for this and the impatient snuffling of horses, the morning is still. While candles flicker in alcoves within, outside a watery sun betrays the shape of tangled boughs. Attendant horsemen, hardened to war, are uneasy. Leaden images, depicting a man and a woman, found discarded in an orchard nearby, suggest enchantment. Why else would the king, promised to a Savoyard Queen, agree to marry an ignoble Englishwoman older than himself, already the mother of two young sons by another man? Why too should he marry in secret?

The wedding service is hurried. Edward will have little enough time to spend alone with his bride while his men are fighting in the North, putting their bodies on the line for him. Once he has put his own body to more immediate use, he too must join them. The chanting ends. Bride and groom kiss. The service is done. The chapel empties. Footsteps recede down the cinder path back toward a walled garden and a brick-laid path. There is no piping to the marriage bed, just a startled cry, then stillness, broken at last by the muted sound of laughter.

5

THE WOODVILLE CONNECTION

Success in war was just one way Edward sought to prove himself; success with women was another. A natural outlet for an unmarried twenty-two-year-old man, unfettered by the same strict moral principles which may have constrained his predecessor. Rather than mere youthful indulgence, however, there might have been something untoward about Edward's methods of ensnaring the opposite sex. The king was held to have lured reluctant partners to bed by falsely promising matrimony. According to popular rumour, several women may have been suckered into some form of pre-nuptial arrangement by him, dishonoured once the king had satisfied his lust. Edward had at least one bastard son recognised and ennobled: Arthur Plantagenet, Viscount Lisle, later a middle-aged jousting partner of Henry VIII. He also had an illegitimate daughter. Even after Edward's marriage to Elizabeth Grey, a seductive widow, older than himself, who is said to have wisely refused his advances until after a secret marriage, the king is said to have maintained a string of mistresses. Of one, Jane Shore, Tudor historian Thomas More later wrote, 'Many he had but her he loved.'

English kings in those days, with a few notable exceptions, took mistresses as a matter of course, so for Edward to be singled out for his sexuality is telling. Henry VIII and Charles II are now popularly seen as England's most celebrated kingly lotharios, but if stories told about Edward's carousals and revelling are true, our first Yorkist king was equally, if not more rapacious. According to one of Edward's biographers, the king was ever to be found 'feasting with his lords [and] engaging in youthful debauchery'.[1] The same writer also claimed that Edward contributed almost nothing to the campaigning in the North of England after Towton, that even when insurrection threatened '[the king's] mind was not even then much bent on war'.[2] Written in a somewhat dismissive manner, comments like this have fostered the perception that Edward was at times a feckless ruler who was happier to delegate the dirty work to others, but – assuming the king not to have been engaged in love-making on a continuously compulsive basis – take no account of the pressing need for the young king to deal with other issues of state.

Doubt surrounds the circumstances of Edward's covert marriage to the Lancastrian war-widow Elizabeth Grey (née Woodville), a woman with doubtless erotic appeal seeking to secure her financial future after the death of her husband in battle. That the king married a near penniless subject, rather than the daughter of a rich and powerful foreign prince, meant that the marriage had to be kept under wraps for a time to prevent an immediate backlash from the old nobility. Edward's biographer, Professor Charles Ross, has asserted that the king's marriage into a large, grasping family from the minor nobility substantially contributed to the eventual downfall of the House of York, but takes issue with what he calls 'modern attempts to read a political motive into the marriage', disagreeing specifically with assertions made by others that Edward's 'immoderate promotion' of the queen's relatives was done deliberately to broaden support away from the Nevilles.[3] Ross sees the traditional story of Edward immediately being smitten by Elizabeth Grey's beauty and marrying for love as a more compelling narrative.

The traditional tale has substantial contemporary backing. Tudor historian Thomas More wrote a version where Edward promised to pursue a lawsuit for Elizabeth, but only if she slept with him first. The legal issue she had got herself entangled with related to dower lands and rents disputed with Elizabeth's mother-in-law. The future queen's late husband, Sir John Grey, had been killed during the last cavalry charge at Second St Albans in 1461, fighting for Queen Margaret. Elizabeth and Sir John had married in 1452 and Grey had sired two sons by her – Thomas and Richard – both very young at the time of their father's death. As much to secure their future as hers, Elizabeth struggled to assert her legal rights and a lengthy and expensive court case beckoned.

Taking advantage of a potentially rich widow was an attractive proposition for men on the make in medieval times. Edward's Lord Chamberlain, Lord Hastings, may have been just such a man. When approached by Elizabeth for financial and legal help, he looked to benefit personally by suggesting that her son Thomas should be betrothed to his own, as yet unborn, first daughter; also, that Hastings should have use of half of any money secured from the dower dispute until Thomas gained maturity. So far this all seems true, but the story then goes on to imply Hastings made the offer somewhat tongue-in-cheek, and that when the feisty Elizabeth laughingly refused him he at once referred her to his friend the king, who she accosted when out hunting. Standing under a tree, since named the Queen's Oak, with young children under each arm, Elizabeth is said to have pleaded her case to Edward. The impassioned king offered to help her, but only on condition she slept with him first.

A contemporary depiction of Elizabeth shows her as very fair with heavy-lidded, downcast eyes. Other portraits show her to have had a longish neck, considered a mark of beauty in those days. Little wonder the king was so attracted to her.[4] A fanciful poem written by Antonio Cornazzano, written in 1468, four years after these supposed events took place, titled 'Of Admirable Women', related how the vulnerable widow, considering herself too base to be a queen but too good to be a harlot, resisted Edward's advances at the point of a dagger. Overcome by her beauty, the king is said to have proposed marriage. A secret wedding was then held at Elizabeth's parent's estate at Grafton, in Northamptonshire, probably in the Hermitage Chapel, where fifteenth-century floor tiles decorated with the arms of Woodville and York have been unearthed in modern times. The wedding reputedly took place on May Day morning, 1464.

The truth probably differed. Elizabeth may have first met Edward in the late spring of 1461 while formally in mourning, at least two years earlier than the supposed meeting under a tree and almost three years earlier than the wedding. Edward spent two nights at Stony Stratford on his way back from Yorkshire after the Battle of Towton. Elizabeth's father's home lay nearby. From Stony Stratford, Edward is known to have sent word to his cousin Bishop George Neville in London that he had decided to 'pardon, remit and forgive Lord Rivers [Elizabeth's father, Richard Woodville], of all manner [of] offences and trespasses of him done against us'. As mentioned before, Lord Rivers and his son Anthony had fought on the Lancastrian side at Towton. Until recently they had been among the king's foremost enemies. Circumstantially, the king's blanket pardon may have been elicited at the special request of River's comely daughter, who Edward cannot have helped but be attracted to. Additionally, Elizabeth did not laughingly reject Hastings' later offer to help her: she signed a formal contract with him on 13 April 1464, an agreement that has since been described as a hard bargain, favouring Hastings more than it did Elizabeth. Having already met Elizabeth several times, the king might have sought to seduce her, but he would not have threatened to harm her in the way suggested by Cornazzano. However, had she not resisted his appeal for immediate sexual gratification she might never have become his queen, just one of his many mistresses.

That Edward's proposal of marriage came out of the blue is supported by the fact that Elizabeth closed on the business deal with Hastings in mid-April, something which she would not have done had there been marriage to the king in the offing. Edward's offer and her acceptance of marriage must logically have occurred after this, circumstantially supporting the May Day date.[5] If the king's wedding did occur on or around May Day, it took place at the height of Henry Beaufort's insurgency, just a week after the Battle of Hedgeley Moor and a fortnight before the Battle of Hexham. Edward would have needed to keep the Nevilles on side throughout this dangerous period and he knew that their support might be placed at risk had they learned of his marriage plans. Other than carnal motives, there were practical reasons why the ceremony had to be rushed and kept under wraps. The problems in the North also help explain why the king's time with his bride was cut short.

Although we can never really know the truth of what occurred or the precise dates, if the marriage did take place in secret the way near contemporary historians suggest, few can have witnessed the event: probably just Elizabeth's mother, a priest, a few unnamed attendants and a youth paid to chant, as was the custom of the time. After consummating the marriage, the king is said by the chronicler Robert Fabyan to have left Grafton, returning a few days later in the guise of Lord River's guest. The chronicler claimed that the king 'nightly to her bed was brought, in so secret a manner that almost none but her mother was of counsel'. Elizabeth's mother, Dowager Duchess Jacquetta, would have been best placed to know the truth of this. Enemies later claimed she actively encouraged the liaison and that she used dark arts to bewitch Edward. Witchcraft was much feared in medieval times. When the twenty-year-old Henry VI was presented with evidence, elicited through torture, of a plot to kill him using sorcery, the alleged perpetrator, a cousin, was hung, drawn and quartered.

Did Edward immediately regret the marriage? Probably not!

The fact he kept the union a close secret for several months is not necessarily an indication that he sought to annul it, as has sometimes been suggested; rather, it indicated that he was waiting for the right time to make a clean breast of it. That it was a love match first and foremost appears borne out by the fact the pair spent much more time together than was considered usual for a king and queen at the time, and probably not merely to avoid the expense of maintaining separate households. Edward's disclosure of the marriage was made all the more difficult because there existed little or no precedent for a medieval king to marry a mere subject – especially not a near destitute widow of a former enemy, older than he, with two fatherless sons. Perhaps the nearest example of something similar had occurred when Edward III's son, the Black Prince, wed the twice-married noblewoman Joan of Kent.

Although much has been made of Edward marrying beneath him, it must also be remembered that Elizabeth's mother, Jacquetta of Luxemburg, was a dowager duchess, once upon a time second only to Margaret of Anjou in female rank in England; she was a woman who could trace her ancestry back to Charlemagne, and was said to have been descended from a mythological serpent goddess named Melusina, a magical protectress with links back to the time of the French Crusader kings of Outremer. Jacquetta and her family had not lived a straitened existence. Not until Elizabeth's husband's death and the withholding of the monies and land comprising her widow's dowry did her eldest daughter face potential hardship. It is also probably the case that Elizabeth's extended family was already one on the rise, even before her engagement to the king. That Elizabeth had borne two strong sons already could also be spun positively in favour of the marriage. Edward needed a wife of proven childbearing potential – someone strong, attractive and fertile. We know now that marrying outside of a close-knit European royal family would have had positive genetic outcomes, but this would not have been a consideration in medieval times.

Edward announced his marriage to his council in September 1464. The need to do so had by this time become urgent because of pressure exerted on him by Warwick, among others, to agree to a match with a foreign princess. This was the normal matrimonial outcome for a monarch, done to gain hefty dowries and forge alliances – something particularly important for a king saddled with enormous debts and belligerent neighbours.[6] As early as October 1461 a match had been proposed with Mademoiselle de Bourbon, sister-in-law of Charles, Count of Charolais, a man, like Henry VI, descended from John of Gaunt (Edward III's third son), who upon the death of his father, Philip, Duke of Burgundy, would become better known as Charles the Bold. The match was at the time seen as a way the Yorkists in England might distance Charles from supporting his Lancastrian cousins, but in the end nothing came of it.[7] Instead English ambassadors had set about opening negotiations with the French, in part in the hope of extending the truce which had held since the previous year. The proposed peace accord relied on Edward marrying the French king's sister-in-law Bona, the daughter of the Duke of Savoy. Warwick had encouraged the French king into believing Edward to be as keen as he in securing a lasting bond between the two countries through marriage. Presumably Edward must too, for a time, have been complicit in this.

Edward's announcement of his marriage to Elizabeth Grey must have come not only as a bombshell to Warwick but as a major embarrassment to the English government because of the snub to the French. A planned peace conference to be held at St. Omer had to be cancelled. For a time there was fear that King Louis XI of France would support a renewed Lancastrian insurgency. The chronicler Jean de Waurin stated unequivocally that Elizabeth was not Edward's match, saying, 'However good and however fair she might be ... her mother, the duchess of Bedford [Jacquetta], had married a simple knight, so that though she was the child of a duchess and the niece of the Count of St Pol, she still was no wife for him.' Edward's councillors, possibly his mother too, sought ways of dissolving or invalidating the union. Duchess Cecily doubtless pointed out to her son that while love was best kept for sport, marriage should remain strictly business. Thomas Habington, in his History of Edward IV (published about 1640 by Thomas's son, William), stated that Edward's mother went so far as to challenge the legality of Edward's marriage on the basis her son was already contracted to another, namely Lady Elizabeth Lucy, by whom he had had a bastard child.[8]

Historians have since seen Edward's withholding of the facts from his chief minister as evidence that he feared the reaction of his powerful cousin; that Warwick was greatly displeased was borne out by the chronicler Warkworth's statement that there arose great dissension ever more between the king and Warwick. The disclosure of marriage triggered a change in the relationship between the two men. Edward was from then on required to assert himself more forcibly to get what he wanted and to promote his new in-laws. It was this breakaway from Warwick's shackles that would prove in time to be the true making of him, but the affront to the earl's standing in France and the broader international ramifications of the marriage would spark a further outbreak of civil war.

Louis XI and the Earl of Warwick had been close in a comradely sense for a considerable time. John II of Aragon once described Louis as 'the inevitable conqueror of all negotiations', testament to the king's winning ways and adept diplomacy; so it is not surprising Warwick was so taken by the French monarch. Being of the same generation as Edward's father, Louis had fought against York and Lord Talbot at the Siege of Pontoise on the Seine in 1441. Appointed lieutenant general two years later in 1443, he had then successfully led 1,500 men-at-arms and a heavy siege train against the English at Dieppe, where 300 English soldiers lost their lives. French collaborators in the town were promptly hanged by him. It was against the Swiss, however, that Louis, at the time aged just twenty-one, won his greatest military accolade. At the Battle of Bale (23 August 1444), in alliance with the Holy Roman Emperor, his polyglot force of Gascons, Bretons, Walloons and Spaniards crushed part of a large Swiss army intent on laying siege to Zurich. At one point he led his men into battle with his leg pinned to his saddle by a crossbow bolt. News of the victory stunned all of Europe. Louis for a time sat imperiously astride the Rhine, strong enough to dictate terms to the Austrians – terms by which his countrymen gained much of Alsace.

It was in 1458, however, that Louis probably first encountered Warwick. Louis was by then in rebellion against his father, Charles VII, and as a consequence had struck up an accord with the gallant and unscrupulous Warwick, Captain of Calais. Warwick tacitly agreed to oppose English support for the French king against Louis's ally Philip the Good of Burgundy, and it was probably for this near-treasonable connivance that Warwick had been recalled by Henry VI's government in the autumn of that year, leading to the brawl at Westminster and the hurried mobilisation of forces in the spring of 1459, mentioned earlier. There may even be a good case to be made for Louis being the indirect catalyst for much of what occurred a year later. After the Battle of Northampton Louis had eagerly received the first reports of hostilities across the Channel from papal legate Coppini, who reported that 'everything is [now] in Warwick's power ... he has done marvellous things'. That Louis, who remained at loggerheads with his father, actively sided with the Yorkists was borne out when Warwick faced Margaret of Anjou's army at Second St Albans. Fighting men sent from Louis and Louis's Burgundian allies fought in Warwick's army. The Frenchman's banner, bearing the image of the Virgin Mary, was not only held aloft in Hertfordshire, but also in Yorkshire at the Battle of Towton.

When Louis gained the crown of France – an event that occurred soon after Towton – it might have been supposed a reconciliation with England would follow, but it was not until the spring of 1464 that French envoys first broached the offer of marriage between Louis's sister-in-law Bona of Savoy and Edward, plus a generous dowry and the blessings of peace. For his support in this regard, Louis had held out the promise of a continental lordship to Warwick, as a consequence of which Warwick was heavily invested in the proposed marriage pact from the outset. Louis was said by Milanese observers to have been so eager for peace with England that 'every day he prays to God and the Virgin Mary to grant him this boon'. As early as 3 October 1463, Louis had pestered the attendants of Warwick's brother Bishop George Neville for details about the character of England's new king, who, he said, he wished 'all good fortune'. He reminded them of the military support he had provided to the Yorkists when he and they had stood 'in common cause', ominously adding that now he and Edward had become rival kings he feared for their future friendship.

A year later, in late September of 1464, word reached Louis that Edward had taken an English wife and that he was honeymooning with her at Reading Abbey. Even then the Frenchman did not immediately give up his quest for a marital alliance. Warwick's agent, Robert Neville, assured Louis that the headstrong, lusty Edward would most likely be forced to abandon his unwise marriage. It was only later, when it became clear this would not happen, that Louis resignedly wrote Edward off as a fool – one who had possibly engineered his own undoing. On the positive side, the first stirrings of domestic strife in England caused by Edward's unwise marriage meant that the English government was unlikely to be able to mount any immediate military threat to the French had they been of a mind to. This allowed Louis to concentrate on pacifying his own turbulent nobles and prepare for an inevitable conflict with his mortal enemy, Charles the Bold, Count of Charolais. With Philip the Good's health ailing, the aggressively ambitious Charolais would in the early summer of 1467 succeed to the duchy of Burgundy. Even before that, however, rivalry between the two men would result in an outbreak of acrimonious warfare.

Unlike his wife, Jacquetta, Elizabeth's father, Richard Woodville, Lord Rivers, came from modest gentry stock. A younger son, he had made his career soldiering and had been promoted to the rank of knight banneret in 1442 or thereabouts. The title 'banneret' described an officer with responsibility for leading a troop of knights into battle: the equivalent of a squadron leader in modern-day terms. Pre-dating Edward's own covert marriage by almost three decades, Woodville had shocked Henry VI's court when admitting to having secretly married Jacquetta of Luxemburg in March 1437 without the king's permission. Being the widow of the Duke of Bedford, Jacquetta's marriage to a mere knight caused a great scandal at the time. Woodville was lucky to get off with just a hefty fine. Once the initial shock had worn off, Henry became taken with the pairing. He is said to have viewed Richard Woodville and the Lady Jacquetta as the handsomest couple in his kingdom. They were later feted as the handsomest family too, with a clutch of beautiful children in train. The marriage proved the making of Richard, linking him in a familial sense to not only the English royal family, but also to the continental royal houses of Luxemburg, Burgundy and Anjou, enabling him to live well beyond the means to which he had become accustomed. Moreover, the children from his marriage were paired with others from England's noble houses: their son Anthony was betrothed to Lord Scales's daughter and their eldest daughters, Elizabeth and Jacquetta (named for her mother), were married off to Sir John Grey and Lord Strange respectively. To cap it all, in the spring of 1448 Henry raised Sir Richard to the peerage as Lord Rivers. Two years later he became a knight of the garter.

Edward had got to know Rivers, Jacquetta and Anthony Woodville well even before his stay at Stony Stratford in 1461. All three had for a time been with him at Calais the year before.

They had been seized during one of Warwick's raids on the Kent coast. Their abduction may have been violently carried out and the brave Jacquetta is said to have admonished her captors for their effrontery in holding her against her will. Once ensconced at Calais, Warwick and Edward are claimed to have berated Rivers for gathering a hostile fleet at Sandwich to oppose them and to have also verbally chastised Anthony. Most modern historians now doubt the veracity of such tales, however. Rivers, his wife and son, after a period of awkwardness, probably struck up a friendship or an understanding of sorts with their captors. Once wind and tide allowed, the dowager duchess was packed off to England and Lord Rivers and his son were released soon after the Yorkist earls invaded the mainland in June 1460.

Given the intermittent nature of Edward's involvement in military affairs after Towton and his constant travelling back and forth across England, it would have been unlikely had he not visited Rivers and Jacquetta when stopping overnight in Northamptonshire, staying at or near Grafton on the main London road. As earlier asserted, this must have been how he came to properly know Elizabeth and first fell under her spell. He might also have renewed his acquaintance with her brother Anthony. Both men had been in their late teens while at Calais, so Edward would have had much in common with Anthony Woodville. Both were of a martial mindset, although in Anthony's case this may have been taken to idealistic, quasi-religious extremes. He would later become motivated to wear a hair shirt. Although anecdotal stories tell of Edward accusing Anthony of being an upstart, it is possible their meeting at Calais helped seed the later union of their families.

Anthony fought at Towton on the Lancastrian side, was wounded and on first accounts feared killed. Nevertheless, he and his father were among those men pardoned by Edward a few weeks later. By the winter of 1462, Anthony, now with the title Lord Scales, was serving as one of Edward's top commanders in Northumberland.

Well before Edward's marriage to Elizabeth Grey, the Woodvilles would appear to have been a family on the rise, basking in the king's favour.

Edward's rule was fortuitously bolstered in the summer of 1465 when Henry VI was apprehended. Evading capture after Hexham, Henry had gone on the run. While the battle raged he had remained hidden nearby at Bywell Castle. Once the coast was clear he left the castle in such haste that he forgot to take with him his bejewelled hat. Montagu's men discovered it later, after they occupied the castle. Not until a year after this did Henry fall into Edward's hands, being apprehended in Ribblesdale in Lancashire by three of Edward's knights: Sir James Harrington, Sir Thomas Talbot and Sir John Tempest. All were well recompensed by Edward. Harrington's father and brother had fallen at Wakefield fighting alongside Edward's father, so for him Henry's capture was personally gratifying as well as rewarding. For such an apparently dreamy and unworldly monarch, Henry had made a good job of distancing himself from danger for the best part of four years, constantly on the move up and down the Lothian-Northumberland coast. Now, securely bound, strapped to the stirrups of a horse, the hapless monarch was taken back south and locked-up for safe keeping in the Wakefield Tower, within the Tower of London, behind walls fifteen-feet thick. He was treated well at first. Edward made sure members of the royal household attended on him and allowed him visitors, but over time care for him tailed off. The pro-Lancastrian John Warkworth alleged that by the year 1470 Henry was 'not worshipfully arrayed as a prince [should be], and not so cleanly kept as should seem such a prince [to be]'. With Henry's son alive, nothing could be gained by Edward engineering Henry's death. On the contrary, the objective was to keep the old king alive, since his death, should it occur, would have resulted in Edward of Lancaster becoming a rallying point for the Lancastrian old guard and for others disaffected with Edward's regime.

Lancaster travelled with his mother, Margaret, to Lorraine in August 1463. He would remain there with his small, impoverished retinue for the next eight years, most of the time at his grandfather's castle of Koeur, near St Mihiel-en-Bar. Fellow exile Sir John Fortescue, a lawyer in his early seventies, remembered the prince ever 'seated on fierce and half-tamed steeds, urged on by his spurs', and the Milanese ambassador to France reported the prince to be a spirited youth who talked of nothing other than cutting off the heads of his enemies and making war on them. A victim of circumstance, such unambiguous displays of violence may have masked a deep, growing insecurity. Lancaster had witnessed at first hand the brutal aftermath of Second St Albans: a traumatising experience for an eight-year-old. Tellingly, it was he who had been made to pronounce judgement on Sir Thomas Kyriell and Lord Bonville before their execution.

Sir John Fortescue was a dyed-in-the-wool Lancastrian, who wrote a number of forceful propaganda pamphlets when abroad making a strong case against Henry VI's usurpation by Edward. Fortescue argued that the Yorkist claim to kingship was invalidated because it relied on descent from Edward III through the female line. He maintained that in natural law, ratified by the Bible, women were excluded from the royal line.[9] He also contended that Henry's rule was absolute and that he should continue to exert 'full regal authority over his subjects', hereditary right being the deciding factor. A supporter of William de la Pole during the great revolt of 1450, Fortescue had subsequently taken a leading role in attainting the Yorkist rebels at the infamous 'Parliament of Devils' in the winter of 1459. Surviving the carnage at Towton two years later, he had joined others who accompanied the Lancastrian royal family to safety first in Scotland and then on the Continent.

On 24 July 1465, a month or so prior to Henry's capture, Elizabeth's coronation took place at Westminster. Plans for it had been set in motion immediately after the Christmas festivities ended. The formal coronation might have been put on hold by Edward to allow time to organise an appropriately attended state occasion. In particular he wished to stress his wife's noble credentials on her mother's side. Envoys were sent to Philip the Good, Duke of Burgundy, to arrange an appropriate delegation of members of Jacquetta's extended family, specifically the duke's uncle, Jacques de Luxemburg. On 14 April Edward wrote to the Mayor of London, formally announcing the date of his 'most dear and most entirely beloved wife's coronation ... Sunday before Whitsunday next coming'.

Edward was in London on 23 May to create thirty-nine knights of the Bath to mark the occasion. Elizabeth followed him there the next day, making a stately procession from Sheen Palace at Richmond to the Tower to spend the night there, as dictated by tradition. Her route took her across London's celebrated bridge. In those days London Bridge was an edifice lined with dwellings: a bustling suburb in its own right. The road across was sanded for the occasion and rotting traitor's heads were removed from poles along the way to improve the ambiance. The following morning Elizabeth was escorted into Westminster Palace by the Bishops of Durham and Salisbury. The Dowager Duchess of Buckingham bore the queen's train, along with two of Edward's sisters and Elizabeth's mother, Jacquetta. The dukes of Clarence and Norfolk and the Earl of Arundel proceeded her. In line with custom, Edward did not attend. The queen was led to the throne with great reverence and solemnity. Significantly, a number of former Lancastrian stalwarts took part in the proceedings, an indication that Edward's marriage into a once avowedly pro-Lancastrian family might have served to help mend divisions. The coronation ceremony concluded with a tournament graced by a number of Burgundian knights from the retinue of Jacques de Luxembourg. The honours of the day, however, went to an Englishman, Thomas, Lord Stanley – Edward's champion and a fighting man of some renown. There is no evidence that Stanley had fought at Towton.

Being reluctant to declare his hand so early in the game, he had most probably remained in Lancashire until the dust of battle settled. He had built up a good run of form in this regard: in the autumn of 1459, Margaret of Anjou had ordered Stanley to raise troops to intercept the Earl of Salisbury's forces, but when the rival armies clashed at Blore Heath, Stanley had failed to commit his 2,000 troops to battle; it was also later alleged that he deliberately prevented Lancastrian reinforcements from Cheshire reaching the Queen and covertly reinforced Salisbury instead.[10]

The Woodvilles quickly became England's nouveau rich, though not all of them directly benefited from the king's political patronage, as is sometimes claimed. Edward was astute enough to only place political power in the hands of men capable of wielding it. On balance, no more was done to improve the standing of the Woodvilles than might reasonably have been expected for in-laws in such circumstances. The extended Woodville family were said to be large, clannish and greedy – even so, this is a charge that might have been made by jealous onlookers about any sizeable, but relatively obscure, family lucky enough to have been married into royalty. Elizabeth's father, Lord Rivers, gained an earldom. Anthony, by now a close colleague of the king's and already ennobled with the title Lord Scales, became an influential figure at his brother-in-law's court. In November 1466 he was made governor of the Isle of Wight and keeper of Portchester Castle, in Hampshire. This placed him in control of the important Solent seaway access point to Portsmouth and Southampton harbours.

Rivers' other children benefited too. The earl's son, Lionel, became Bishop of Salisbury; another son, the twenty-year-old John Woodville, was knighted and gained a prior's appointment. John also took the hand of the sixty-five-year-old Dowager Duchess of Norfolk in marriage, an outcome which, given the enormous difference in age between bride and groom, caused a degree of scandal. Worse, the aging duchess was Warwick's favourite aunt, so the indignation which was aroused greatly angered her already ruffled nephew. Five Woodville daughters were married off in all: one of these, Katherine, to the young Henry Stafford, grandson and heir of the Duke of Buckingham, very 'near the king and of his blood royal'. Elizabeth was awarded custody of the young man and was granted subsidies from his Welsh lands to pay for his maintenance. With his proud royal pedigree, Stafford is said to have later come to resent his marriage to a mere Woodville, claiming he had been married below his station. Also probably true is that Warwick may have regarded Stafford's marriage as a block to his marrying the boy to one of his own two daughters, both of whom remained unattached even though they were among the wealthiest heiresses in the land.[11] The queen also made sure her eldest son Thomas, from her marriage to Sir John Grey, profited. In 1466, shortly after the birth of her first daughter to Edward (a baby girl named Elizabeth), she paired him with Anne Holland, child-heir to the renegade Henry Holland's vast estates. Elizabeth paid a large sum of money to secure the match. This was once again much to the annoyance of Warwick, who had harboured plans for one of his own nephews to marry the girl. Professor Ross has suggested that so numerous were the Woodville clan that they in effect cornered the domestic, high-end marriage market.

Sensibly, Edward cast additional awards the Nevilles' way too. Warwick gained territorial grants in Westmorland and the wardship of the young Viscount Lovell, heir to a number of baronies. Bishop George Neville became Archbishop of York as well as Lord Chancellor of England. The Archbishop's investiture took place at York in September 1465 with much pomp and ceremony. There were reputedly 6,000 guests, including two dukes, two earls and three bishops at the high table and thirty-one abbots at the second table. Warwick acted as steward. Coming so close after Elizabeth's coronation, many saw such an ostentatious display of grandeur as a belated attempt at one-upmanship by the Nevilles – another sign to observant contemporaries that the king's marriage had proved divisive.

Because the queen was understandably conscious of her position, she demanded much formality and protocol in day-to-day affairs. That Archbishop Neville's inauguration had been so sumptuous may therefore have rankled with her. The size of Edward's household was modest and may not have been as extensive as either Warwick's or even the Duke of Clarence's, something which again the queen might have been ruffled about. Its extent in the early 1460s has been estimated at around 550 officials and servants, split almost equally between a 'downstairs' commissariat, responsible for provisioning and headed up by a steward, and an 'upstairs' with attendant knights and esquires, bodyguards, ushers, grooms, valets, pages, boatmen, chaplains, heralds, pipers, trumpeters, astrologers, jesters, choristers and the like, all under the authority of the king's chamberlain. The queen's household would, though smaller, have been a mirror image of her husband's, but with the addition of ladies-in-waiting and other female attendants. The size of her waiting-staff has been estimated at around 100. Elizabeth had been forced through lack of money to cut back on numbers in comparison to her predecessor, Margaret of Anjou, yet she did not go without, spending in excess of £1,000 on her wardrobe in one particular year, as well as lesser amounts on medicines, entertainment, gold and furs.[12]

Elizabeth's formal manner may have been fostered by her high-born mother, Jacquetta, who coached her daughter to display herself to best advantage. This was not done to simply show off, but to bolster her daughter's authority. On one occasion, shortly after the birth of her first child to Edward, Elizabeth was described by a foreign observer as dining in state with much pomp and ceremony, seated on an expensive golden chair. The occasion may have been to honour the newly born baby princess, whose safe arrival was seen as 'a sign that God had blessed the marriage and dynasty'.[13] Elizabeth's mother, Jacquetta, and the king's sister, Margaret, had to stand some way off and not until the queen had eaten her first dish were they allowed to be seated. The observer recounted how all the ladies and maidens who served the queen were of noble birth and had to kneel before her as she ate. Three hours were spent dining in this way. Dancing followed the banquet. Elizabeth sat while her sister-in-law Margaret of York stepped out in stately fashion with two dukes. Among the throng of attendant ladies were eight duchesses and thirty countesses.

Although Warwick had at first appeared to take the setback of the king's marriage in his stride by graciously escorting Elizabeth when she had somewhat nervously made her first ceremonial public appearance at Michaelmas 1464, he did not attend her coronation. This omission has sometimes been seen as the first outward display of resentment at the rapid rise of the Woodvilles, but may in reality have been nothing more sinister than a clash of diaries: the earl was abroad with the lords Hastings and Wenlock on an embassy to Burgundy when the coronation took place. However, not only did Warwick become progressively side-lined at council, he also discovered that the Woodville connection had moved the goalposts with respect to foreign policy. Whereas Warwick was, as previously noted, pro-French, Edward's instincts were to play the French and the Burgundians off against each other. If anything, the king may have now been more inclined to side with the Burgundians.

High tension existed between Louis and his enemy Charles the Bold, Count of Charolais, at all times. On 16 July 1465, at Montlhery, on the north bank of the Loire, astride the road from Paris to Orleans, Louis's and Charolais's armies clashed. With Duke Philip the Good seriously ill, Charles the Bold had become the de facto ruler of Burgundy and had bolstered his forces opposing Louis XI's expansionist aims with troops supplied by his allies John II, Duke of Bourbon, and Francis II, Duke of Brittany, creating the famous 'League of the Common Weal [good]'. In total the French king's enemies assembled a coalition force 20,000 strong. Louis's army was smaller, perhaps 15,000 men all told, comprising his bodyguard of Scots and a household regiment from his own provincial base, as well as other units of men-at-arms and crossbowmen. Flanking the main body of his army were the mounted lances of Pierre de Breze, Margaret of Anjou's old ally. At the height of the battle Louis was unhorsed but cried out, 'Have no fear, today the victory is ours!' Men around him are said to have fought hand-to-hand 'like rabid, raging dogs'. Even after the two sides had fallen back artillery continued to boom across the corpse-strewn battlefield, described ever after as 'the field of tears'. Because the battle ended indecisively, and although it proved a military check to Charles as well as to Louis, Paris was soon placed under siege by Charles's coalition forces. To end the siege Louis was forced to cede to him control of Picardy and a number of important Somme bridging points, like Abbeville, as well as the duchy of Normandy to one of his own rebellious brothers. They were humiliations which could only be expunged by a renewal of the war at some later date.

Warwick was soon on hand to commit England to a non-interventionist policy, promising on his own volition that Edward's government would not intervene should Louis seek to reconquer his lost territories, including parts of Normandy still claimed by the English throne. He promised too that should a Warwick-led government come to power in England he would militarily support the French in their continuing struggle with Charles of Charolais, implying a coup of sorts being raised against Edward. That Warwick was of a mind as early as the autumn of 1465 to oust or outface the king, speaks volumes with respect to the chasm that had opened up in relations between the one-time partners, betokening civil war to come.

6

INFIGHTING

Unlike the pro-French Earl of Warwick, Edward was for a time happy to play one international neighbour off against another, this notwithstanding his mother-in-law's familial links with the Burgundians becoming energised since his marriage to Elizabeth. On 25 September 1465 the stakes were raised, when Charles the Bold, Count of Charolais, sent emissaries to the English court to seek the hand of Edward's sister Margaret. The following April, Edward despatched Warwick and the lords Hastings and Wenlock to Burgundy to commence formal marriage negotiations, not only for his sister, but also for his brother George, Duke of Clarence. Edward hoped the latter might gain the hand of the widowed count's only daughter, Mary of Burgundy. It was probably at this meeting that Warwick formed his alleged antipathy to the Burgundian duke, although, on the face of it, the two men appear to have got along well enough. Warwick was doubtless a consummate diplomat when he wished to be. He may already by this time have harboured designs of his own for his daughter Isobel to marry George of Clarence (known henceforth in the narrative simply as Clarence), so was probably not minded to push too hard for the second match. In the meantime, Edward concluded a holding truce with France that would last until March 1468.

For a time matters settled amid a round of cautious diplomatic exchanges, but that an accord had been struck between the English and the Burgundians was underlined in the autumn of 1466 when Edward's brother-in-law Anthony Woodville engaged in a much celebrated joust with Antoine, the Bastard of Burgundy, at Smithfield in London. Antoine was the illegitimate son of Philip the Good and therefore Charles the Bold's natural brother. The contest was a sure sign of the warm friendship that was growing between the English king and the Burgundian royal house. Like other talented royal bastards, Antoine was trusted to carry out his master's bidding to the letter, so was a considerable diplomatic asset for the Burgundians.

Being by law unable to inherit land, illegitimate sons posed no threat to their father's titles or their legitimate brothers' claims; they could therefore be relied upon in matters of diplomacy and war to act unconditionally in the interests of the state. Antoine had fought against the French at Montlhery the year before and his martial qualities had been much lauded. Positioning himself conspicuously in the centre of the Burgundian line, his banner – a blue barbican on a yellow background – had fluttered bravely in the hot breeze before battle commenced. His bodyguard that day had comprised a group of mounted archers dressed in red jackets and adorned with the white cross of St Andrew. 500 English bowmen, said to be 'the flower of the Burgundian army', backed him up. According to Philip de Commines, after the fiercely fought battle (briefly described in the last chapter) Antoine's banner emerged from the fray 'so shredded that it was not a foot long'.

Not only did the tournament at Smithfield broker good relations with Burgundy, it also helped establish the Woodvilles as a family with strong royal credentials – not simply 'parvenus', as some claimed. Chivalric pageantry in medieval times focused attention on noble connections, so we can be sure the hand of Jacquetta of

Luxembourg was at work in the planning and preparation. The programme should have encompassed a full week's jousting, but was ended prematurely when news broke of the death of Duke Philip the Good. Even before this, Antoine's charger had been killed. Hand-to-hand fighting on foot had been banned by Edward because he feared a fatal outcome: 'After two or three strokes at the most,' reported *The Great Chronicle of London*, 'the king cast down a baton which he held in his hand and commanded them to be disarmed.' The report concluded by saying the day ended 'indifferently of honour'. The following Sunday Edward threw a great feast as a tribute for his Burgundian guests, attended, it was said, by between fifty and 100 ladies of which the least noble was the daughter of a baron.

Warwick worked tirelessly to maintain increasingly strained Anglo-French relations. In January 1466 he reiterated his unwarranted promise to the French that English troops would not intervene should Louis annex those parts of Normandy that had fallen outside the French king's control. Given that Edward was more minded toward a pact with Burgundy at this time such a promise was probably a treasonable offence. Warwick was repeating the same subversive behaviour which had alienated him from Henry VI's government in the late 1450s.

Sent again to France by Edward in May of the following year – in part to provoke the Burgundians into closing a better deal with England – the earl was extravagantly hosted by Louis at Rouen. Warwick arrived accompanied by a large and impressively armed, 200-strong entourage and was received as if he were a head of state. Once again he was offered generous personal inducements to settle an alliance with France. The French king backed up his overtures with gifts to the earl of a golden, gem-encrusted cup. Other members of the English party were given commemorative coins and plate. On top of this, Louis proposed the payment to Edward of an annual pension of 4,000 marks if an alliance between their two countries was sealed. All these negotiations and promises were made in public, but in private Louis is reputed to have made the observation that Warwick might have done better to keep the pliable Henry VI on the throne, rather than work through the unpredictable Edward. Louis relied on Warwick calling the shots but was having doubts as to the earl's ability to do so. Warwick is said to have assured his host that everything was under control and that his master would fall in line with whatever was agreed.

Going further out on a limb, Warwick may also have raised the possibility of Edward's sister Margaret of York marrying someone in the French royal family rather than Charles of Burgundy. At this time no firm agreement of marriage between Charles and Margaret had been reached. It was a suggestion energetically seized upon by Louis, who identified no fewer than four potential partners for her. Spread by Warwick and the French king's agents, rumours were soon circulating in diplomatic circles around Europe that Edward and Louis would together attack Burgundy. Milanese observers whispered of plans whereby Edward would renounce his ancient claim to the throne of France and support a joint Anglo-French invasion of Burgundy, in consideration of a yearly subsidy and improved trading arrangements. A partition of the Low Countries would grant Holland, Zeeland and Brabant to Edward's brother Clarence and the whole of Flanders to Louis. All such considerations must have been in play during Warwick's sojourn at the French court. Some aspects of the negotiations entered into may have been with Edward's tacit nod – firm details are lacking.

How far Warwick really bought into the positions he took also remains unclear. Nevertheless, when he returned to England in June he got a nasty shock, discovering his brother Archbishop George Neville had been high-handedly dismissed from the post of Lord Chancellor of England by Edward and that French envoys despatched by Louis had been diplomatically cold-shouldered. Additionally, the match between Princess Margaret and Charles the Bold (until then on hold) had in Warwick's absence all but been agreed upon.

Edward's loss of patience with Warwick's brother may have been a knee-jerk reaction to the archbishop's opposition to his foreign policies, made worse by personal affronts to the queen and members of her family. Normally relaxed and easy-going – a man who disliked unpleasantness for its own sake – Edward nonetheless had a fiery temper, usually vented against those of noble rank who angered or disappointed him. Though more often stressing the king's good nature, contemporaries sometimes touch on this aspect of Edward's character. As well as his build, Henry VIII may have inherited his propensity for untoward bouts of rage from his Yorkist grandfather. Such outbursts were probably rare, however. More marked were the king's man-management skills. Dominic Mancini claimed that if Edward came across a newcomer at court who appeared overawed by the king's 'royal magnificence' he would lay a kindly hand upon his shoulder to put him at his ease. He was said to have 'liked to have all comfortable about him'. Later, in 1473, he kindly placated the agitated Sheriff of Devon, saying, 'Ye sit still and be quiet.' With respect to the heavy-handed dismissal of Archbishop Neville, in the king's defence his cousin had probably gone too far when voicing opposition to the entente with Burgundy. That and the insult of his expensively staged inauguration at York must have proved his undoing. Edward could not countenance a conspiring and indulgent chancellor any more than he could a devious first minister, but was not yet strong enough to confront Warwick directly.

The Neville propaganda machine was soon busy at work attacking Jacquetta, the enabler of the Burgundian match, as well as others from the Woodville family. On 12 July 1467 the dowager duchess was mentioned by name in a petition drawn up by Kentish dissidents who spoke against 'certain seditious persons which have caused our said sovereign Lord and said realm to fall in great poverty of misery, disturbing the administration of law, only extending [their efforts] to their own promotion and enriching'. With echoes of Jack Cade's remonstrance in 1450, threat of direct action loomed. At Coventry at the turn of the year, Edward had with him a bodyguard of 200 heavily armed knights and men-at-arms, indicating he may have feared a rising of some sort. Warwick had at last been outed as a traitor in the pay of the French. Confessions to this effect had been made to Lord Herbert by a captured French agent. Summoned to explain himself in person to the king, the earl obstinately refused to travel so late in the year. Bad weather may well have been a factor, so Edward sent an emissary to Sheriff Hutton Castle to reason with the earl, but a second formal summons made by the king on 7 January 1468 was also rebuffed. Warwick claimed he had reason to fear meeting Edward face to face while Lord Rivers, Anthony Woodville and William Herbert were in attendance, implying concern for his safety. Ironically this was a replay of responses made by Edward's father when summoned by Henry VI to account for himself prior to First St Albans – a point that cannot have been lost on York's son. That Warwick felt he could defy Edward in this way speaks volumes for the earl's arrogance and willingness to broker disharmony.

Warwick probably dared to disobey the king because he knew he retained strong support in the land, nurtured by his extravagant hospitality and generosity and his penchant for out-and-out populism – the same traits that had helped catapult the Yorkists to power. He was an astute politician, albeit one who at times overreached himself. Warwick cannot have been naïve enough to consider a Burgundian alliance as necessarily any worse or better than a French one, nor can he have failed to realise the commercial importance of strengthening ties with the Burgundians. He had, however, become seduced by Louis into believing that more could be gained by England allying with France than with Burgundy. He had also been angered at the high price demanded by Charles as a dowry for Princess Margaret. The sizeable sum of 200,000 marks had been asked for; Edward had difficulties raising a first instalment. The Woodville-inspired alliance with Burgundy was in Warwick's view proving to be an unnecessarily expensive one, especially when the French king's counter-offer of a pension for Edward was taken into account. Clarence was probably angered too. The promise to him of captured Burgundian imperial provinces should Edward ally with France and the fact that his own proposed wedding to Mary of Burgundy was on hold, if not altogether shelved, rankled.

When finally persuaded to appear before the king at Coventry in the New Year, Warwick was excused his earlier failure to attend court and was received gracefully by Edward. In return Warwick covered up his disappointment at his brother's sacking from the post of Lord Chancellor. By this time Edward had found reasons to reject the accusations made by Herbert's captured French agent. Openly at least, he dismissed the reports against Warwick as baseless provocation on the French king's part. Whether he really trusted his cousin to remain loyal is not known with any certainty – the likely answer is probably not. The two men's heavily stage-managed reconciliation probably occurred after the formal announcement to Parliament of Princess Margaret's wedding to the Duke of Burgundy on 17 May 1468. A month earlier Edward had paid the first portion of his sister's dowry – 50,000 marks – along with the despatch to Charles the Bold of an expensive ring.

Edward and Warwick's reconciliation owed much to Archbishop George Neville's mediation. It seems effort was being made all round to restore good relations. To underline the accord, Warwick escorted Princess Margaret from London to the Kent coast for embarkation to the Continent. He even had her ride pillion on his horse. The duchess-to-be sailed from Margate on 24 June for Sluys. Two days later she met her fiancé, Charles, for the first time. The couple were married a week later in the church of Notre Dame, at Damme, near Bruges. Those in the crowds lining the streets to witness Margaret's grand entry were reportedly much taken by their new, tall, elegant duchess, whose stately build and demeanour may have reflected her brother's. Festivities stretched out over ten days. Anthony Woodville attended the wedding on behalf of the queen and broke eleven lances when combating Adolf of Cleves as part of the wedding celebrations, an occasion that was marred only by Antoine, the Bastard of Burgundy, crying off after breaking his leg.

Like Warwick, Edward could also play the populist card when it suited him. Just after a thirty-year Anglo-Breton alliance had been sealed in June 1467, he openly declared his intention to invade France to recover England's lost territories. Lord Rivers announced to Parliament that an amicable accord with the dukes of Burgundy and Brittany, 'the two mightiest princes beholden to the crown of France', had successfully been concluded and that the time was ripe to bring the French, England's ancient enemy, to account. The commons voted Edward a substantial sum to bolster his aggressive foreign policy. Edward was described by one Milanese observer as 'a poor man' who had promised 'to live of mine own ... and not to charge my subjects but in great and urgent cases'. War with France was just such a case.[1] Described by Professor Ross as a 'classic [medieval] anti-French stance', Edward's foreign policy mirrored that of many late-medieval English kings.[2] Possibly the chest-beating was just bravado, designed to maintain the pressure on the French and keep the Burgundians on side during a period of worsening trade relations, caused by a four-year prohibition on imports of finished English cloth. The policy nevertheless probably went down well with the majority of Englishmen. Although the Burgundians were distrusted by the English, the French were actively hated – something Edward appreciated better than Warwick.

Louis's immediate response to Edward's declaration was to spread anti-Yorkist smear stories that he had himself rejected offers for the twenty-one-year-old Margaret of York to be married into the French aristocracy. He claimed she was no virgin and had already given birth to a bastard son. On hearing this an infuriated Charles the Bold ordered that anyone found spreading such lies in his provinces would be thrown into the nearest river. Meanwhile, Warwick's agents fomented anti-Burgundian feelings in London. Only at the last minute was a plot to attack the Flemish-mercantile community in Southwark prevented by London's authorities. Warwick also fanned the flames of resentment against the Danes and the Hanseatic League. Both were alleged by him to have engaged in piracy against English shipping. A costly naval war resulted, a clever move on Warwick's part, deflecting attention and resources away from potential French targets.

Edward's threatened invasion may have worried Louis XI a good deal less than the possibility the English might provide the Bretons with mercenaries and military supplies and make war by proxy. Duke Francis of Brittany had commenced hostilities against Louis in the autumn of 1467 with the aim of conquering Normandy, but after a period of heavy fighting a shaky truce of sorts had held. In the summer of the following year Louis massed troops along their shared border and renewed fighting broke out. Edward's reluctance to rush to the support of his Breton allies was soon exposed. He hesitated before committing a promised 7,000-strong expeditionary force, commanded by Anthony Woodville. Without this support Francis was forced to yield to French pressure and conclude a formal peace treaty, ratified in September 1468. Burgundy followed suit, concluding a peace deal known as the Treaty of Peronne with the French the following month.

With his homeland encircled by potential enemies, as far as Louis was concerned the only good neighbour was a weak one. Even when preparing for war with the Bretons and Burgundians he found time to man and equip a force, led by the exiled Jasper Tudor, for a sortie into Wales – a diversion designed to tie down English troops. The invaders landed at Harlech before marching across North Wales and retaking Denbigh Castle, setting up a court there in Henry VI's name. A newsletter from France dated

2 July 1468 boasted of Jasper Tudor putting 4,000 Englishmen to death, but more plausibly added that Jasper was 'gathering as many partisans there [in Wales] as he can [to confront King Edward]'. The invasion eventually came to nothing. Harlech Castle fell to William Herbert on 14 August 1468. Jasper and his entourage hurried back to France. It was for this military success that Edward rewarded Herbert with the earldom of Pembroke.

A revenge foray into Southern France planned by Edward then failed to materialise when reports of Margaret of Anjou concentrating troops at Honfleur diverted the bulk of Edward's fleet away from convoying an army and instead to maintaining preventative patrols along the Channel. Other than the expulsion of Jasper Tudor, all that Edward managed to accomplish during this period was the recovery of the Channel Island of Jersey and the securing of treaty arrangements with another of Louis's enemies, John II of Aragon.

A terminal breakdown in relations between Edward and Warwick did not occur until two years after Archbishop Neville's denouement as Lord Chancellor. Trust between the two men eroded gradually, with periods of rapprochement. Warwick is said to have maintained an impenetrable veil of deception throughout, but it is unlikely Edward can have been entirely duped. Although he was, arguably, trusting and accommodating by nature, he was not a fool. Growing distrust of Warwick persuaded Edward to contest any important appointments which might favour his rival. For instance, when one of Warwick's cronies, Sir John Langstrother, was nominated to become the Prior of the Hospital of St John of Jerusalem in England – an important and prestigious appointment normally reserved for a royal councillor or a premier baron of England – Edward tried to impose his brother-in-law Richard Woodville in the post instead. Nevertheless, that the king still hoped to win back the loyalty of his difficult cousin is indicated by him sending Warwick to Burgundy on a diplomatic visit in the spring of 1469,

EDWARDVS IIII

1. Edward IV, described by Tudor historian Sir Thomas More as 'princely to behold [and] of body mighty'. (Courtesy of Ripon Cathedral)

2. The Bargate at Southampton where Richard, Earl of Cambridge, was executed with two other noblemen on the eve of the Agincourt campaign.

3. York's enemy Edmund, Duke of Somerset, was appointed Constable of Carisbrooke Castle – pictured here with the medieval motte in the background – in 1456; it was a military posting which reflected the government's faith in his ability to confront a possible French invasion of the south coast.

Above left: 4. Statue of Henry VI at Canterbury Cathedral.
Above right: 5. Statue of Margaret of Anjou and Edward of Lancaster. (Courtesy of Deborah Esrick)
Below: 6. Titchfield Abbey ruins, near Fareham in Hampshire. This impressive Tudor house incorporated the former abbey where Henry VI and Margaret of Anjou first met.

7. Edward's childhood home, Ludlow Castle, Shropshire, a prestigious marcher stronghold overlooking a loop in the River Teme, protected by steep cliffs down to the river to the south and west. This view is taken looking from high ground to the south, beyond the river.

8. Ludlow Castle, looking south-westward from the battlements of the gatehouse keep to the gorge of the looping River Teme.

9. The gatehouse keep of Ludlow Castle. Note the trace of masonry (centre) which betrays where the original entrance and drawbridge were positioned.

10. 'Lord Saye and Sele brought before Jack Cade' – Cade's rebellion set the tone for the later events of the Wars of the Roses. (Courtesy of the British Library)

11. The fight at Wakefield, where Edward's father and brother Edmund were killed, was described as 'a sore battle' fought in the south fields between Sandal Castle, depicted here, and Wakefield Bridge.

Above: 12. The Broadgate at Ludlow, through which Richard, Duke of York, Edward and the other Yorkist earls probably fled after the stand-off with Henry VI's army at Ludford Bridge on 13 October 1459.
Left: 13. Micklegate Bar at York, where the heads of Richard, Duke of York, his son Edmund and the Earl of Salisbury were displayed after the Battle of Wakefield.

Right: 14. Part of the ruined gatehouse at Wigmore Castle near Ludlow, from where Edward rode to victory at Mortimer's Cross in February 1461.
Below: 15. Another view of the ruins of Wigmore Castle showing the conical Norman Motte.

Above: 16. The River Lugg at Mortimer's Cross. Its banks would probably have been frozen on the morning of the battle, and perhaps the river was too. The river likely anchored Edward's left flank.
Below: 17. Part of the battlefield of Mortimer's Cross as it appears today, looking north-west toward Edward's left flank from the old Hereford Road.

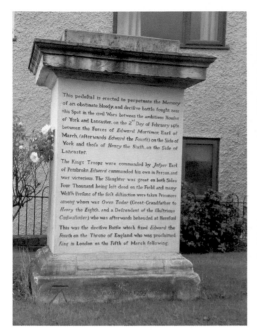

Above left: 18. The monument at Mortimer's Cross. The final wording reads, 'This was the decisive battle which fixed Edward the fourth on the throne of England who was proclaimed King in London on the fifth of March following.'
Above right: 19. Ancient waymarker at Mortimer's Cross.
Below: 20. Diorama of the Battle of Mortimer's Cross, showing the embattled Yorkists being assailed by the Earl of Wiltshire's Irish vanguard.

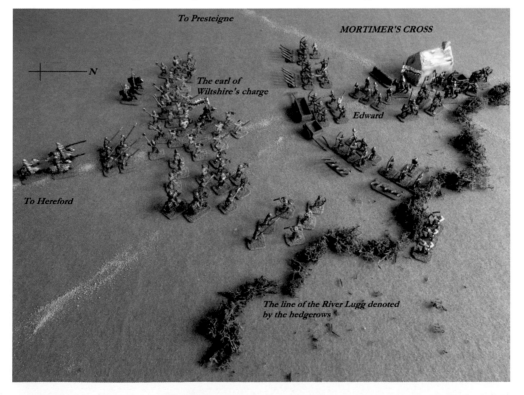

21. Diorama of the Battle of Towton, showing the imagined situation just prior to the Yorkist rearguard becoming involved in the fighting.

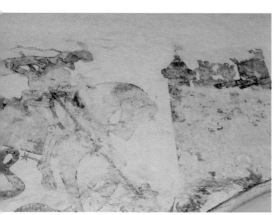

Left: 22. Fifteenth-century depiction of St George and the Dragon at Nether Wallop Church in Hampshire. A pageant which included a scene inspired by this was laid on when Edward visited Bristol not long after his coronation. (Courtesy of the vicar and church wardens)

Right: 23. Harlech Castle in Wales, the last stronghold to hold out against Edward, which finally fell to his forces in August 1468.

24. Elizabeth Woodville, whom Edward IV married in secret, putting love above the interests of the state.

25. Southampton's medieval walls, from where the Earl of Worcester had decapitated and impaled bodies of his victims hung after the Battle of Empingham.

26. Remains of the medieval walls at Sandwich, which was attacked by the French in 1457. Along with Calais, Sandwich was part of England's front-line defences against the French.

27. The old harbour frontage at Sandwich, scene of the Yorkist earls' return in 1460. It was also from here that Edward IV sailed when invading France in 1475.

28. Diorama of the Battle of Barnet at the point of Edward's attack, showing the overlap on the king's left flank and the corresponding overlap of Warwick's left.

29. The gatehouse of Beaulieu Abbey in Hampshire, where the Duchess of Warwick sought sanctuary after learning of the death of her husband at Barnet.

30. The tidal Beaulieu River as seen from beside the medieval abbey.

Left: 31. Burgundian pikeman and wife from the late fifteenth century. Men dressed much like this may have supplemented Edward's forces at Barnet and Tewkesbury. *Right:* 32. The Santa Maria at Funchal Harbour, Madeira. This ship is a replica of a fifteenth-century carrack, the sort of 'full-rigged' vessel employed by medieval navies. One such was described as 'orrible, grete and stoute'.

Left: 33. The Buttermarket at Canterbury, where the mayor of the city, among others, was executed in the presence of King Edward after the failed Kentish risings in the summer of 1471.
Right: 34. Statuette of a knight in Gothic armour from the second half of the fifteenth century.

Above: 35. Tewkesbury Abbey, close beside the battlefield of Tewkesbury. The more extensive medieval abbey grounds witnessed a great deal of fighting and a number of Lancastrians sought sanctuary within its precincts.

Below left: 36. 'The Children of Edward IV Parted from their Mother' – a dramatised nineteenth-century depiction of Elizabeth Woodville being convinced to surrender the princes to their uncle, Richard of Gloucester. (Courtesy of the British Library)

Below right: 37. Statue of Edward IV at Canterbury Cathedral – an imagined and much leaner depiction of a king who would grow fat in his mid-thirties.

Above: 38. The Tower of London, where Henry VI was imprisoned before being murdered on Edward's orders and where Edward's sons, the princes, were last seen.
Below left: 39. Statue of Richard III, England's most enduring bogeyman. (Courtesy of James Nicholls)
Below right: 40. Statue of Henry VII at Canterbury Cathedral. Enjoying a credible claim to the throne, Henry, as a young man, was not someone Edward IV could allow unfettered liberty of movement.

something he would not have done had the two men been openly at each other's throats. This prearranged visit was probably made to return the chivalric honour of the Golden Fleece – a Burgundian copy of the English equivalent Order of the Garter – bestowed on Edward by the Burgundians the year before. On Edward's behalf Warwick welcomed Charles as a newly made knight of the Order of the Garter. A formal adornment ceremony occurred later in January 1470 at Ghent.

Having wedded Edward's sister and now wearing the Garter, Charles the Bold had become closely attached to England's Yorkist king, but this did not make him a hard-and-fast supporter of the House of York. Charles put Burgundian interests before anything else. He was neither Yorkist nor Lancastrian, but hard-nosed and pragmatic enough to lay any Lancastrian familial loyalties to one side when dealing with the English. At his court were two prominent Lancastrian exiles: Edmund Beaufort, now styling himself Duke of Somerset, and Henry Holland, Duke of Exeter. Both were distant cousins of Charles's and were diplomatically kept out of the way during Warwick's state visit in April 1469; however, that there were high-ranking enemies of Edward's in Burgundy and France at the same time (two states ever teetering on war) underlines the complexity of the political situation on either side of the North Sea.

The final breach between Edward and Warwick occurred when Edward refused to sanction the marriage of Clarence to Warwick's daughter Isobel. Warwick's desire to see his eldest daughter married into the royal family was the logical outcome of the Woodvilles bagging most other eligible candidates, but it suited Clarence's interests too. The young and ambitious duke aspired to an elaborate lifestyle and needed the money which Isobel had access to in abundance. Clarence's household may have been grander even than Edward's and came at enormous cost. As we have seen, at one time Edward may have planned for his brother to marry into the Burgundian royal family, something Warwick had likely been tasked to progress when bestowing the award of the Garter on Charles at St Omer. A foreign match proved, however, to be less financially attractive to Clarence than the hand of Isobel Neville, an heiress to great fortune. The duke may also have harboured residual ambitions of gaining further dukedoms abroad, courtesy of Louis XI, and maybe even one day of gaining the kingship of England – an ambition not completely untoward, given that Edward had so far sired two daughters but no son (the king's second daughter, Mary, had been born in 1467). Should Clarence marry Isobel and should she promptly give birth to a son, Edward's authority and legitimacy might be threatened. Being the heir presumptive to the throne meant that Clarence was always likely to be a focus for discontent and insurrection: something Edward must have foreseen.

It was around this time too that rumours of Edward's own illegitimacy first surfaced – other than as idle speculation. Allegations that Edward's mother Cecily had engaged in an affair with a common soldier named Blancborgne in Rouen and that Edward was the result became rife. Having been born abroad during wartime added credence to the tale. The chronicler Mancini went so far as to claim Cecily had earlier spread the story herself in a fit of anger when learning of her eldest son's covert marriage to Elizabeth Grey. At odds with this, the Tudor historian Polydore Vergil recounted how the king's mother was deeply shocked when hearing the rumours and tried to get the purveyors silenced. One of them was probably her own son Clarence. Unsurprisingly, relations between the king and his brother rapidly deteriorated. Shakespeare's portrayal of the young duke as false and flighty may or may not have merit, but what seems clear is that Clarence at some point became a willing pawn or active agent in facilitating Warwick's plans to gain an Anglo-French accord and, if necessary, replace Edward. Although feigning embarrassment when confronted by Edward about the now proposed Clarence-Isobel match, Warwick went over the king's head anyway and secured through his brother Archbishop George Neville a papal dispensation for the marriage to go ahead.[3] Soon plans were being put in place in secret for the wedding to proceed. Edward, if aware of what was afoot, found himself powerless to intercede. There was no legal precedent for a king vetoing such a marriage, since no marriage act had yet been passed.[4] Edward must have known what was going on, however, since he wrote to his brother and cousin asking them to deny that they were 'of any such disposition towards us as the rumour here runneth'.

The wedding between Clarence and Isobel eventually took place with great pomp and ceremony on 11 July 1469 at Calais, where any diktat from Canterbury interrupting the proceedings could not apply. Archbishop George Neville officiated and five knights of the garter attended. A line had been drawn in the sand. Warkworth summed up the situation this way,

> The Earl of Warwick took to him in fee many knights, squires and gentlemen as he might, to be strong; and King Edward did [the same] that he might enfeeble the Earl's power. And yet they were accorded many diverse times: but they never loved together afterward.

From Calais, Warwick and his new son-in-law issued a proclamation denouncing Edward's key advisors. Their manifesto targeted Lord Rivers, Jacquetta, Anthony Woodville and other members of the queen's family specifically, charging them while in government with 'making great impositions on the commons so that honest men were made to fear for their livelihood, and sometimes for their very lives'. It was said that the commons 'grouched sore'. The chronicler Warkworth claimed that the people looked for prosperity and peace, 'but it came not'. He added that England was 'brought right low, and [that] many said King Edward had much blame'. This was probably stretching the truth. Economic conditions remained largely out of Edward's direct control, and may even have started to improve with the ending of the Burgundian embargoes. With a few notable exceptions Edward had also done well in maintaining law and order.[5]

In a dramatic rerun of the invasion of the Yorkist earls in July 1460, Warwick and Clarence landed in Kent from Calais at the head of a small armed force of veterans on 16 July 1469, less than a week after the duke's marriage to Isobel. Much remains uncertain from this time, but that Edward took the threat of an insurrection seriously is attested by an urgent summons to arms in his name to his commanders in Wales and the South West, specifically to his powerful allies William Herbert and Humphrey Stafford, the newly made earls of Pembroke (created 27 May 1468) and Devon (created 7 May 1469). He also sent letters to the Midland towns for armed support. One of these, written just a week before the wedding in Calais to the authorities at Coventry, requested 100 archers from the city. Almost simultaneously a major rebellion, probably inspired by Warwick and Clarence as a diversion, flared up in Lancashire.

Throughout these weeks of uncertainty Edward retained a relaxed demeanour, finding time to set off on pilgrimage to the shrine of Our Lady at Walsingham near Norwich, a visit which had been planned for some time. The shrine was associated with birth, so the king, whose wife Elizabeth had just given birth to a third daughter – named Cecily after Edward's mother – doubtless had a fourth pregnancy in mind for her. Edward and his entourage were 'worshipfully received' in Norfolk by Sir John Paston. In an attempt to impress his royal guest, Paston, of Lancastrian leanings, dressed his household staff in expensive blue and yellow livery, presumably Yorkist colours. With the king were Anthony and John Woodville, his brother-in-laws. Both men received expensive gifts from their host. Edward then spent a week with Elizabeth and their two eldest daughters, Elizabeth and Mary, aged three and not quite two respectively. He travelled with them by boat to Fotheringhay Castle along the River Nene. After the recent rigours of childbirth Elizabeth was probably exhausted throughout. In medieval times the only palliative for the pain of childbirth was prayer and a period of recovery much longer than today. Baby Cecily had been left in London to be nursed when Elizabeth rejoined her husband to sexually renew the quest for a son and heir, explaining the choice of Walsingham for their pilgrimage.

The only intimation that confronting civil strife was on Edward's mind as well as procreation were the summonses for military support, already mentioned, plus orders for banners and standards to be made ready at Nottingham and for an additional 1,000 jacks (body protection) to be despatched into the East Midlands. As further reports came in confirming growing troubles in the North, it soon became apparent that the rebels were targeting the king's extended Woodville family specifically. Given their unpopularity in the land, Warwick could readily stir up dissent by targeting them as the villains of the piece. Rightly fearing the worst, Edward ordered his father-in-law and brothers-in-law to seek safety in sanctuary or outside the kingdom. He sent Elizabeth and the children back to Norwich, via Peterborough, Wisbech and Lynn, under strong escort. Edward continued his progress into the East Midlands, girding himself for the campaign ahead. He reached the security of Newark Castle on or around 10 July; this was a day or so before Clarence's wedding to Isobel Neville in Calais, and a week or so prior to Warwick and Clarence's unopposed landings in Kent. Edward had not yet linked up with his advancing forces, however, when on 26 July 1469, at Edgecote in Warwickshire, the flamboyantly named Robin of Redesdale fired off the first salvoes of renewed conflict.

Edgecote

The true identity of Robin of Redesdale is not known for sure, but he was probably a Neville surrogate, likely one of Warwick's northern relatives: either William Conyers, a retainer of the

Nevilles, or William's brother, Sir John Conyers, an experienced soldier. The latter had been with Robert, Lord Ogle, at the Siege of Carham in 1461. Though favoured by Edward, Ogle, like Conyers, was ever Warwick's man. Whoever Redesdale was in reality, he made his mark as a general at one of the wars' most dire fights.

Shorthand for crusading rebel or rabble-rouser, the names Robin and Jack were favoured pseudonyms for medieval opposers of misrule. Jack Cade, Jack Amend-All and Jack Straw are other examples. There had been an earlier rebellion in Yorkshire inspired by another man also using the name Robin of Redesdale, and an insurgent using the name Robin of Holderness had also periodically been up in arms. Little is known of these earlier disturbances. In the words of Professor Charles Ross, the sources are 'meagre, confused and contradictory ... both the character and chronology of these rebellions remain thoroughly obscure'.[6] Modern academic opinion favours the sobriquet 'Robin' to have been bestowed on a collective of individuals rather than a single man, perhaps of the Neville affinity in North Yorkshire in general. Supporting this assertion, one of Warwick's relations, the earl's cousin Henry Neville, was killed in one of the exchanges.[7] However it was Montagu, Warwick's brother, who confronted the Holderness rising and ruthlessly put it down, so not all members of the Neville clan can be implicated.

Most probably, Warwick's involvement in the current insurrection was not at first suspected by Edward. As late as 22 May, prior to the wedding in Calais, the earl had been appointed to head up a commission to look into the causes of northern disquiet. If Warwick was stirring up trouble in the North he was – to use a modern phrase – 'operating well under the radar', using proxies in a manner designed to circumvent the activation of any immediate royal redress. Today we might use the term 'hybrid warfare' when describing acts like these: acts designed to surprise, confuse and wear down an opponent. Warkworth referred to the final Redesdale rising as a more all-encompassing event than the others, describing it as a 'whirlwind from the north ... a mighty insurrection of the commons'.

In response to Edward's call to arms, William Herbert and his brother Richard raised a large force of Welsh spearmen and set off into the midlands to confront the rebels. After an initial skirmish to secure a crossing over the River Cherwell, they marched toward Banbury in Oxfordshire to join up with Humphrey Stafford and his corps of West Country archers. Had the loyalist commanders not failed to coordinate their actions their combined force would have posed a formidable challenge to rebel intent. Chroniclers explained the generals' failure to successfully combine forces variously as a misjudgement or a misfortune. Warkworth stated that the two Yorkist armies 'fell into variance for their lodging': in other words, they became too-far separated when billeting for the night, perhaps after an argument of some kind. De Waurin considered the Yorkist commanders to have underestimated the proximity of the main rebel force approaching from the north-east and failed to concentrate in time. More imaginatively, Tudor historian Edward Hall claimed Devon had a pressing date with a fair damsel, leaving his allies in the lurch. Whatever the truth of it, Robin of Redesdale proved quick to press home his advantage.

The resulting battle was probably fought near Danes Moor, south of the Cherwell, in the parish of Edgecote.[8] The Herberts' Welshmen faced Redesdale's rebels across a small tributary stream, flowing south to north. They took casualties from rebel archery, which, being spearmen, they could not return. Both sides were playing for time: the Herberts were awaiting Stafford's belated approach, while Redesdale awaited the arrival of a mounted reinforcing army of Calais veterans. These men had been brought over to England by Warwick and were by this time clattering up Watling Street from London to threaten the Herberts' flank. Numbering around 500, they were said to be accompanied by 'all the rascals of Northampton and other villages about'. Against this nucleus of newly arrived, well-trained soldiery, the Herberts' already badly shot-up spearmen stood no chance. Welsh Road to the north of the Cherwell is said to have witnessed their flight. Bards lamented the fallen: 168 men of worth and an uncounted number of common Welsh foot soldiers died at Edgecote, the battle being considered in Wales as a national calamity.[9] William Herbert and his brother Richard were executed the next day at Northampton on Warwick's direct orders: acts of spite carried out unlawfully since they were not done in the king's name.

It seems William Herbert's rise may have been a significant factor in driving a wedge between Warwick and the king from the very start of his reign. In particular, Edward's grant of attainted Lancastrian lands to Herbert in 1461, immediately after Towton, angered the earl. Warwick also resented a grant of estates at Dunster in Somerset to Herbert's eldest son, who had married Edward's sister Mary in September 1466. The jealousy felt by Warwick at this grant and prestigious marriage may even have been the trigger that encouraged the earl to back Clarence's bid to marry Isobel. That William Herbert would become a marked man was then all but guaranteed when he ganged up with Edward to strip Archbishop George Neville of the chancellorship in June 1467. Warwick and Clarence's joint proclamation named him, along with the Earl of Devon and Lord Rivers, as foremost among their mortal enemies.

Rivers and his son John fled for the Welsh border but were apprehended at Chepstow in the Forest of Dean and executed at Kenilworth Castle by Warwick's henchmen on 12 August. Humphrey Stafford also fled west but was captured by commoners and executed at Bridgwater on 17 August. No trials were enacted. Instead a proclamation charged all these unfortunates, along with others killed at this time, of causing 'our said sovereign Lord and his said realm to fall in great poverty of misery, disturbing the administration of the laws, only intending to their own promotion and enrichment'. Although inclining more toward personal rivalry than popular will, these were charges echoing those raised by Jack Cade's insurgents during the government purge of 1450. The insurgents' other main Woodville target, Elizabeth's brother Anthony, managed to evade arrest. Ever afterwards the knight is said to have harboured a distinct loathing for the Duke of Clarence. Edward's brother may have been directly culpable for much of the bloodshed. Rather than a malign, twenty-year-old bit-player he could have taken a much more active role in the rebellion than is often supposed.

Elizabeth was in Norfolk when she heard the news of her father and brother's deaths. Frightened and appalled, she too is said to have held Clarence primarily accountable. The queen and her children hurried back to London to join her mother, Jacquetta, who must also have been in fear for her life. Jacquetta was later placed under arrest when accused by one of Warwick's followers of practicing witchcraft. A leaden effigy of a man or woman – broken in the middle and held together with wire – had been produced by her accuser as evidence of intent to harm; who the intended target was has never really been made clear. Almost certainly the whole affair was a frame-up but was a dangerous development nonetheless. Kentish troublemakers were also up in arms and there was rioting serious enough for the Duke of Burgundy to threaten armed intervention to protect Flemish mercantile interests. Worse still, taken by surprise by fast-moving events, Edward was taken into custody by Archbishop Neville's henchmen at Honiley, near Warwick, ostensibly for his own protection. For reasons that remain obscure, Edward's armed retinue had dispersed and the king initially welcomed his cousin's men as much needed bodyguards. Only later did it become apparent he was under house arrest.

Edward is sometimes portrayed as acting uncharacteristically indecisively throughout the insurrection of 1469, but that is to underestimate the problems he faced when presented with deliberately obfuscating, incomplete and contradictory intelligence.

He may have thought he was dealing with a series of unrelated, localised threats and would have expected the Herbert and Stafford forces to be able to hold off any immediate rebel attack. He also remained unaware that a strong force of Calais regulars had been added to the mix. During his earlier campaigning the enemies he faced had been obvious ones; the battles had been fought by and large in a set-piece manner and on his own initiative. In 1469, however, there had been a slow build-up of dissent in the North, with no obvious indication of a coup involving the king's brother and his Neville cousins. Even today there is no compelling narrative that accurately describes the build-up and aftermath of Edgecote, or why Edward was caught so flat-footed. Events would have remained confusing for Edward right up until the time he was seized and placed under house arrest at Warwick Castle. From there he was taken north and for a time secured behind Middleham Castle's twelve-foot-thick walls.

Like Henry VI, Edward had become a captive king. The Woodville hegemony at the heart of Edward's government had been broken. What next for Warwick, the puppetmaster now holding centre stage? With Edward effectively a captive at Middleham, the queen's mother's liberty curtailed, several of the male Woodvilles dead and two of Edward's key supporters executed, Henry VI in the Tower and Warwick's new son-in-law waiting in the wings there was all to play for. The stage was soon reset, but not to Warwick's liking. Without a king on hand to arbitrate disputes, Edward's close ally John Mowbray, Duke of Norfolk, laid siege to Caister Castle near Yarmouth in Norfolk, forcing its surrender after a two-month siege. Built just a few decades earlier by Sir John Fastolf, a veteran of the Hundred Years War, the castle had dissolved to the Paston family who were supporters of Henry VI, but its ownership had remained hotly disputed. In the North, meanwhile, resurgent Lancastrian dissidents arose, crying out for the restoration of Henry VI.

The rebel leader in the North was another relative of Warwick's named Sir Humphrey Neville, but was not a Warwick surrogate. The twenty-two-year-old, staunchly Lancastrian knight had fought at Towton alongside his father, who died there. Humphrey had then avoided the debacle at Hexham and had maybe even assisted King Henry's getaway. He was with Sir Ralph Grey at Bamburgh Castle when negotiating terms of surrender in June 1464, somehow again avoiding retribution. He became an outlaw, operating in the remote north, from time to time causing serious disturbances of the peace. Upon Edward's capture after the Battle of Edgecote, Humphrey seized his opportunity to intensify his campaign of violence, rallying men from several shires to King Henry's banner. Without Edward's backing, Warwick found himself too weak to confront this threat or adequately police the country. He called an emergency parliament on 22 September 1469, a forum which, tellingly, foreign observers at first thought might see Edward toppled and the Duke of Clarence enthroned, but he struggled to attract backers. The earl's self-seeking behaviour had proved off-putting even to his own brother Montagu, who distanced himself from Warwick politically. The earl soon found that he could not govern convincingly without the backing of the lords of England and there was as yet no real appetite for reinstating Henry.

Although Edward allegedly remained compliant during his brief period of house arrest, Warwick was too weakened to prevent the king gaining his liberty. Edward's release occurred suddenly and was described by a contemporary as in a manner 'almost miraculous and beyond all expectation'. Exactly how the king finessed his escape from Middleham to Pontefract remains unclear. Historian Polydore Vergil claimed the king bribed his gaolers 'with plentiful and large promises'. Edward Hall, on the other hand, claimed that Edward was never really closely confined in the first place, but was able to hunt and amass a host of friends and supporters at nearby Pontefract before reasserting himself as king. Throughout he is said to have remained calm and optimistic. The episode highlights Edward's famously imperturbable nature. The supporters who rallied to the king included Henry Bourchier, Earl of Essex; Sir John Howard; Lord Mountjoy; Lord Hastings; and the king's youngest brother, Richard of Gloucester. Within days of gaining his freedom and for the time being putting thoughts of squaring accounts with Warwick to one side, Edward joined forces with his recent enemy to confront the rebels. Sir Humphrey Neville and his brother Charles were brought to battle and defeated at some forgotten northern battlefield. Both rebel leaders were captured and taken back to York, bringing the revolt to an end. They were executed on 29 September.

Being on the campaign trail together, albeit in trying circumstances, may have persuaded Edward toward leniency with respect to recent events. If the plotters' actions were not overlooked, they went largely unpunished. Warwick's main loss was to have the Welsh lands he had illegally seized from the murdered William Herbert transferred to the young Richard of Gloucester. Seeking to draw a line under the matter, a general pardon was announced by the king's new government early the following year. That Edward remained on guard and that matters remained far from resolved is indicated by later chroniclers claiming the king to have harboured suppressed feelings of fury at his cousin and brother's 'over-daring deed'. Polydore Vergil later imagined the trio of conspirators 'raging and fuming' that they had been thwarted. There were, of course, a number of political casualties. One was Sir John Langstrother, the Prior of the Hospital of St John of Jerusalem, who had been appointed Lord Treasurer of England by Warwick after Edgecote. Edward had him removed from both posts. Only when the knight swore an oath of fealty – something considered to be setting a dangerous precedent by an order which jealously guarded its independence – did Edward allow him to regain the priory post. That Edward went so far as he did in suppressing his anger is perplexing to a modern audience and may have seemed so to contemporaries too. Clearly the king wished to avoid a damaging, full-scale civil war and hoped to conciliate all parties, but he was to be disappointed. Factional in-fighting had become all but inevitable.

Returning to London in October 1469, Edward was warmly greeted by the mayor, aldermen and 200 apprentices, all finely turned out and keen to demonstrate their loyalty after the recent rioting. Archbishop George Neville and John de Vere, Earl of Oxford, rode out to join him, hoping no doubt to ingratiate themselves, but in a display of renewed royal assertiveness they were sent back to their estates and told to wait on the king's pleasure. Edward's first action on arriving back at London was to have the charges of witchcraft against his mother-in-law, Jacquetta, dropped. No lawsuit was taken against her accuser however. Like others at this time, he gained pardon as part of an Act of Atonement passed in February 1470. Elizabeth, Jacquetta and Anthony Woodville, as well as the other surviving members of the Woodville family, must have been deeply put out at Edward's reluctance to press his advantage and have miscreants more publicly held to account. Adding insult to injury, Lord Montagu's son, another George Neville, was betrothed to the infant Princess Elizabeth and had the vacant title of Duke of Bedford bestowed on him. Montagu gained a marquisate for remaining loyal during the recent insurrection. His elevation and his son's betrothal to the Princess Elizabeth may have upset the queen, who cannot have been other than shocked at the idea of her daughter one day marrying the nephew of a man who had murdered her father and brother.[10] After narrowly surviving the murderous purge of his family, Anthony Woodville was another who was hardly likely to allow Warwick and Clarence's actions to go unavenged in the longer term, but in the meantime, like his sister, he had to take his lead from Edward.

The king clearly wished to retain Montagu's services and good favour. A marquisate outstripped an earldom, so on paper at least the newly made grandee outranked his brother Warwick, who remained a mere earl. Montagu was also granted extensive lands in the South West, formerly held by the murdered Humphrey Stafford. Stafford's death had left a power vacuum in an area where the Yorkist writ ran thin. Edward now looked to his militarily talented cousin to control the region on his behalf. The betrothal and titles may also to some extent have been made to placate Montagu for his imminent loss of the earldom of Northumberland, something now necessary to allow young Henry Percy – son of the 3rd Earl of Northumberland, killed at Towton – to re-inherit his birthright and act as a counterweight to Neville power in the North. Although on the face of it a snub to the Nevilles and their affinity, difficulties in navigating northern politics without the steadying hand of a Percy at the tiller demanded this. The earlier risings in Yorkshire involving Robin of Holderness may have been a siren call for the reinstatement of a Percy lord to the earldom of Northumberland, explaining why Montagu had gone to such pains to suppress them.

Henry Percy was released from the Tower of London on 27 October 1469 and did homage to the king at Westminster. It was not, however, until 25 March 1470 – once the full extent of Warwick and Clarence's treachery had become apparent – that he was formally confirmed as 4th Earl of Northumberland, with full custody of his dead father's estates, and not until the summer of 1470 did he finally replace the Nevilles as controller of the East and Middle Marches toward Scotland, the traditional Percy fiefdom. The Percy reinstatement and the loss of his earldom did, however, have the unwarranted effect of turning Montagu against Edward. The marquis is said by Warkworth to have seethed with resentment, saying somewhat disingenuously that he now would have 'little more than a magpie's nest to maintain his estate with'. His marquisate and the extensive land grants in the West Country seem to have been set to one side when this statement was made. For this reason, if no other, Edward's apparent softly, softly approach was doomed to fail.

The deals done in the aftermath of Edgecote and the positioning that went on remain a puzzle to this day. They were no less puzzling for Edward's contemporaries. Sir John Paston claimed the king spoke well of the Duke of Clarence and the Earl of Warwick in public, but not in private. Was this the politician in Edward coming out, putting the nation's best interests before those of his immediate family? Or did he genuinely desire to mend the damaging rift that had opened up? Edward needed the Nevilles, as well as the Percys and the Stanleys, to remain loyal subjects if at all possible, so that he could maintain control in regions of the country which remained disaffected to him – no more so than in the ancient kingdom of Northumberland in the North East, a region once described as akin to a foreign country to southern-based kings. Dating back to Norman times, monarchs had only ever ventured north at the head of large armies. Loyal marcher wardens like the Stanleys, Percys and Nevilles – the heads of whose families were virtual kings in their own right – had to be feted as well as cajoled. Edward's father had been killed in Yorkshire. Even after Towton, northern rebels had continued to threaten the king's authority. For the outwardly placid Edward, maintaining his hold on the North and keeping all parties on side was proving to be a near-impossible task. With hindsight the protagonists might be seen as circling each other like boxers, looking for openings, never allowing their guard to slip. Because he had failed to act decisively against Clarence and Warwick and now having also alienated Montagu, the king had become vulnerable: a fact not lost on foreign princes watching from the wings.

7

RAVENSPUR

Unconvinced by Edward's apparent good grace in letting matters rest and fearing delayed retribution, Warwick was soon plotting his next move. The following year another rebellion flared, this time in Lincolnshire. Anticipating modern tactics of denial and deception, Sir Robert Welles became his stalking horse. An out-and-out rebel, Welles called himself the 'great captain of the commons of Lincolnshire'. He had proclamations made throughout the county calling 'every man to resist the king'. This time Edward was ready. On 7 March 1470 he hurried north from Essex at the head of a sizeable army, one which included a strong detachment under the command of John Mowbray, Duke of Norfolk. Two days later he was at Huntingdon. Edward's growing reliance on Mowbray was commented on by the Lancastrian Sir John Paston, who complained to a correspondent, saying, 'while our duke [Norfolk] is thus cherished with the king, neither you nor I shall have a man unbeaten or slain in this country'.

Sir Robert Welles's father, Lord Welles, was also implicated in the rebellion. Edward had him seized and urged him to send word to his rebel son to stand down and submit to royal mercy. The king threatened otherwise to have the unfortunate lord and his associates executed, saying that 'they for their said treasons should have death, as they had deserved'.[1] While at Stamford, Edward was assured of support from Clarence and Warwick, as related by the chronicler of the rebellion.

> Of most noble and rightwise courage [Edward] with all speed purposed to go upon his said rebels, [and] early on the Monday, before dawn, drew himself to the field and marched towards Stamford; and at his coming [he] set forth his vanguard toward his said rebellion [rebels], and based himself and his fellowship in the town, where came afterwards a message from the said duke [Clarence] and earl [Warwick] … certifying the king that they were coming towards him in aid against his rebels, and that night they were at Coventry, and on the Monday night they would be at Leicester; whereof the king delivered them with letters of thanks [written] of his own hand.[2]

Despite Edward's threats against Lord Welles these promised reinforcements had not materialised by the time Sir Robert opted to fight. Fearing himself to be outnumbered and unsure who to trust, Edward had no choice but to carry out the promised executions. Lord Welles was beheaded under the king's banner along with another rebel nobleman named Thomas Dymmoke. This unsavoury episode highlights Edward's ruthlessness when pushed to the limits. In the wake of the earlier spate of killings instigated by Warwick after Edgecote, the act has sometimes been claimed to mark a point of departure from Edward's earlier, more relaxed style of leadership, but the executions carried out after Mortimer's Cross and the heavy cull of Lancastrians after Towton belie this: Edward always had the capacity to act in a cold-blooded manner.

Empingham

Welles is said to have gambled on defeating the king before harm could come to his father, hoping, it was said, 'to have set upon the king in Stamford [on] the Monday night [12/13 March 1469] ... destroy him and his host, and so rescue his father's life'. Instead, rather than wait to be attacked, Edward sent his vanguard forward to pin the rebels, then brought up his main body of troops to crush them. On 12 March at Empingham, five miles to the west of Stamford, the king is said to have put the rebels to flight when he 'loosed his guns upon them'. Belligerent cries in the enemy ranks of 'A Clarence! A Clarence! A Warwick!' left no doubt who was behind the revolt. Men captured after the battle were found to be wearing the Duke of Clarence's livery. Some are said to have attempted to divest themselves of such damning apparel, earning the battleground the nickname 'Lose-Coat Field'.[3]

Although one of the lesser known battles of the Wars of the Roses, there may have been considerable loss of life at Empingham. A wood near to the battlefield is still known to this day as 'Bloody Oaks'. Cannon and royal household troops pitted against ill-equipped rebel levies probably made it something of a one-sided affair. Even so, the battle was also among the wars' most decisive. An officer's helmet left on the battlefield contained incriminating evidence against Warwick and George of Clarence: material later described by Warkworth as a 'matter of the great seduction, and the very subversion of the king and the commonwealth of all this land with the abominable treason that ever were seen or attempted'. When examined, probably under torture, Sir Robert Welles and a number of other rebel leaders acknowledged Clarence and Warwick to have been 'the chief provocateurs' of the insurrection and that their purpose had been to destroy Edward and place Clarence on the throne. The news of these confessions was of enormous political import once. With others, Sir Robert was executed at Doncaster 'before a multitude of the king's host'. The rebellion in Lincolnshire was over but the great split in the Yorkist ranks was now clear for all to see.

Edward formally summoned his brother and cousin on 17 March, just a few days after the battle, to answer the charges made against them, but there could no longer be any patching over the cracks. Neither man dared appear. At York the king received only the submission of Lord Scrope and a number of other northern insurgents. Although there could now be no doubt of Warwick and Clarence's treachery, Edward offered to act compassionately should they at once submit to his mercy. His offer was not taken up and therefore the two men were formally proclaimed traitors.

The renegades first fled across the Pennines to Manchester, hoping to garner the support of Thomas, Lord Stanley, Lancashire's powerful but cautious guardian: a man who had so far kept to the sidelines as the Yorkist government imploded. Unwilling to declare his hand so early in the game, he rebuffed them. In the build-up and aftermath of Empingham too few men of consequence came forward to constitute a force capable of confronting Edward. The runaways next headed south, making an initial detour into the Midlands to secure their families, and then another at Bristol to park the earl's artillery train, before riding hard for the coast.⁴ Edward detached Anthony Woodville to head them off. At Southampton Anthony took possession of some of the traitor's ships, including Warwick's great flagship the *Trinity*. Warkworth's Chronicle mentions a fight occurring, but it seems unlikely Warwick or Clarence were present: the earl and duke, their wives, siblings and main supporters had by this time already veered west. They did, however, come close to being apprehended at Exeter, where Mowbray was said to have pursued them with an impressive retinue, but they somehow managed to keep one step ahead of their pursuers and successfully embarked from Dartmouth for the Continent. Having narrowly escaped the clutches of the king's men and put to sea, they were then repulsed at Calais by John, Lord

Wenlock, who had up until that time been one of Warwick's close allies. Seeing the way the wind was blowing in England, he now backed Edward.

Warwick's fleet in the Channel must have been sizeable. Some of his ships moored at Southampton, Portsmouth and Sandwich managed to avoid seizure and succeeded in rendezvousing with the earl's Devonshire contingent while at sea. Among them was a flotilla commanded by Thomas Neville, one of two bastard sons of the late Lord Fauconberg, both of whom had up until now been serving in Warwick's navy. The combined force managed to capture and take in tow upwards of fifty vessels, many of them Burgundian; they were prizes which Warwick hoped would raise money to help fund mercenaries and weaponry on the Continent. An outraged Charles the Bold ordered his naval commanders to intercept the English squadron and soon Warwick's ships were being harried along the northern coast of France by Burgundian and English warships, the latter under the command of John, Lord Howard. While at sea, Isobel, Duchess of Clarence, gave birth to a stillborn child. It was a sad and debilitating event which must have added to the heightened sense of dejection enveloping the fugitives. The party finally made landfall at Honfleur on 1 May 1470. On hearing of their safe arrival in Normandy, Louis XI sent messages to ensure they were accorded every honour.

Warwick's desperate cruise brought Burgundy and France to the brink of war. The earl's subsequent trade and ransoming of captured vessels elicited a strongly worded ducal missive from Charles the Bold, which spoke of the Earl of Warwick and the Duke of Clarence being rightly expelled from England by King Edward for their 'seditions and mischiefs'. It spoke also of the pair's great 'enmity and hostility' to Burgundy. In the missive, Charles made reference to letters he had written to Louis XI requesting that the French king deny the English refugees safe havens in Normandy and that he prevent the sale of captured vessels and their cargoes. Louis sent back an appropriately worded expression of his desire to maintain the friendship of the duke, but turned a blind eye to Warwick's captains continued harassment of shipping in the Channel. Prior to this the exiles had 'refreshed, reinforced and provisioned' themselves at Honfleur and other ports in Normandy.

The Duke of Burgundy later claimed there to have been at least three of his ships taken that bore his ducal coat of arms, later stripped and sold in Norman ports. Throughout, Warwick's captains and crews got the better of the pursuing squadrons and captured yet more ships. On one occasion Warwick's fleet threatened the Dutch harbour of Sluys. On another it attacked and plundered a Zeeland boat. Bellicose cries of 'A Warwick and a Clarence!' were said to have rung out. French vessels sent to intercept them were claimed at the ducal court to have attacked Burgundian ships instead. In one of many letters sent by Charles the Bold to King Louis's ministers, dated 29 May 1470, the duke discarded diplomatic niceties and added a postscript saying, 'The ships which you say were sent by the king against the English have now attacked my subject's ships on their return to their territories; but, by St George, if anything can be done, with the help of God, I shall do it, without waiting for your leave, nor your explanations of judicial decision.' Charles later ranted at French ambassadors, saying, 'When anyone we have reckoned as our friends makes friends with our enemies, we commend them to all the hundred thousand devils in Hell.' Burgundian balladeers railed that 'Louis had met his true kin [and that] he and Warwick were brothers under the skin'.

In England a number of Warwick's associates were taken captive during round-up operations jointly carried out by Anthony Woodville and John Mowbray. These unfortunates now faced the full weight of law. Edward's fearsome enforcer John Tiptoft, Earl of Worcester, was brought back from across the Irish Sea to adjudicate and was soon hard at work, ordering the rebels to be 'hanged, drawn and beheaded at Southampton' and for their naked bodies to be impaled and hung by the legs from the city walls. It was a gross and demeaning spectacle, resonant of the worst excesses of the wars between Christians and Ottoman Turks – one for which Warkworth claimed 'the people of the land were greatly displeased'.

After some initial diplomatic difficulties had been overcome, Warwick and Clarence received an honourable reception at Louis XI's court at Amboise, on the Loire. It was by now clear to Warwick that the opportunities opened by the Clarence-Isobel match must now be shelved. Without full French-military support there was no likelihood of Warwick making a comeback in Edward's England and Clarence's bid for kingship was never likely to attract French backers. However, the Kingmaker had come prepared: he had his daughter Anne ready and waiting in reserve and soon the unlikely prospect of a marriage between Henry VI's son, Edward of Lancaster, and Warwick's younger daughter was being mooted at the French court.

Such a marital alliance may first have been suggested as early as three years before. There is a story of the French king and Margaret of Anjou's brother, John, Duke of Calabria, carousing one night and of the duke drunkenly calling Warwick a downright, double-dealing traitor who could not be trusted further than he could be thrown. Louis is said to have responded to the duke's diatribe by instead praising Warwick for favouring an Anglo-French alliance, saying that although undoubtedly a slippery customer the earl had ever been a friend of France. Having been conspired against all his life, Louis may have been comfortable dealing with someone like Warwick, a man who acted entirely out of self-interest. Mollified by the French king's remarks, the Calabrian duke suggested that Louis, with Warwick's support, sealed by a marriage between Edward of Lancaster (the duke's nephew) and one of the Earl of Warwick's daughters, might seek to place Margaret of Anjou (the duke's sister) and Henry VI (his brother-in-law) back onto the English throne. Such a match, he said, would provide the best assurance of peace between the two countries. This 'great enterprise of England' dreamed up by a drunken duke for the benefit of his sister and nurtured by Louis ever since, now appeared as if it might at last see the light of day.

Throughout these eventful years Margaret had remained steadfastly determined to one day wrest back Lancastrian control in England. In the months prior to Henry's capture she had appealed to the King of Portugal for military support, assuring him of Henry's good health and that her husband continued to remain safely out of the hands of the Yorkist rebels. In February 1465 she had once again badgered Louis XI for military support, claiming with justification that Edward and Warwick had come 'to very great division and war together'. Unwilling to risk a head-on conflict with Edward, Louis had had to disappoint her. Now, when approached by Louis regarding the marriage of her son to Warwick's daughter, she was initially horrified at the idea, but on consideration was forced to conclude it to be the best chance of seeing her son one day crowned King of England. Understandably, she made Warwick aware of her reservations and of her ill-feeling toward him. Formalities involved the earl remaining on his knees before the queen at Angers for some considerable time, forced to beg her forgiveness for past trespasses. Obsequiousness paid off: his prostration occurred on 27 July 1470 and the nineteen-year-old Edward of Lancaster and Warwick's fourteen-year-old daughter, Anne Neville, were betrothed three days later. Their marriage took place at Amboise in December 1470, after formal Papal dispensations had been secured (they had a common ancestor in John of Gaunt). By this time Warwick and Clarence were already back in England. They had lost no time in making preparations for a another invasion of England with Louis's help and backing. With good reason to remain distrustful, Margaret had delayed her son's marriage until after the earl and duke's departure; by ensuring Lancaster did not join them until King Edward had been defeated and her husband, Henry, had been restored to the throne, she hoped to better protect him from any change of allegiance on Warwick or Clarence's part – neither man had proven himself trustworthy in the past and she was wise to bear this in mind.

Warwick did not simply wait until the time was ripe to return to England. He again fomented dissent in the North to divert Edward's attention from his planned invasion of the south coast; Lord Fitzhugh – a man dismissed by Edward from the lieutenancy of the West March toward Scotland when dismantling Warwick's grip on the North – was encouraged to lead the revolt and create disturbances in Cumberland and the North Riding of Yorkshire serious enough to require Edward's personal involvement. By the time the king had advanced within striking distance of the rebels, the insurgents had taken fright and melted away across the Pennines into the wilds of Cumberland and to safety. Fitzhugh later sued for pardon, which the king somewhat surprisingly granted.

Edward could take comfort that not only had he quickly stamped out this insurrection, he had also successfully secured Calais and strengthened defences along the south coast. That part of the English fleet which had remained loyal to Edward was operating off the Normandy coast, bolstered by a blockading Burgundian squadron under the overall command of Henrik van Borselen, Lord of Veere and Walcheren. Additionally, an insurrection by Warwick sympathisers in Southampton had been crushed with the help of a party of Dutch sailors. During the affray, cries of 'A Warwick!' were met with exclamations of 'Burgundy, Burgundy!'

For once, however, the weather told against the king. Allied patrol ships were buffeted by gales and forced to break their cordon; it was a weakening of the blockade which enabled Warwick's returning fleet, escorted by French warships, to take advantage of favourable winds once the storm abated and to weigh anchor at Saint-Vaast-la-Houge and then set off unopposed for the coast of South Devon. Crucially, Warwick and Clarence's landings at Plymouth and Dartmouth occurred just three days after Fitzhugh's pardon. Edward was still in the far North when the landing took place. Distance, like the weather, worked against him. Moreover, men who might otherwise have backed him either switched allegiance or kept their heads down.

With Warwick's invading force was John de Vere, Earl of Oxford, a man who Edward might earlier have hoped would remain loyal to him. Having generously put to one side a history of de Vere opposition to the Yorkists (both de Vere's father and brother had earlier been executed by Edward, as previously related), the king had made the earl a Knight of the Bath at Elizabeth's coronation. Since then de Vere had served him faithfully as Lord Great Chamberlain of England and for a time was also chamberlain to the queen. Like Henry Beaufort in 1464, the nobleman's loyalty proved paper-thin. In November 1468 he was imprisoned for plotting against Edward. Pardoned on 15 April 1469, he rebelled for a second time and mobilised his forces against the king during the Edgecote campaign. He later joined the main grouping of rebels at their base in France.

Once back in England de Vere travelled to Essex to raise the eastern counties, before rejoining Warwick in London. Edward's old enemy Jasper Tudor was another Lancastrian who journeyed back to England at this time. He made for Wales, stopping briefly at Hereford where he was reunited with his twenty-three-year-old nephew, Henry, a boy whose fate had for some time hung in the balance. In 1462 Edward had granted Henry Tudor's wardship to the late William Herbert. The boy had been brought up at Raglan Castle in Monmouthshire and it appears that Herbert had the marriage of his elder daughter in mind for him. How close in a quasi-familial sense the young man became to his guardian is not known; the fact that Henry accompanied Herbert on the Edgecote campaign of 1469 may have been a security measure on the latter's behalf rather than a comradely sojourn. Enjoying a credible claim to the throne, Henry Tudor was not someone Edward could allow unfettered liberty of movement. Margaret Beaufort had pressed the king on more than one occasion to allow her son the freedom to join her, but had each time been refused. After Herbert's execution

– an event which Henry may have witnessed – the young pretender remained with Herbert's widow at Weobley in Herefordshire. All the while Margaret engaged with Edward's government in fevered debates over his future.

The reliability of John Neville, Marquis of Montagu, now became all important. Should he remain loyal to Edward, or even maintain a neutral stance, there was every chance the king might be able to join forces with him to confront the unwelcome arrivals. Edward's misjudgement of Montagu now became apparent. Ennobling Henry Percy at the marquis's expense had proved too bitter a pill for Warwick's brother to swallow. Though Montagu had probably never had any hand in fomenting unrest in the North up until now, upon Warwick's invasion the marquis declared for his brother and mustered an army. Warwick's energetic diplomacy had not only brought this powerful sibling on side, Lord Stanley, notorious for sitting on the fence, was also now persuaded to throw in his lot with the rebels. Edward was suddenly faced by a dangerous coalition of forces intent on his destruction: Warwick and Clarence in Devon, Lord Stanley in Lancashire, Jasper Tudor in the Welsh Marches, John de Vere in East Anglia and Montagu in the East Midlands. The immediate threat to Edward came from the last. Montagu had concentrated a large army – thought by the authorities at Coventry to number in the tens of thousands – within a mile or so of where the king's much smaller force lay. Had it not been for intelligence of the enemy's proximity gained from a runaway from the marquis's army, Edward might have been overwhelmed.

With Edward was his youngest brother, Richard of Gloucester; Lord Hastings; Anthony Woodville; Lord Saye (whose father had been executed by Jack Cade in 1450); and a number of other knights, squires and retainers. Retreating eastwards, Richard of Gloucester may have been detailed to organise a rearguard defence against Montagu's advancing forces. If true, his endeavours in this regard allowed the king's main force to retire to [King's] Lynn in Norfolk largely unmolested.

Edward was now intent on seeking temporary exile in Burgundy, where he hoped his sister and brother-in-law would rally to his support.⁵ Harried by de Vere's East Anglian outriders, as well as Montagu's men from the East Midlands, Edward nearly drowned in the waters of the Wash. It was the nearest he ever came to being killed while on campaign. Avoiding a further clash on land, ships were found to transport the royal party and the king's small flotilla set out for Flanders at the beginning of October, attacked en route by Warwick's privateers and pummelled by seasonal gales. A somewhat abject and weather-worn Edward eventually put ashore at Texel on the Dutch coast on 3 October, to be generously cared for and provisioned by the Duke of Burgundy's governor, Louis de Gruuthuse, a man who would later be rewarded with an English earldom by a grateful Edward.⁶ Richard's ships followed on behind, eventually making landfall at Weilingen in Zeeland. By mid-October the two brothers were reunited at The Hague. At around the same time, two of Edward's men-at-arms arrived at Hesdin Castle in Artois to impart the news of the Yorkist king's arrival at the head of an estimated 2,000 men.

Through intermediaries Edward pressed his brother-in-law Charles for immediate support. Disappointingly for Edward, the duke proved reluctant; fearful of providing the French king with an excuse to declare war and not being entirely supportive of Edward – a man who the duke may have considered a spent force – Charles held back from making any firm commitment. He may have also been put out by Edward's unexpected arrival at the head of an army. Reputedly he declared in private that he would have rather seen the English king killed by Warwick's rebels than arrive mob-handed and unannounced in the Netherlands. Though the Burgundian duke may have distrusted the Earl of Warwick, he was not averse to a Lancastrian restoration as such. Through the good offices of the exiled, thirty-two-year-old Edmund Beaufort – the self-styled Duke of Somerset – and Henry Holland, Duke of Exeter, he may even have hoped to sway any future Lancastrian administration at Westminster away from declaring militarily against his duchy. A run-down English army and a defeated king parked in the Netherlands was an unwelcome outcome for him.

Warwick now needed to rule through Henry VI, so the Lancastrian king was restored to the throne on 3 October 1470, the very same day Edward and his followers landed in Burgundy. After the earl's failed Lincolnshire rebellion the previous year, the distrusted Sir John Langstrother had been stripped by Edward of his quasi-military responsibilities with the Knights Hospitaller and imprisoned in the Tower of London. Warwick's return now saw him placed back in high office. He was reappointed Lord Treasurer on 20 October. What is more, at the earl's behest Henry VI acknowledged the right of the Order of St John to gain independence from the Crown, at the same time reconfirming Langstrother's appointment as Prior of the Hospital. Earlier than this, on 8 October, Louis XI received a letter from Warwick thanking him for his support, saying, 'Please to know that by yours and God's, for which I don't know how to thank you enough, this whole kingdom is now placed under the obedience of King Henry my sovereign lord, and the usurper Edward driven out.' Two days later John de Vere proudly bore the Sword of State before the restored king in procession to St Paul's for Henry's ceremonial crowning.

Even before Warwick's arrival in London the wretchedly attired Henry had been escorted from the Tower by the Bishop of Winchester, attended among others by George, Duke of Clarence, and the newly freed Sir John Langstrother. Once the dishevelled and bemused monarch had been cleaned-up and re-apparelled, he was led to the Palace of Westminster where great reverence was shown him. All who loved him were said to be 'full glad' to have him back as king. How much Henry understood of what was happening is unclear. De Commines described the king as being 'as mute as a crowned calf' throughout, and another observer likened the frail king to 'a shadow on a wall'. Nonetheless, Henry's simple piety won over many men of all classes, nobility and commoners alike. Warwick's largesse did so too. He styled himself Lieutenant of England and placed himself in charge of an interim administration pending the arrival of Margaret of Anjou from France. Clarence was confirmed as Lieutenant of Ireland – a reward for his support in helping to orchestrate Henry's restoration. Clarence also retained a number of other honours and this gave rise to mounting opposition from disinherited Lancastrians with whom the duke remained unpopular.

At a parliament convened on 26 November, Edward IV was formally declared a usurper. Both he and Richard of Gloucester had their lands placed under an Act of Attainder. Ambassadors from France were warmly received at Henry's court. Warwick brazenly condemned the absent Edward, 'late Earl of March', as an oppressor. To neutral observers it must have seemed ironic coming from the man who had done most to promote England's first Yorkist king. The pro-Lancastrian chronicler Warkworth claimed England to have been brought 'right low' under Edward's rule, with trade mentioned especially as being impeded. The deposed king's covert marriage – portrayed by Warwick and Clarence as unseemly, if not downright illegal – also now told against Edward. Henry's past failings, however, were brushed aside.

Jasper Tudor was soon on hand at Westminster. With him was his nephew, the thirteen-year-old Henry Tudor. The future king was formally presented to his uncle on 27 October. Henry VI allegedly prophesised that one day his nephew might replace him on the throne. Although this overly prescient claim is now considered to have been made-up by Tudor historians to promote Henry VI's sanctification, there may be a kernel of truth in it. The status of the king's own son was still in question and Henry may have doubted his wife's resolve in continuing to press the prince's case to be restored to the succession. Henry Tudor was also at last reunited with his doting mother, Margaret Beaufort. Not until November, after substantial land grants had been bestowed on them and Jasper had been reconfirmed as Earl of Pembroke, did the Tudors return to Wales.

Parliament was convened on 25 November. Archbishop George Neville presided. Henry's restoration (formally known as his readeption) was confirmed. Early the following year, other previously exiled Lancastrians flooded back to England. Among them were Henry Holland, Edmund Beaufort, Edmund's younger brother John, two other earls and many knights, squires, gentlemen and yeomen. Henry Stafford, the sixteen-year-old Duke of Buckingham – a ward of Edward's wife Elizabeth up until this point – was now transferred to the custody of his mother, the dowager duchess, and her husband, Lord Mountjoy. A brief reckoning ensued. John Tiptoft, Earl of Worcester, was its most celebrated target. Tried by John de Vere, whose father and brother had died at Tiptoft's hands, there could never have been any doubt as to the outcome. Once he had been executed, Tiptoft's head and body parts were buried at Blackfriars.

Throughout the Lancastrian recovery Warwick appeared on the surface to be in control of the situation, but it proved impossible for him to reinstate previously attainted Lancastrians without at the same time alienating those who, like him, were now ex-Yorkists. These were the very men who had gained most from the seizure of their former enemy's lands and titles, Warwick himself included. On top of this, Parliament was loathe to vote money to meet obligations made by Warwick to open hostilities against Burgundy. To do so would have alienated the rich London merchant class whose wealth and very livelihoods depended on a robust trade with the Low Countries. Fulfilling the promises made to Louis XI would in the end prove more difficult than Warwick had imagined.

The earl was in an invidious position. With hindsight it is hard to see how he would have fared under a fully revived Lancastrian administration, even though he was now Edward of Lancaster's father-in-law. Charles the Bold may have seen this problem coming. It was he, not the French king or Margaret of Anjou, who encouraged men like Henry Holland and Edmund Beaufort to return to England to take control of the situation there. He encouraged them if necessary to replace Warwick, who the duke rightly distrusted. Charles considered Henry Holland to have the familial pedigree to become a potential replacement to Henry VI should Edward remain languishing in the Netherlands and should Margaret of Anjou's bid to restore her son to the English succession fail because of his alleged bastardy. Both Charles and Holland were descendants of John of Gaunt, and Henry Tudor's later toppling of Richard III in 1485 would prove that even the most tenuous claim to the throne might in the right circumstances be made strong enough to capture it.

It might have been expected that Edward's sister Margaret would have played a more commanding role in influencing her husband to back her brother, but it appears she hardly ever saw the duke. Margaret and Charles quickly settled into a domestic routine which kept them at arm's length.[7] Charles probably saw more of his cousin Edmund Beaufort than he did his wife – in a comradely sense, of course. He and Edmund had been firm friends for some time. They had fought together against the French at the Battle of Montlhery in 1465 and again at Liege two years later. Edmund's presence at Bruges had encouraged other Lancastrian noblemen of a martial mindset to join him in exile there too. As late as September 1468 the self-styled English duke had been serving in the Burgundian army, receiving expensive gifts from his mentor, including warhorses. Charles's bond with the Beaufort family may have derived from a sense of kinship, again through a shared descent from John of Gaunt. Even so it seems unlikely Charles would have supported Edmund over his own brother-in-law had he not been convinced that the latter had lost control of England to France's ally Warwick, raising for Charles the threat of a war on two fronts. Even before the Battle of Empingham the

Burgundian duke had made finance available to fund an invasion force under Edmund Beaufort's command. Only when it became clear that Edward's regime had survived the threat from Warwick and Clarence, had an assembling Burgundian fleet on the island of Walcheren in Zeeland stood down – and only now, after Edward's flight and Henry VI's restoration, did Edmund Beaufort, Holland and others return to England, armed and harnessed at the Burgundian duke's expense.

What of Edward's queen, who was seven months into another pregnancy when the king fled the country? On hearing the news of her husband being forced into exile, she took refuge first in the Tower of London with her three children and her mother, Jacquetta, where rooms for her 'lying-in' had been lavishly prepared in advance. Tapestries had been hung, floors thickly carpeted and the windows draped, but, concerned for her and her family's safety, she forsook her luxurious surroundings and stole away instead to the great Sanctuary at Westminster Abbey, probably leaving the Tower at night by boat. Though a safer refuge, the Sanctuary was a large, gloomy building with thick, rag-stone walls and an austere church built above it in the shape of a cross. It housed around fifty tenements, many occupied by the dregs of society. The queen is said to have arrived there 'in great penury and forsaken of all friends'.[8] To have abandoned the comforts of her apartments in the Tower for the relative starkness of the Sanctuary's bare walls and stone floors indicates the queen genuinely feared for her life and for the safety of her mother and three children: her daughter Elizabeth was aged five, Mary aged four and Cecily was still just a one-year-old baby.

Prior to her leaving the Tower, Kentish rebels, stirred up by Warwick's anti-Burgundian rhetoric, had 'assembled in great companies ... waxing wild' on the outskirts of London, emptying gaols and looting the homes of Flemish merchants. Polydore Vergil later wrote that everywhere was despoiled and that 'sword and fire raged all over'. To the east of the Tower, from its upper windows, a drunken throng of rioters could plainly be seen. An anxious Elizabeth wrote to her followers urging them not to resist Warwick and Clarence's coup in case the rebels should seek her out 'to despoil and kill her'. She dreaded the same ferocious backlash that had already seen her father and brother butchered. She probably need not have feared unduly: there was no precedent, yet, for a consort or royal children to be targeted by dynastic rivals and, not wanting his new regime to be tarnished at the outset by the unnecessary spilling of blood, Warwick acted chivalrously toward Elizabeth. In Henry VI's name he despatched Lady Scrope to attend on 'the late queen' and provided her with weekly deliveries of mutton and beef. With Elizabeth was her midwife, a woman named Marjorie Cobbe, retained for her long-term services with an annual pension of £10 awarded for life. In spite of the cramped and insanitary conditions, Marjorie delivered the exhausted queen of a healthy baby son on 2 November. Elizabeth named him Edward after his father and hurriedly arranged for his baptism.

Meanwhile, international relations between Burgundy, France and Warwick's England remained on a knife-edge. On 13 November 1470, less than a fortnight after the birth of Edward's son, Louis formally revived earlier plans for the dismemberment of Burgundy, instructing his ambassadors in England to settle an agreement with Warwick for direct military support in exchange for the captured provinces of Holland and Zeeland. These were both provinces earlier prised from the Bavarians by Duke Philip the Good of Burgundy during the war of 1425–8. Margaret of Anjou was formally received with much pomp and ceremony in Paris the same month and acclaimed 'the true Queen of England'. A formal French declaration of war against Burgundy followed on 3 December 1470. The excuse for war was that Charles had broken his treaties in conspiring with Edward IV, that he had ostentatiously worn the English Garter and had at the same time refused homage to King Louis. Also that he had molested French merchants at trade fairs and sent forces 'with banners raised ...

armed and accoutred' to ravage Normandy. These raids, in fact, were reprisal attacks made by Dutch sailors, attempting to stem Warwick and Clarence's buccaneering exploits. The Dutchmen's battle cry when sacking the Norman coastal settlements had been, 'For Burgundy and King Edward!'

The first direct act of war occurred when French troops occupied the strategic Somme border crossing at St Quentin sometime in December. Rather than immediately deploying for battle, both sides fell back to exchanging warlike proclamations. On 4 January 1471, Louis angrily accused Charles of allying himself with 'Edouard de la Marche, soi-disant [one-time] king of England'. A month later, after the bloodless capture of Amiens, he promised any Burgundian who defected to him would be accorded full privileges of French citizenship, with lands, revenues and rights guaranteed. A formal treaty, signed between Warwick's government in Westminster and France in mid-February, coincided with the only Burgundian victory of the campaign: the capture of the small town of Picquigny on the Somme. Sir John Langstrother may have been the treaty's author. The English contribution to the campaign was negligible. Restricted to raids made on Burgundian territory from Calais, they proved to be of little more than nuisance value, and the French king could, with some justification, be disappointed that Warwick's government had not done more to bolster the allied war effort.

Warwick wrote to Louis on 12 February 1471 saying he hoped to soon be with the French king in person at the head of a strong English contingent. Later the same month the French king received another despatch confirming that the English Parliament would soon approve a ten-year pact with France and that Warwick was manning and provisioning a powerful fleet to cross the Channel. Yet another letter from the earl followed, saying, 'Sire ... I will see you very shortly, if God pleases, for that is my whole desire. Entirely your humble and loyal servant. R. Warrewyk'. The earl was clearly playing for time. He was struggling to find the money necessary to pay his troops and loath to denude the South East of England of troops while Margaret of Anjou and her son remained in France. In a similar vein, Louis was disinclined to allow the royal couple leave of passage to England until the earl's promised army materialised on the battlefield. A dangerous catch-22 situation had developed.

Up until this point Charles the Bold had merely paid Edward a small monthly allowance. He kept his brother-in-law very much at arm's length. If not cold-shouldered, Edward remained under strict diplomatic quarantine; however, in January 1471, upon opening hostilities with France, the duke at last formally received his brother-in-law at court. On 31 December the Burgundian government had decided to provide Edward with the sum of £20,000 to cover the expenses for 'the king of England and his followers to depart from my lord the duke's lands to return to England'. From Charles's perspective, if nothing else, a Burgundian-backed Yorkist foray into England was a way of diverting Warwick from supplying Louis with more troops, thus deflecting hostilities from the duke's own borders to the English countryside. Although inspired by selfish motives, this intervention on the duke's part proved decisive. Without it Edward might have continued to languish in exile, kept at arm's length interminably. The power struggle in England would then have been played out between the loosely pro-French Warwick clique and the Lancastrian champions Edmund Beaufort and Henry Holland, both parties being uneasy allies against Edward while at the same time surrogates for competing foreign princes.

Relying heavily on the duke's help, Edward was able to procure thirty-six ships from the merchant guilds of the Hanseatic League, as well as money, military supplies and approximately 1,200 mercenaries. The main reason the Hanse affiliates were happy to bankroll Edward's invasion force was to hit back at the Earl of Warwick, whose acts of piracy had in the past proved so costly to them. In one year alone, 1458, the earl had seized eighteen fully laden Hanse ships bound for Lubeck simply because they had failed to salute the English flag. The powerful Hanse merchants had long memories. They were not an organisation to be crossed with impunity.[9] Letters requesting support were also sent by Edward to other overseas allies: in particular to the Duke of Brittany, a descendant of the de Montfort's; and to the staunchly pro-Yorkist government in Dublin.

Foreign observers doubted Edward's chances of success. The Milanese ambassador to Burgundy famously compared the king's plans to being ejected by the back door, then trying to get back in again through a window. Once more bad weather became a factor, but this time it worked in Edward's favour, levelling up what had occurred the previous year. Contrary winds forced Warwick's blockading fleet back to harbour and this enabled Edward's forces to embark from the port of Flushing in Zeeland – after a nine-day pause, 'awaiting good wind and weather' – and to make an unopposed though dispersed landing at the port of Ravenspur on the Humber, a place lost now to coastal erosion. Edward's ships were driven ashore by recurring gales and scattered up and down the coast on or around 12 March. By coincidence (certainly not by design) this was the same spot where Henry of Bolingbroke, later to be King Henry IV, had landed before usurping the throne from Richard II in 1399.

Edward's initial plan had been to land and advance through East Anglia, but upon arrival at Cromer in Norfolk he had been deterred from landing by warning letters received from the pro-Yorkist Thomas Bourchier, Archbishop of Canterbury. Additionally, the king's scurriers, led by Sir Robert Chamberlain and Sir Gilbert Debenham, had returned from scouting inland with ill tidings. According to the author of the *Historie of the Arrivalll of Edward IV*, the East Anglian countryside was 'sore beset by the Earl of Warwick, and his adherents, especially by men loyal to John de Vere, Earl of Oxford'. Another local peer who actively raised forces against Edward was Lord John Scrope of Bolton, a man who switched sides on a regular basis throughout the Wars of the Roses. Edward might have hoped for substantial offsetting support from John Mowbray, but the duke had been arrested on Warwick's orders when Edward's ships first appeared off the East Anglian coast. Everyone who Warwick suspected of harbouring Yorkist sympathies had been rounded up and brought to London under guard.

In Yorkshire few supporters materialised. Memories of recent battles, Towton in particular, remained fresh in people's memory. The earlier Yorkist presence had seemed to northerners akin to an occupying force and now Edward was not welcome. It was only when he moderated his stance – employing the well-prepared ruse (previously spun by Henry of Bolingbroke in 1399) of addressing the local authorities as simply the son of the late Richard, Duke of York, alleging he had come home to claim his dukedom and not the kingdom – that the impasse was breached. To add authority to his claim Edward announced that he had come to Yorkshire on the advice of Henry Percy, Earl of Northumberland, and by his leave. On one occasion he was even obliged to show the authorities a letter from the earl to prove that what he said was true. The author of the *Arrivalll* – a surprisingly un-partisan account written at Edward's behest – described how 'the people of the country, which in great number, and in several locales, were embattled ready to resist him from challenging for the realm and the crown [but now, at Northumberland's behest, were] disposed to content themselves, and in no way annoy him, nor his fellowship'.

Edward's small army might have attempted to cross the Humber and gain the Lincolnshire bank, avoiding travelling inland, but with the weather remaining unpredictable and after their recent unpleasant experiences afloat they were loath to do so. What is more, none wanted to withdraw from Yorkshire 'through fear' – such a 'note of slander they were right loath to suffer'. Instead they resolved to boldly march on York. Heading eastward, Hull closed its gates to the returning king and the City of York's authorities initially followed suit. According to de Waurin, Richard of Gloucester became so enraged by the cold reception he and his brother received in Yorkshire that he threatened to execute two local dignitaries when resisting the king's appeals. The cry everywhere was for King Henry and Edward of Lancaster. Many of York's inhabitants were to be seen wearing the Lancastrian prince's livery badge, the ostrich feather, and for a time Edward did so too, for safety's sake. Once agreement had been reached for York's gates to be opened, only Edward, Richard and their respective bodyguards were allowed access into the city overnight – the rest of the army encamped outside the walls. Montagu might have led troops from Pontefract Castle to oppose the king, but he refrained from doing so. He may have been cowed by reports of Edward's small professional army and by the Earl of Northumberland's resolute, if passive, support for the returning king: 'Noble men and commons in those parts were towards [Henry Percy] and would not stir with any [other] lord.' Quoting Julius Caesar, the author of the *Arrivalll* claimed Edward considered all those who were not against him to have been for him: a pointed reference to Percy's stance.

Edward's diplomatic missions to Henry Percy from Burgundy had clearly borne fruit. From Burgundy the exiled king had sent his personal envoy Nicholas Leventhorpe to plead for Percy to remain loyal, or at least remain neutral. He had reminded the earl that it was only the year before that he had had his Percy lands and rights restored by Edward. As pointed out by Leventhorpe, should Warwick prevail in King Henry's name, the earl would most likely lose his title in favour of Montagu. The truth of this had become apparent when Warwick made sure his brother Montagu was reconfirmed by Parliament as Warden of the Eastern March, replacing Henry Percy in the post. The upshot was that upon Edward's return an uneasy stand-off between Percy and Montagu ensued, allowing Edward's embryo army to march south unmolested.

Edward first set off towards Wakefield, leaving Pontefract Castle 'on his left hand'. Not until his army had almost reached Nottingham, via Doncaster, did significant reinforcements arrive – although some supporters, one-time retainers of his father's, may have rallied to him. Those that joined him on the road from Doncaster included contingents led by Sir William Dudley, Sir William Parr and Sir James Harrington. There were also others led by Sir William Stanley. Many of the newly arrived men hailed from the North West of England, the total force numbering around 600. The arriving soldiers were described as 'well arrayed [and] dressed for war'. Other arrivals were men led by Sir William Norris, retainers of Lord Hastings', who joined the king's army at Nottingham. Thomas, Lord Stanley, appears to have remained behind in Lancashire. Always a good weathervane of shifting fortunes, the lord was hedging his bets. He did no more than request his brother William to carry his good wishes to Edward, but may well have sent much the same message to Warwick by another's hand.[10]

Sir William Stanley had fought with Edward's uncle Salisbury at Blore Heath in 1459 and had afterwards fled with the Yorkist earls to Calais. Like them, he had been dispossessed of his lands by Parliament. Upon Edward's accession in 1461, Sir William's fortunes had been restored. Stanley was knighted and appointed Chamberlain of Chester, Constable of Flint Castle and Sheriff of Flintshire. Not only did he hold down Lancastrian insurgencies in North Wales, he also played a leading part in military operations in Northumberland, bringing with him 400 archers to the Siege of Alnwick in 1462. After the Battle of Hexham he was rewarded by Edward with the lordship of Skipton in Yorkshire, as well as other forfeited Lancastrian lands, so it is unsurprising that he was among the first to rally to Edward's banner in 1471.

Edward's scouts soon discovered 'a great fellowship' of the enemy nearby at Newark, led by John de Vere and William, Viscount Beaumont; the latter's father had been killed by the

Yorkists at Northampton in 1460. After preventing Edward's landing in East Anglia, de Vere had marched his troops into the East Midlands to Newark and had linked up with others of a mind to resist the Yorkist king's return. Among them was the newly returned Henry Holland, Duke of Exeter, who is said to have headed up an impressively armed retinue. Confronted by Edward's superior numbers, de Vere and his allies withdrew back in some disorder toward Leicester. Their rearguard was attacked by the Yorkist van and routed on 3 April. News of this small victory galvanised latent Yorkist support. Lord Hastings, a returnee with Edward from exile, is said to have quickly raised as many as 3,000 men. These fresh troops reinforced the king at Leicester. Meanwhile, Warwick, wrong-footed by Edward's arrival, skulked in the Midlands. He was cautious of committing himself to battle until all his forces had concentrated.

Although strengthened somewhat by the remnants of de Vere, Beaumont and Holland's commands, the earl's calls for support made to his son-in-law Clarence and Edmund Beaufort had so far gone unheeded. Warwick was also awaiting Margaret of Anjou's belated arrival from France. Fortuitously for Edward, her invasion fleet had been delayed by unfavourable winds. Warwick's often quoted appeal to one of Clarence's allies, Sir Henry Vernon – 'Henry I pray you fail not now as ever I may do for you' – evokes the desperate lobbying that went on in an attempt to garner support right up until the eleventh hour. Warwick's ambitions, his very life, lay on a knife's edge. Vernon was prepared to act as a scout and provide Clarence with information concerning the king's movements, but otherwise would play a waiting game.[11]

Always more preoccupied with foreign rather than domestic affairs, Warwick may have neglected to invest the necessary time in building up political support in England. He now struggled to turn populist back-slapping appeal into lances and bows.[12] He had raised the North on numerous occasions, but now even some of his northern Neville retainers declared for Edward. An example was the earlier mentioned Sir William Parr: up until then Warwick's lieutenant in the western marches. The beleaguered earl placed his trust in his brother Montagu and his son-in-law Clarence, plus John de Vere, Jasper Tudor, John Courtenay, Lord Scrope of Bolton, Viscount Beaumont, Edmund Beaufort and Henry Holland. Henry Percy had been excluded by Warwick from a commission. The earl, with others, must have been distrusted, rightly, by Warwick from an early stage. Of these supporters, Lord Scrope – a Yorkist veteran of Towton and Hexham, with war wounds to prove it – had supported the earl in the spring of 1469. Pardoned by Edward, who valued his soldierly qualities, he had once again fallen in behind Warwick after Henry's restoration and had raised troops by commission on the earl's behalf in the eastern counties. However, he now failed to heed Warwick's calls for support. For reasons that remain unclear he took no further part in the campaign. Jasper Tudor and his Welsh forces remained west of the Severn, too far away to intervene, awaiting the long-overdue arrival of Margaret of Anjou. Worse, Beaufort and Courtenay could not stomach an alliance with Louis XI. On two occasions – once prior to leaving Charles the Bold's court, and again at Westminster in audience with Henry VI – the two men had strongly argued against any alliance with France. Warwick's declaration of war on Burgundy had therefore come as a disappointment and a shock to them. When Warwick issued Beaufort with a commission of array and ordered him to march on London, the self-styled duke's and Courtenay's forces advanced no further than Salisbury. Gerhard von Wesel later reported them as riding westwards from London, 'not having taken the field against Edward at that time'. Presumably they were heading for the Dorset coast where Queen Margaret was expected to land.

Clarence's alliance, or, to quote Professor Ross, his 'miss-alliance' with his father-in-law, was also at breaking point. Margaret of Anjou's coldness toward Edward's brother had left the duke in no doubt that once Edward was defeated she would, in

Warkworth's words, 'procure the destruction of him, and of all his blood'. Aptly described by historian Helen Castor as 'a cuckoo in the Lancastrian nest', Clarence, ensconced at Burford in the Cotswolds, had by this time become dangerously isolated. He had betrayed Edward and married one of Warwick's daughters only to find himself sidelined by his father-in-law's latest round of realpolitik.[13] Should Warwick manage to defeat and kill Edward, it was only after the deaths of both King Henry and his son, Edward of Lancaster (who would need to die without issue), that George could even hope to reign as king – and even this formula failed to take into account Clarence's newly born nephew, Prince Edward. Clarence's claim to the throne was, in effect, indefinitely postponed. All he might hope for were promised ducal rights in the Low Countries, but then only should Louis XI, with English help, defeat Charles's forces and overrun Burgundy. This was something that now looked decidedly unlikely. Warwick on the other hand, by successively having married his daughters to Edward of Lancaster and Clarence, had cunningly covered his bets. As a potential 'Queenmaker', he could hope one or other of them might one day reign as queen and that a grandson of his might someday gain the throne. The upshot of all this was that only Montagu, de Vere and Henry Holland could be counted on to provide Warwick with immediate military support.

In the face of Edward's advance, Warwick retreated behind Coventry Castle's strong defences. Edward pitched camp outside and sent detachments of his army – now, with the arrival of the additional recruits already listed and more that had followed since, numbering between 5,000 and 6,000 men – to lay siege to nearby Warwick and Kenilworth Castles. At Coventry, displaying banners, the king challenged his enemy to come out and settle their quarrel 'on a plain field', but Warwick, unsurprisingly, would not budge. The author of the *Arrivalll* stated that 'the king, seeing this [that Warwick would not fight], drew him and all his host straight to [the town of] Warwick, seven miles from thence, where he was received as King, and so made his proclamations from that time forth'.

Even though Warwick had been cornered, the returning king was now engaged in a dangerous stand-off. After first nerving himself to do so, Montagu was at last marching against Edward. Had others not now held back their support, it is possible Edward would have been forced to fall back on the defensive. Aware of the awkward position Clarence was in, Edward's agents and the female members of the king's family lobbied the duke to forsake his father-in-law and reconcile himself to Edward, who they claimed still loved him. Among those who urged Clarence to return to the Yorkist fold were Thomas Bourchier, Archbishop of Canterbury, and the Archbishop's brother Henry Bourchier, Earl of Essex, both of whom were committed Yorkists.

Being a rich man, Archbishop Bourchier had over the years provided not only administrative and spiritual support to Edward and his extended family but financial support too. He had become one of the most powerful men in the kingdom and had been empowered to call and dissolve parliaments in the king's name throughout Edward's reign. In recompense for such good service Edward had earlier petitioned Pope Paul II to promote the archbishop to cardinal. This was achieved in principal in 1467, although it took another six years and another pope before the cardinal's red hat was finally received from Rome. Interestingly, at no point did Edward ever consider lobbying for Archbishop George Neville to be honoured in the same way, and there is a story which relates how the king cruelly teased his ambitious cousin with Bourchier's confirmation letter.

Clarence's wife, Isobel, had travelled back to England from France in advance of her mother, sister and new brother-in-law and must have been on hand arguing the case for her husband to remain loyal to her father. If so, she failed. Intercessions made now bore fruit and Clarence and Edward's forces drew together, uniting near Banbury on 3 April 1471. With his youngest brother Richard at his side, Edward is said to have ridden out 'betwixt both hosts' to embrace the prodigal sibling, and one chronicler mentioned that there was 'right kind and loving language' used.

Four days later, on Palm Sunday – the tenth anniversary of the Battle of Towton – as Edward knelt in prayer at Daventry, clasps boarding up a small, alabaster image of Saint Anne suddenly parted with a great crack, displaying the image of the blessed saint, patroness of fertility. Though probably caused by the wind or a minor earth tremor, to a medieval audience this was seen as God's clear and potent promise that the king's efforts would prosper, both in a military and a familial sense. The timing was spot on. Upon arriving at Westminster on 10 April, after first offering up prayers and prudently securing the person of Henry VI, 'the sanctuaries were opened' and Edward was reunited with his wife and daughters and presented with his new baby son, described in a letter sent by Edward as 'God's precious sending and gift, and our most desired treasure'.[14]

Edward had ridden into London accompanied by his two brothers, Lord Hastings, Anthony Woodville and several other lords. The Yorkist king had made from Cheapside to St Paul's to offer up a mass by way of thanksgiving and it was from there that he travelled to the Palace of the Bishop of London to apprehend Henry VI and the several noblemen attending on him, the most prominent being Archbishop George Neville, Lord Sudeley and the Bishop of Chester. Henry was relieved when confronted by Edward. The old king somewhat naively admitted that he felt safer in his cousin's hands than the Neville's. He had clearly been anxious all the time he had been in Warwick's custody. In a last-ditch attempt to rally support, the world-weary Lancastrian king had the day before been paraded through the streets of London by Archbishop Neville. Few well-wishers lined the pavements sporting Warwick's badge, the ragged staff. Most stayed at home. It was a dangerous time to be abroad. Although prominent Yorkists had earlier been incarcerated in the Tower, the fortress had been stormed the day before Edward's arrival. Warwick's gaolers had been seized and prisoners had been released. With London secured and with Elizabeth and their children reunited with Edward, Clarence attempted to persuade Warwick to give up the fight, but was unsuccessful. The duke had been only too happy to break faith with the Lancastrians, but must have hoped to remain reconciled to his father-in-law. For the sons of York an armed showdown with the Neville brothers had now become imminent.

8

BATTLES FOR THE THRONE

Only when their combined force reached Dunstable on Good Friday, 12 April, did Warwick and his brother John Neville, Marquis Montagu, gain intelligence that Edward had successfully reoccupied London and recaptured Henry VI. Their advance took them to St Albans later the same day. On Easter Saturday their army cautiously advanced southward and occupied the heights at Hadley Green, north of Barnet – the highest point of land between London and York. Von Wesel described how Warwick and his liegemen 'pitched camp a mile beyond the said village [Barnet], right beside the St Albans high road, on a broad green [Hadley Heath]'. Edward must have been well aware of his enemy's movements. On the afternoon of 13 April he led his men from London and quickly drove in outriders of Warwick's army in the town of Barnet before deploying under cover of darkness in a marshy hollow within striking distance of his enemy's main position on Hadley Heath. His field artillery pieces were transported from London to the battlefield on carts. Although it was later alleged that Warwick planned to surprise Edward at his Easter devotions, he probably held out little hope of doing so. This explains why he instead took up such a strong defensive position and awaited Edward's onslaught. Knowing Edward well, he would have counted on the king coming to him and that the king would attack no matter what.

Barnet

The Yorkists may have had as many as 9,000 men at Barnet; they included a contingent of late-arriving East Anglians led by the redoubtable Lord Howard, as well as approximately 500 Flemish hand-gunners. One contemporary account reckoned on 20,000 Yorkists mustering at Smithfield on the outskirts of London the day before the battle, but it appears less than half that number fought at Barnet, the rest remaining behind to guard the city. Warwick's army may have outnumbered the king's but it cannot have been by much, if at all. It also seems unlikely that the earl can have been stronger in light field guns and hand-guns, even though it was later said his 'ordnance of harquebuses and [long-barrelled] serpentines immediately opposite the road coming from Barnet ... fired all night without hitting Edward's followers'.[1] Warwick's hand-gunners appear to have posed as much a threat to themselves as their targets. Eighteen of them burnt to death when their firearms blew up in their faces.

Overnight a great mist fell. Edward ordered his men to keep as quiet as possible. His plan was to attack just before dawn. He may have hoped to avoid a protracted artillery exchange and maybe catch the enemy off guard. Both sides were deployed in the traditional three 'battles' [battalions] in line abreast, but because of the gathering darkness the alignment of the opposing armies was ill-judged by Edward's commanders: the king's right wing overlapped Warwick's and his left wing was itself overlapped. Reconstructions of the battle place Richard of Gloucester in command of the Yorkist vanguard on the right, King Edward with

Clarence in the centre with the main body and Lord Hastings with the rearguard on the left. At Edward's side may also have been his teenage brother-in-law, Henry Stafford. That Clarence was not allotted a command is telling. The middle brother may have been no great soldier, but neither was he fully trusted.

Warwick's army is thought to have comprised divisions, commanded, from their right to left, by John de Vere, Montagu and Henry Holland. There was also possibly a reserve under Warwick's direct command. Gerhard von Wesel claimed that Edward's artillery silenced Warwick's guns and that 10,000 broken arrows later littered the battlefield, but the battle was not decided by gunnery or archery alone; brute force won the day, man-to-man, in a terrifying head-on clash.

Committing his cause and quarrel into the hands of God, Edward launched his attack before the first light of dawn on Easter Sunday, 14 April, closing with the enemy after a short cannonade and exchange of arrows, as detailed in the *Arrivalll*.

> The King, understanding that the day approached near, betwixt four and five of the clock, notwithstanding there was a great mist ... yet he committed his cause and quarrel to Almighty God, advanced banners, did blow up trumpets, and set upon them, first with shot, and then and soon, they joined and came to hand-strokes, wherein his enemies manly and courageously received them.

Hastings' men on Edward's left were hampered by a line of hedgerows, which had to be hacked down before contact with the enemy could be made. Richard of Gloucester's right wing attacked across more open ground and soon began to push the enemy back. On this flank Holland's men were disadvantaged by being overlapped – it was something that is said to have 'distressed them there greatly'. Outflanked and pressed inward toward their centre, they were then further assailed by elements of Edward's 'main battle' in the centre. On the other flank – Edward's left

– the result of the overlapping of the two armies was even more pronounced, this time in Warwick's favour. Here the 3,000 men under Lord Hastings' command were quickly overwhelmed and broken. Soldiers from either side, in flight or pursuit, streamed back from the fighting towards Barnet. Yorkists' horses were taken by Lancastrians and Barnet was looted by de Vere's men. In London early reports of the fighting spoke of Edward's defeat and capture and caused fights to break out in the city.

> On Easter Morning during early mass when every decent Christian man should be turning his thoughts to God, the report reached London that Warwick had won the day and that Edward had been captured. At this many were distressed and many rejoiced so that many ruffians rose up in London and began to brawl.[2]

Concerned that Henry VI might be seized if left in London, Edward had taken the precaution of forcing the now frail, bewhiskered yet gracious, Lancastrian monarch to ride with him to battle, but at the height of the fighting Henry briefly fell into the hands of one of de Vere's lieutenants. For a time he was hurried away along the Great North Road toward St Albans, but because of the foggy conditions this dramatic event, as well as the fate of Edward's left wing, went unnoticed elsewhere on the battlefield. Had visibility been better the sight of Henry's capture and the collapse of the Yorkists' left wing might have panicked the rest of Edward's army and encouraged their opponents. Instead the Yorkist king is said by the author of the *Arrivalll* to have 'manly, vigorously, and valiantly assailed them [the enemy] in the midst and strongest of their battle, where he, with great violence, beat and bore down before him all that stood in his way'. An account that he rode around upon 'his white steed' rallying his men and leading them forward can be discounted: the king fought on foot throughout.

Some of de Vere's men, wearing the earl's livery badge of a radiant star, were mistaken in the fog for Yorkists when returning from their pursuit of Edward's broken left wing and were fired on by their own side. Edward's badge was of similar design – a radiant sun. Cries of treachery added to the confusion of battle. The resulting Lancastrian losses to friendly fire may have been unexpected but did not alone turn the tide of battle. More likely the Yorkist victory owed most to the fierceness of the king's offensive in the centre, coupled with Richard of Gloucester's success on the right. At around eight o'clock in the morning, after three or four hours of fighting, Edward's army emerged triumphant. The king immediately gave thanks to God for his victory that Easter Sunday morning, as related in the *Arrivall.*

> This battle endured, fighting and skirmishing, sometime in one place and sometime in another, right doubtfully, because of the mist, by the space of three hours, or [so] it was fully achieved; and the victory is given to him [Edward] by God, by the mediation of the most blessed Virgin and Mother, our lady Saint Mary; the glorious martyr St. George, and all the Saints of Heaven, maintaining his quarrel to be true and righteous, with manifold good and continual prayers.

Montagu was killed 'in plain battle', fighting to the last. Henry VI was recovered during the pursuit, unhurt and apparently unfazed by all that he had been through. Anticipating defeat, Warwick fought his way back to the rear of his disintegrating army in an attempt to escape on horseback. At some point he must have opted to dismount and fight on foot, possibly at his brother's urging. Tudor historian Polydore Vergil recounted him 'manfully fighting [all the while encouraging and] heartily desiring his soldiers ... to abide this last brunt with valiant courage'. Had he not dismounted he might have escaped the carnage that ensued. Shakespeare's 'proud setter-up and puller-down of kings' was overtaken in a nearby wood and unceremoniously killed and 'spoiled naked', allegedly against orders from Edward and Richard to have their cousin taken alive.[3]

Although described by Warkworth as 'a prince [normally] inclined to show his mercy and pity to his subjects', the slaughter meted out on defeated Lancastrians was unremitting; Edward, angered by Warwick's treachery, was slow to offer quarter. A low-lying area known today as 'Dead Man's Bottom' marks the traditional site of the killing ground. That the battle was hard won is evidenced by a high number of Yorkist knights killed and wounded, the latter group including both Richard of Gloucester and Anthony Woodville. Among Warwick's commanders wounded were Henry Holland and John de Vere, two of de Vere's brothers and William, Viscount Beaumont. In total around 1,500 men were killed. Sir John Paston, who fought with Warwick, estimated in excess of 1,000 Lancastrians fell, implying therefore that the Yorkists lost around 500 men. Gerhard von Wesel, a Hanseatic merchant living in London, claimed it had been the fiercest battle fought in Europe in the past 100 years.

Edward's exhausted men returned to London on the afternoon of Easter Sunday 'with sorry nags and bandaged faces ... some without noses'.[4] Their return was described as 'a very pitiable sight'. Rather than an occasion for celebrating, Edward's reception in London by a gathering of churchmen – the most prominent of whom were the Archbishop of Canterbury and the bishops of Bath, Lincoln, Durham, Carlisle, Rochester, St David's, Dublin, Ely and Exeter – was a prelude to prayers of thanks and much-needed rest and refreshment. The occasion was sombre. Warwick had been Clarence's father-in-law and former ally. He had also at one time been Richard's formal guardian, as well as Edward's mentor in power politics. On more than one occasion Warwick and Montagu had put their lives on the line for Edward; they had endured long periods of hardship on campaign in the North and had been at the forefront in underpinning the young king's fledgling Yorkist regime. Montagu was the victor of Hedgeley Moor and Hexham – battles that had secured the North for Edward. It seems the marquis may have approached the fight at Barnet with reluctance.

A Yorkist badge said to have been found under his armour might have betrayed a lingering affiliation felt for Edward. So too may have the Earl of Warwick, who is said to have come close to seeking a last minute accommodation with Edward; however, having sworn an oath on a fragment of the True Cross at Angers that he would remain faithful to his pact with Margaret of Anjou, he must have been afraid to break his word. Such anecdotes go some way to capturing the mood of resignation in the rebel camp before the battle.

On the same day that Edward and his men returned to London, the corpses of Warwick and Montagu were brought in two wooden coffins and placed on the pavement beside St Paul's for all to view. They lay naked save for a loin cloth covering their manhood. Thousands are said to have streamed past to view them lying there. Archbishop George Neville later had his brothers' bodies removed and transported to the Neville family vault at Bisham Priory in Berkshire, where their father, the Earl of Salisbury, and another of their brothers, killed at the Battle of Wakefield, were already interred. Henry was unceremoniously returned to the Tower and was joined there for a time on Edward's orders by Archbishop Neville.

Of Warwick, the Burgundian Jeane Mielot had written presciently the year before, 'Your fierceness leads you to folly and savage fates ... you shall be miserable dust, a wraith and nothing but a tale.' Burgundian balladeers, in turn, mocked the earl's continental allies.

> Frenchmen ... rain tears and sound alarms,
> For Warwick, your sworn brother,
> Is crushed by force of arms.

When Louis XI was told of Warwick's death he is said to have sighed and stated that none could fight ill fortune.

Defeating the Nevilles removed one threat, but another danger now loomed. On the eve of the Battle of Barnet Queen Margaret and Edward of Lancaster landed at Weymouth. Sir John Paston, a veteran of Barnet, concluded a letter to his mother by saying, 'As for other tidings, it is understood here that the Queen Margaret is verily landed, and her son, in the West Country, and I think that as tomorrow, or else the next day, the King Edward will depart from hence to her-ward to drive her out again'. Gerhard von Wesel claimed the queen arrived with seventeen ships at Falmouth, muddling Falmouth with Weymouth. With Margaret was Sir John Langstrother, who had earlier been sent to France by Warwick to act as her escort, as well as John Wenlock, who, with the bulk of the garrison of Calais, had switched sides on learning the news of Edward's earlier exile. Philippe de Commines noted that all the soldiers at Calais wore Warwick's livery and that Wenlock sported Warwick's device of a ragged staff in his hat. De Commines had been among those who had witnessed at first hand the rapid disintegration of support for Edward in England, relaying back to his Burgundian master that those so recently foremost in the Yorkist king's affections now appeared to be his most bitter enemies.

Margaret's fleet had been ready to sail from France even earlier than Edward's had from Flanders, but Louis XI had not allowed her to leave until Warwick had declared war on Burgundy. Unfavourable headwinds had then kept her bottled up in harbour until Saturday 13 April, too late to intervene to reinforce the earl. It was yet another meteorological assist for Edward. Had she arrived in England in time to rally to Warwick's support, bringing Edmund Beaufort and others with her, the Battle of Barnet may have had an entirely different outcome.

Upon reaching Cerne Abbey in Dorset she received the triple tidings of Warwick's death, Clarence's treachery and King Henry's recapture. Her spirits sank. Edward Hall later retold how 'when she heard all these miserable chances and misfortunes, so suddenly, one in another's neck, to have taken effect, she, like a woman [was] all dismayed for fear'. The author of the *Arrivalll* described her as 'right heavy and sorry'. Arriving separately at Portsmouth,

Warwick's immediately terrified countess took ship down the coast to the River Beaulieu and sought sanctuary at the Abbey of the same name. The author of the *Arrivalll* saw this as a defection, but the duchess had no reason to trust Queen Margaret or her Lancastrian associates and her retreat to Beaulieu was likely made while in the depths of despair.

For Henry's queen and her son, however, all was not lost. Soon a considerable body of troops, including 'the whole might' of Devon and Cornwall, had rallied to them. Prominent were the forces raised by Edmund Beaufort and John Courtenay. Until then these men had been stationed on Salisbury Plain, having taken no part in the fighting north of London, so they were fresh troops. Lancastrian spirits rose. Margaret had been on the verge of returning to France, but was now persuaded by Edmund Beaufort to strike north to rally support from Wales and Lancashire. The two noblemen – both with strong West Country connections – attracted additional recruits, but perhaps not as many as they had hoped for; Clarence had earlier led an army 4,000 strong out of Somerset to reinforce King Edward.

The Lancastrian forces concentrated at Exeter and a fortnight was spent there making preparations for the coming campaign. Commissions of array had earlier been sent out from France. An example is a letter from Edward of Lancaster to a certain John Daunt of Wotton-Under-Edge in Gloucestershire, requesting that the latter join the prince with 'all such fellowship as you can make in your most defensible array against Edward, Earl of March, the King's great Rebel, our Enemy'.[5] Not all summoned proved willing to join up. Written requests for support from the Midlands went largely ignored. One to the authorities at Coventry was forwarded on to Edward by the city burghers and received by the king while at Abingdon. News of Warwick's death and defeat persuaded men who might otherwise have thrown their support behind Margaret of Anjou and her son against doing so. An example of this was when forty archers who mustered at Salisbury at Edmund Beaufort's bidding joined up with King Edward instead. Nonetheless, Edward faced a considerable challenge. Troops that he had disbanded after Barnet had to be hurriedly recalled, commissions of array had to be raised and the royal artillery train, augmented by pieces captured at Barnet, had to be mobilised. Orders for armed support were issued to fifteen counties. On 19 April Edward left London for Windsor, where he kept the Feast of St George. His army mustered at Windsor or thereabouts. Five days later, on 24 April, after learning of the Lancastrian army's intention to strike north, he set out. His mainly mounted force made a series of energetic marches, determined to bring on a decisive battle. By 29 April his vanguard was at Cirencester, well positioned to intercept any northerly move by the Lancastrians into the Severn Valley. The enemy objective was the bridge at Gloucester. Margaret and her son were intent on crossing into Wales where their ally Jasper Tudor was raising men. Tudor had been commissioned to do so by Henry VI on Warwick's orders on 30 January, well before the earl's death at Barnet. Once having linked up with Jasper Tudor, the Lancastrians might then have planned to head into the North West of England where they could anticipate further substantial support materialising.

Clever manoeuvring on the part of the queen's commanders enabled them to give Edward the slip at Sodbury Hill, the site of a Neolithic hill fort near Chipping Sodbury. Edward's scouts for a time believed the Lancastrians intended to offer battle there, causing Edward's lead troops to concentrate to the east of Malmesbury. The opposing army deftly bypassed them and made for Berkeley Castle, fourteen miles south-west of Gloucester. Here the Lancastrians briefly rested before continuing their march. Some additional support arrived from Bristol, swelling their ranks, but to Margaret and her son's anger and dismay, upon arrival at Gloucester on the morning of 3 May, they found the bridge barred to them by forces loyal to Edward. There was not time for them to organise an attack on the town and force a river crossing. The next fordable point was a further twenty-four miles distant at

Tewkesbury. With Edward's forces closing on them, there was no time to lose.

Already weary to the point of exhaustion, the Lancastrians set off again. Following close to the banks of the Severn, their way was described in the *Arrivalll* as across 'foul country, all in lanes and stony ways, betwixt woods, without any good refreshing'. Edward's pursuing troops were also suffering. The day was sunny and hot and water for horses was scarce. The fine weather did at least allow his army to make a detour across the high western scarp of the Cotswolds to Cheltenham; for this reason his scouts managed to keep Margaret's rearguard in sight throughout the long day. Both armies arrived at or near Tewkesbury that evening, just a few hours apart. The Lancastrians had covered almost fifty miles in the space of thirty-six hours or so, with very little time to rest. The footmen in particular are said to have suffered grievously and were now exhausted. Edward's mainly mounted force had covered in excess of thirty miles that day alone, refreshed only with 'such meat and drink as he had' – in other words, just the few provisions they had brought with them. The Yorkists encamped at the village of Tredington and the fields round about; the Lancastrians made camp closer to the abbey and town.

Tewkesbury

The crossing of the Severn at the Lower Lode at Tewkesbury was a tidal ford, only passable at low water. No matter the state of the tide, with the Yorkists behind them, an undisturbed river crossing was no longer an option for the Lancastrians. According to the *Arrivall* the river level was not really the issue, rather it was 'because they [the Lancastrians] knew well that the king ever approached toward them, nearer and nearer, ever ready, in good array and with field guns, to have pursued and fallen upon them if they would travel any further'. The queen's commanders prepared for what in military terms might best be described as a static defence, deploying on a ridge of high ground (which cannot today be identified) to the south of the town.[6] Warkworth described their position as 'in a close even at the town's end [with] the town and [Tewkesbury] Abbey at their backs'. Very little now remains of Tewkesbury Abbey apart from the church. Much of the site was levelled in 1830. The coming fight was once dubbed the 'Battle of the Gastons'. The Gastons was a large field on the southern slopes of Holm Hill, where once stood a castle, long fallen into ruin. In those days the ground thereabout was much less even than it is today, so any approach made by the Yorkists from the south or south-west would have been made across undulating ground, dotted with hedgerows, ditches and orchards.

The size of Edward's army is not known for sure, but was probably much smaller than the one he led to victory at Barnet. Payroll records identify 3,436 mounted archers being present, so there were unlikely to have been many more than 5,000 fighting men in the Yorkist army. Because of the pace at which they had ridden, few supernumeraries, if any, accompanied them. Margaret's army is said by her enemies to have been larger, but 'mainly footmen', presumably billmen and spearmen. The implication is that the Lancastrian army was under-strength in missile-men, archers in particular. Another consideration is that, as at Barnet, Edward had far stronger baronial support than Margaret. Even if he did not enjoy superior numbers the overall fighting quality of his army was probably better than the Lancastrians.

Secondary accounts divide the Lancastrian force into the three traditional battles, with the serial turncoat Lord Wenlock (sometimes Warwick's man, sometimes Edward's man, never yet the queen's man) and the better-respected Sir John Langstrother co-commanding the main body of the army under the notional command of Edward of Lancaster, and with Edmund Beaufort and John Courtenay leading the vanguard and rearguard respectively.[7] Given that the Lancastrians appear to have occupied the higher ground, Edward, of necessity, had to marshal his army 'in plain view' of the enemy, probably within long range of any Lancastrian missile-men. He personally maintained direct command of his 'main battle' in the centre. Once again Clarence was denied a command. Richard of Gloucester commanded the vanguard, positioned this time on the left. Lord Hastings had the rearguard. The order of battle was reversed from Barnet; as a reward for distinguishing themselves at the last fight Richard's men were assigned to lead the main assault, supported by Edward in the centre.

A newcomer to the Yorkist army since Barnet was John Mowbray, Duke of Norfolk, who led a strong contingent. Broken at the earlier battle, Hastings' men, including Edward's stepson Thomas Grey, Marquis of Dorset, were held back in reserve, possibly under cover. Because of the possibility of Lancastrian troops being deployed out of sight in wooded ground on the Yorkist left, Edward detailed 200 mounted men-at-arms to take up a position a quarter of a mile from the main army to screen this open flank. If no ambush was sprung the commander of the detachment was given leave to put his squadron to the best use possible, as this extract from the *Arrivall* explains:

> Thinking to purvey a remedy in case his said enemies had laid any ambush in that wood, of horsemen, he chose out of his fellowship 200 spears and set them in a plump [clump], together, near a quarter of a mile from the field, giving them charge to have a good eye upon that corner of the wood, if case that any need were, and ordering them, if there were no ambush, to employ themselves as they thought best at the most opportune moment.

The Lancastrians' main advantage lay in holding the higher ground and also, possibly, hard cover provided by the partially broken-down walls of the former castle. It was said that the Lancastrian army held a 'marvellous strong ground' fronted by 'evil lanes, and deep dykes, [with] so many hedges, trees, and bushes, that it was right hard to approach'. To the east were fishponds and the deep and muddy Swilgate Brook which formed an almost impassable obstacle for any attacker encroaching on this flank. Carts and wagons would have been defensively arrayed across the army's front, plus makeshift ramparts formed from the branches of felled trees. The queen's few archers and what field artillery her generals had managed to commandeer and retain – some pieces were lost en route when Gloucester's men fell on the Lancastrian rearguard – put the masonry provided by the former castle's exposed foundations to good use as cover, while infantrymen armed with pole weapons took their place in support behind. If the Lancastrians held fast and brought Edward's assault parties under short range fire from archery and cannon it would be difficult for the Yorkists to carry the position. Edward nevertheless determined to do so.

Capitalising on his strength in guns and bowmen, the Yorkists opened an immediate artillery bombardment and ordered the advance of Richard's archers of the vanguard, who 'so sore oppressed [the Lancastrians] ... with shot of arrows that they gave them right a sharp shower'. It was probably this intense missile fire that drove Edmund Beaufort to launch a desperate and in hindsight unwise counter-attack; in doing so his forces gave up the security of their barricades. Polydore Vergil claimed the self-styled duke was overly hasty in 'drawing his men [forth] against the advice of the other captains', a claim substantiated by Warkworth who reported how, at the head of his division, Beaufort had gone 'out of the field, by which the field was broken'. The *Arrivall* adds further detail:

Edmund, called Duke of Somerset, having that day the vanguard, whether it was that he and his fellowship were sore annoyed in the place where they were, as well with gunshot as with shot of arrows, which they could not abide, or else, of great heart and courage ... advanced aside-hand the king's vanguard ... and came into a close, even afore the King where he was embattled, and from the hill that was in one of the closes, he set right fiercely upon the end of the King's battle.

Although apparently reconnoitred in advance 'by certain paths and ways ... afore purveyed', Beaufort's attack proved premature – a prelude to disaster. Edward quickly exploited his opponent's mistake by bolstering his brother's force with men from the main body. At their head he is said to have 'full manly, set forth even upon them, entered and won the ditch, and hedge, upon them, into the close, and with great violence put them up towards the hill, and so also the king's vanguard, being in the rule of [commanded by] the Duke of Gloucester'. The king's counter-stroke was ably backed-up by the commander of the squadron of mounted troops placed by him to screen the army from attack from the woods. The author of the *Arrivall* recounted how the commander of the unit of spearmen deployed on the extreme left flank of the Yorkist army, 'Seeing no likeliness of any ambush in the wood-corner, seeing also good opportunity to employ himself well, came and broke on, all at once, upon the Duke of Somerset and his vanguard, aside-hand [from the flank], unadvised'.

Edward followed up this success by launching a general assault, breaking down any residual opposition with the balance of the forces to hand; these probably included the men of Lord Hastings' division, who up until now had been unengaged. Lancastrian resistance was half-hearted at best: 'In the winning of the field, such as abode hand-strokes [hand-to-hand fighting] were slain incontinent ... the most part of the people fled away from the prince.' Some of those who fled were drowned when driven into deep water in meadows 'fast by the town'. This was probably a millstream to the rear of the Lancastrian position. The slaughter extended westward, from the later-dubbed 'bloody meadow' below Holm Hill to the banks of the Avon, where mass grave pits were afterwards dug. Those killed included Edward of Lancaster, John Courtenay and Edmund Beaufort's younger brother John. Edward of Lancaster was said by Warkworth to have been hacked down when 'fleeing to the town ... slain in the fields'. A made-up Tudor account later said he called on his brother-in-law, the Duke of Clarence, for succour at the moment of his death. Lord Wenlock was alleged to have had his brains smashed in with a war-hammer by Edmund Beaufort. It seems Tudor commentators sought to scapegoat Wenlock for failing to support Beaufort's ill-judged attack in an attempt to blame the Lancastrian defeat on human frailty rather than God's design.

Edmund Beaufort, with other fugitives from the battle, fled to the abbey church. Local tradition has it that the fighting continued on the day of the battle as far as the nave of the church and that Abbot Strensham, celebrating Mass at the high alter, bravely intervened to end the killing and assert temporary sanctuary for the surviving Lancastrian runaways. The amount of blood spilt in that holy place so unsettled the religious community that the abbey church was later reconsecrated. A parish church several miles away at Didbrook was also claimed to have been 'notoriously polluted by violence and the shedding of blood', so it seems some fleeing Lancastrians sought sanctuary further afield. At some point a formal procession was organised within the abbey church for the Yorkist victory to be celebrated. Edward also found time to knight a number of men who had distinguished themselves in battle. Lord Hastings' two brothers, Richard and Ralph, were among them. This ceremony is said to have taken place at 'Knight's Field', several miles to the east of Tewkesbury, near the village of Grafton, beside Bredon Hill, a place that has since been described as 'a jewel in a jewelled plain'.[8]

Edmund Beaufort, among others, was later dragged from the abbey precincts on Edward's orders. The king was in no mood to defer to Church privilege. The self-styled earl had languished in the abbey for forty-eight hours or so before being removed. He was afforded a trial of sorts. The king's brother, Richard of Gloucester, in his capacity as Lord High Constable of England, and John Mowbray, Earl Marshal of England presided. Beaufort and fifteen others, including Sir John Langstrother, were executed in the marketplace. Their bodies suffered no dismemberment. Instead their corpses were 'licensed to be buried' intact. Langstrother's corpse was conveyed to the hospital of St John at Clerkenwell for honourable interment. Edward's actions in denying the men sanctuary has since been described as 'despotic in the extreme', but religious experts had ruled the abbey unable to legally provide sanctuary.[9]

With Edmund Beaufort's execution and the death of Edward of Lancaster, Lancastrian hopes appeared to have been crushed and the Yorkist triumph seemed complete. Margaret of Anjou and her companions were captured three days after the battle. Henry's queen had taken refuge in 'a poor religious place', either Little Malvern Priory or Evesham Abbey, but was later captured somewhere nearer to Tewkesbury. With her when taken were three recently made widows: the queen's fourteen-year-old daughter-in-law Anne Neville, the Countess of Devon and Lady Katherine Vaux. It was while in hiding that Margaret must have learned of the death of her son and the execution of her champion, Edmund Beaufort. That she left the priory and travelled back toward the scene of the fighting could indicate she wished to gain firm corroboration of what had occurred. Stories claiming she had been present at the battle and had watched the disaster unfold from the tower of Tewkesbury Abbey are untrue. Another fireside tale that can be discounted is that Edward of Lancaster survived the battle and outfaced Edward, only to be struck down by a knife wielded by the king's brother, Richard of Gloucester.

Edward reached Coventry on Saturday 11 May. Margaret of Anjou was brought to him there. She is reputed to have castigated him for the death of her son, much to Edward's annoyance. She had little to lose in doing so. Her plans, it seemed, were in ruins. Only now did she receive the news of the arrival of another great army at large in England, this one led by the late Lord Fauconberg's bastard son Thomas Neville, but if Margaret momentarily held out any hope of a turnaround the sources are silent. There was also rioting in the North and it was probably with respect to this that Edward wrote to his supporters requesting additional troops be sent into the Midlands. Much to Edward's relief, however, Henry Percy, with a small bodyguard described as 'not arrayed in the manner of war', brought Edward news in person that there was now no longer any need for the Yorkists to continue northward as the nascent risings there had been nipped in the bud. As a reward for his loyalty the earl had the wardenship of the East March restored to him, as well as a lifetime constableship of Bamburgh and the justiceship of the king's forests 'beyond the Trent'.[10]

London

Since 1463, the year of his father's death, Thomas Neville, with another of his illegitimate brothers, had served at sea with Warwick and had spent his time harassing Burgundian shipping. During the period of Henry VI's restoration he had kept up a patrol of the English Channel, glorying in the impressive title 'captain of the navy of England and men of war both by sea and land'. If Warwick had detailed him to blockade the Burgundian ports to hamper any attempt made by Edward to re-invade England, Thomas had abjectly failed. On top of this he had arrived back in Kent too late to reinforce his uncle in the lead up to Barnet. It was not until late April that his force of Calais regulars and volunteers sailed up the Thames to threaten London – a waterborne rerun of earlier Kentish insurrections. Warkworth reckoned Thomas to have had 20,000 men under arms, all 'good men, well harnessed' and led by deputies loyal to him, but a figure a quarter of this size would probably be more accurate.

From Sittingbourne in Kent, Neville wrote to London's mayor and aldermen asking permission to pass through the city, claiming he had come only to 'seek out and oppose the usurper of the throne'. In reality his intent must have been to re-establish or secure custody of Henry VI. The London authorities, aware by this time of Margaret of Anjou's defeat at Tewkesbury and backed-up by forces under the command of the wounded Anthony Woodville and Earl of Essex, refused him entry. It was a bold move which left the ball firmly in Thomas Neville's court as to what to do next: bypass London and strike westward or mount an immediate attack on the capital's defences?

On 12 May, hoping to force a way into the city, Neville opened a cannonade against the Southwark end of London Bridge and destroyed a newly built gate. In parallel to this happening, more of his men were ferried across the river in an attempt to gain the north bank, but in fierce hand-to-hand fighting the assault was driven off by the determined London citizenry. Next day Neville marched westward to Kingston, seeking an easier river crossing. Instead he found bargeloads of men ready and waiting to oppose him. Rumours of Edward's imminent return probably then persuaded him to fall back to his ships to the east of London Bridge. Thomas Neville was too good a soldier to risk being sandwiched between a returning, triumphal army and the stubborn Londoners.

He gave an assault on London one last shot, however. On 14 May his forces stormed Kingston Bridge and Aldgate. The incursions were only beaten back when Anthony Woodville, at the head of London's defenders, bravely sallied out from a postern gate of the Tower and drove the rebels back to Stepney and Poplar with heavy losses. Under fire from guns mounted on the Thames embankment, the rebel ships were forced to withdraw downstream. Neville and his core Calais contingent fell back to Canterbury four days later. The writer Thomas Mallory – at the time a prisoner in Newgate Prison – later used Neville's attack on the capital as inspiration for a fictional onslaught on the Tower of London in his alliterative poem set in the days of King Arthur and the Knights of the Round Table, making reference to the booming of great guns and of the determined forays launched against the city walls using scaling ladders. Edward's queen and daughters most likely witnessed these events at first hand.

Edward arrived back in London on 21 May. At his side rode Henry Stafford, Duke of Buckingham. The teenage duke was now the veteran of two major battles. Edward's bloodied gauntlet travelled on ahead of him, a token received by Queen Elizabeth as proof of her husband's victory and safety. Next day the king knighted London's mayor and ex-mayor, as well as a number of the city's aldermen, for their resolve in the face of Thomas Neville's attacks. Most of the army which had fought at Tewkesbury had by this time dispersed, so new commissions of array were sent out in the face of the renewed, albeit blunted threat from Kent.

Soon after this Henry VI was murdered. His killing probably took place in the Wakefield Tower at the Tower of London, the monarch's normal place of imprisonment. The seventeenth-century historian William Habington claimed the murder was committed 'in the dark ... as an act of state' and this seems a more likely explanation than an official report which claimed Henry died 'from pure displeasure and melancholy'. Margaret of Anjou had been drawn through the city in a cart in advance of Edward's army, suffering the same sort of humiliation that the ancient Egyptian queen Cleopatra had avoided only by poisoning herself before her enemies could take her. Shortly before his death Henry may have watched the sorry spectacle of his defeated wife being paraded before London crowds unfold from one of the Tower's windows.

Richard of Gloucester has ever since been implicated in Henry's murder. Philip de Commines mentioned rumours at the time of the duke's involvement. Warkworth also indirectly implicated Richard by claiming he was at the Tower when Henry died. Richard may have been there, but so too probably was Edward, and it must have been on the king's orders, not his brother's, that the unfortunate Henry was despatched, likely garrotted or bludgeoned to death. The Milanese ambassador in France considered Edward to have ordered Henry's death to 'crush the [Lancastrian] seed' forever. In the event, there was really no reason to keep Henry alive, but every reason to see him dead. Rather than a wanton deed, the old king's murder might better be spun as done in the public good and for the future stability of the realm; an action in keeping with the Machiavellian principle that it is better to remove one individual than allow discord to spread in the many. Edward was enacting a necessary toughness.

Henry's body was brought via Cheapside to St Paul's on a bier on the afternoon of 22 May, where it lay uncovered overnight for all to see. Next day the body was moved to Blackfriars, then on to Chertsey for burial. Blood was allegedly seen to issue from the nose of the corpse onto the pavement at St Paul's and again at Blackfriars; the discharge would have alerted a medieval audience to the fact that the king's murderer was to be found nearby.[11] According to Warkworth, when Henry was finally interred 'a blazing star three foot high by estimation appeared in the west' as if symbolising the dead king's heavenward ascent.

Pursued to the coast of Kent, Thomas Neville threw himself on the king's mercy after surrendering his fleet of forty or more warships to Richard of Gloucester. He gained a full pardon at Richard's hands. Edward was also in Kent at the time, securing the City of Canterbury and making arrangements for the re-officering of Calais. On 29 June he granted his brother, Richard Neville, castles at Middleham, Sheriff Hutton and Penrith. Two weeks later Richard was given all the Neville lands in Yorkshire and Cumberland. These grants represented the establishment for York's youngest son of a great northern power base. Thomas Neville accompanied Richard when the latter rode north. Possibly it was hoped that the presence of Fauconberg's bastard might help win over former Neville retainers to their new overlord. Well aware he now faced delayed retribution, Richard's companion almost immediately upped and fled. He was apprehended at Southampton, hoping to gain a ship which would take him into exile. After a violent scuffle he was taken back north and executed at Middleham Castle on Richard's orders.

In September that year Edward was again in Canterbury, taking with him from London a host of supporters and well-wishers. The event was described as a great pilgrimage of thanksgiving. Sir John Paston wrote, 'The King and Queen and much other people are ridden and gone to Canterbury; never so much people was seen in pilgrimage before at once, as men say.' Perhaps the royal couple took time out to view a magnificent set of stained glass which depicted them at prayer. The glass portraiture had first been ordered by Edward after news of Henry VI's capture in June 1465 had been received. Upon the birth of the royal children, the order had been added to. Whether the panes had been installed in the north-west transept of the cathedral beside the Martyr Chapel by the summer of 1471 seems unlikely; more probably they remained works-in-progress.[12] Escaping the attentions of Cromwell's iconoclasts, the series of panes remain in situ today. They show Edward and Elizabeth plus their two ill-fated sons, Edward and Richard, and their five daughters, Elizabeth, Cecily, Anne, Katherine and Mary, at prayer.

It was at this time too that Thomas Neville's accomplice, Canterbury's mayor Nicholas Fount – 'a creature of Warwick's' – was drawn along Canterbury's rough, cobbled streets on a hurdle from the castle to the main gate of the cathedral and in the presence of the king executed as a traitor. Not many other gory examples of retribution such as this were carried out: fines far outstripped gaol terms or executions in the aftermath of Tewkesbury. The *Great Chronicle of London* went so far as to conclude that Edward wished to hang men who had opposed him 'by the purse' rather than by the neck, an approach later used to even better effect by Henry VII. Sums paid in Essex and Kent came to £250 and £1,700 respectively and were described as lump sums paid as communal fines. The Cinque Ports and places like Coventry, where rebels had also been harboured, had to buy back their liberties and privileges as well.[13]

It was also probably true that after Tewkesbury more men were pardoned than punished. The king was looking to build trust and harmony rather than to erect executioner's platforms and gallows. With justification Edward could feel proud at what he had achieved. No other English king save Ethelred II in the eleventh century had won back a lost kingdom through force of arms, and none had won the right to kingship in battle on two separate occasions.

9

THE KING'S BROTHERS

Edward's brothers George and Richard were respectively just ten and eight years of age at the time of the Yorkist takeover in 1461. Both were too young to play any part, but old enough to be aware of the risks the family faced. When London was briefly threatened by Margaret of Anjou after her victory at St Albans, they were hurried off to Burgundy for their better security, housed away from the Burgundian capital to save Duke Philip the Good's diplomatic blushes. The Burgundian duke – father of Charles the Bold – wished to appear neutral with respect to events unfolding across the North Sea. After Towton the international status of the two boys dramatically improved. They were invited to the ducal court at Bruges and presented to Duke Philip before travelling back to England to attend their brother's coronation. George was now second in line to the throne – in the words of his biographer, 'of immediate importance' in the kingdom.[1] His title, Duke of Clarence, was chosen specifically to underline his royal credentials; so too was his award of extensive estates. Still a minor, he remained living for a time with his sister Margaret at Greenwich Palace on the south bank of the Thames, east of London. Richard was meanwhile placed in the household of the Earl of Warwick, probably remaining under the earls' protection – variously at Middleham, Sheriff Hutton and Warwick – until the age of sixteen. Setting aside the close ties he developed with the earl's family, he then allied himself with his brother Edward, a man he is said to have looked up to with something akin to hero-worship.

The comparison between the shorter, slight and misshaped Richard with the tall, strongly built Edward must have been marked, but the two men were close and made a good team. Shakespeare's description of Richard as 'not shaped for sportive tricks, nor made to court an amorous looking-glass … Deform'd, unfinish'd' we know now to have some merit, but suffering from a deformity of the spine did not prevent him from marrying, governing on Edward's behalf and energetically pursuing warlike agendas. Whether Warwick ever sought to inveigle Richard as he did Clarence is not known for sure, but seems unlikely. Being younger than Clarence and fanatically fond of Edward made Richard a less promising target for the earl's ambitions.

Richard's first-recorded official function on behalf of his brother was in presiding at the trial of two traitors, Henry Courtenay and Thomas Hungerford, at Salisbury, in January 1469. The men were alleged to have plotted the death of Edward in league with agents of Margaret of Anjou. Both were executed. In the summer of the same year, just prior to the Battle of Edgecote, Richard was at the king's side when embarking on pilgrimage to Walsingham in East Anglia. When so many men appear to have sought Edward's downfall, it might come as a surprise to Richard's casual critics to know that he remained among his brother's most loyal supporters. Possibly the two men shared Edward's brief period of semi-informal house arrest at Middleham Castle. If so they must have spent many hours together in conversation, planning how best to bring their wayward brother Clarence back into the family fold. The two brothers were again together in the autumn at London. On this occasion Edward entrusted Richard, aged just seventeen at the time, with the constableship of England, replacing the king's murdered father-in-law, Lord Rivers, in the post. The deaths of several of the king's allies after Edgecote made a major territorial reassignment a pressing requirement. In particular royal authority needed to be re-established in Wales after William Herbert's death. Edward unhesitatingly awarded Richard with the substance of the deceased's offices in Wales, as well as other official responsibilities in Gloucestershire. In effect this placed his youngest brother in control of the Welsh Marches and the principality itself. It was while Richard was asserting his authority there that the Battle of Empingham was fought, so it is unlikely that he took any part in the fighting.

Only after the Earl of Warwick's death did the more grasping side of Richard's nature assert itself; by then he, like Clarence, was being driven by the need to establish himself as a great nobleman in his own right. The tensions that this created in the royal family brought the country once again to the brink of civil war. Dispute first centred on the division of the Neville spoils. Clarence was married to one of the two richest heiresses in the kingdom: Isobel Neville. Richard sought to emulate this by marrying Isobel's sister, the recently widowed Anne Neville, now a fulsome sixteen-year-old girl, described by her biographer in retrospect as 'an unhappy pivot of destiny'.[2]

Anne was Richard's second cousin and probably someone well known to him from childhood. Clarence, her brother-in-law, had her under his guardianship and was probably hopeful that he would inherit the bulk of the forfeit Neville territories, including Anne's portion, without challenge. How Anne viewed her brother-in-law after Clarence's defection back to Edward is, of course, not known, but since it had led to her father and husband's deaths she had every cause for anger. Richard wasted no time securing Anne from wherever Clarence secreted her.[3] He smuggled her away, placing her for safe keeping in sanctuary at the Church of St Martin le Grand in London. Did Anne go willingly? She may have gone kicking and screaming for all we know!

Sir John Paston was among those who witnessed what followed. He recounted in one of his many letters that Edward was soon forced to intercede between his brothers, adding that the resulting meeting was 'not [conducted] all in charity'. Probably indifferent to Anne's eventual marital fate, George nevertheless demanded the lion's share of her inheritance, setting in motion a longstanding legal battle. Edward might have passed an Act of Attainder on the Neville's lands and titles, bringing them within the remit of Crown patronage and thus avoiding this, but this would not have given a future beneficiary a solid, long-term hold over them. This was because a future Act of Parliament might reverse the attainder. A better way forward was to rely on marriage and time-honoured laws of inheritance. Once title was established it could not readily be overturned.

The *Croyland Chronicle* speaks of 'violent dissensions' between Clarence and Richard and of Edward sitting in judgement while each man put forward his legal arguments. For young men not long out of their teens, contemporaries were impressed by the depth and scale of the debate, where 'many arguments, with the greatest acuteness, were put forward'. In the end only an uncomfortable compromise sealed matters: Clarence gained the confiscated territories of the earls of Devon, Salisbury and Warwick, and was made Lord Great Chamberlain; Richard forfeited the chamberlainship but was granted leave to marry Anne – this occurred in the spring of 1472, but without the necessary papal dispensation. Richard also gained the territories of the now exiled John de Vere, Earl of Oxford, but, crucially, not the Countess of Oxford's. He had, as earlier mentioned, been awarded the Neville lordships of Middleham, Sheriff Hutton and Penrith. Anne was confirmed as legally entitled to inherit her father's northern lands, so in effect these came to Richard too.

A major bone of contention was the argument about what should become of Clarence and Richard's mother-in-law's substantial landholdings. Despite desperate pleas made to Edward to honour her legal rights, the Countess of Warwick – under close guard at Beaulieu Abbey for the best part of two years, at Edward IV's 'right sharp commandment' – in the end saw her vast estates in the Midlands become forfeit, divided between her two son-in-laws as if she were deceased and therefore had no say in the matter. It was a deed that has since been described as a hard-nosed act of appropriation on the part of York's sons, mitigated only by the subsequent kindness shown to the dowager countess by Richard, who, during the exceptionally hot, dry summer of 1473 – a year of poor harvests and 'a bloody flux' – persuaded the king to allow the duchess the freedom to accompany him to Middleham so that she could be at her daughter's side during her confinement. Even this small consideration on his brother's part is said to have caused Clarence a great deal of anxiety. He would rather have seen the countess languish in Hampshire than allow Richard to have the possession of her person, since this might prove to be an advantage when the shares of her estates were divided up. Richard's potential ulterior motives have, of course, been questioned by his detractors, and an equally good case can be made that the countess was cajoled by Richard into trading imprisonment at Beaulieu for something very similar at Middleham Castle.

Another countess was also targeted by Richard. Through a mix of threat and persuasion he managed to strip the Countess of Oxford of her estates. Rights to these were formally released to him on 9 January 1473. Even Edward considered his brother to have acted harshly and probably illegally in forcing the countess's arm. This was later borne out when the king warned off a potential purchaser from buying the duchess's old town house from Richard, saying, 'The title of the place [may] be good in my brother's hands [but it would be hard for another] to keep it and defend it.'⁴ Cynical realism would appear to have been another facet of Edward's character.

On account of the jealousies engendered by all this legal flummery, by the winter of 1473 the country – much of which was flooded after an autumn of torrential rain – was again verging on civil war, as expounded by a Paston correspondent:

> The world seems queasy here [in London]; most that be about the king have sent hither for their armour, and it is said for certain that the Duke of Clarence makes himself as big as he can, showing how he will deal with the Duke of Gloucester, but the king intends, in eschewing all inconveniences, to be as big as both, and to be a stifler between them.[5]

Edward's intervention may have prevented armed conflict between his two brothers, but also served to harden attitudes with the royal family. Elizabeth took Richard's side over Clarence and may have influenced Edward in this direction too. It seems threats were aimed at Clarence while sweeteners went to Richard. An example was a grant of Barnard Castle in County Durham and land in Derbyshire and Hertfordshire to Richard. The Hertfordshire lands would later be exchanged by Richard for landholdings in Yorkshire, including the important lordship of Scarborough Castle. Parliament also ruled that the late John Neville's son, George, Duke of Bedford, be barred from any claim on his father's estates, which meant that Richard was able to incorporate them into his own northern landholdings. This final act of aggrandisement was formally passed into law in February 1475.

Edward may have set out to treat his brothers equally, but the upshot of all this territorial dismembering was that Richard emerged as the second most powerful man in the kingdom and by far the most powerful man in the North East, a region that had proved so troublesome for Edward in the past. Apart from the king's own landholdings only those of Henry Stafford, the young Duke of Buckingham, may have exceeded Richard's in size and wealth. Richard became in effect Edward's 'Lord of the North'. The only areas north of the Trent where his rule did not run unopposed were in Lancashire and Cheshire, where Lord Stanley's interests juxtaposed. Elsewhere important local nobles, like Henry Percy, proved more malleable and deferred to the duke. Edward also granted Richard two of the commanding Great Offices of State: Lord High Constable and Lord High Admiral of England. Clarence never gained equivalent political office. Because of this relations between him and Edward chilled. It may be that Edward had never really forgiven his brother for earlier treacheries. Certainly Elizabeth and other members of her family had never done so. Now blamed for almost sparking another bout of civil war, Clarence was stripped of his ownership of Tutbury Castle in Staffordshire, his principal seat, something the duke is said to have greatly resented.

Other than his brother Richard, Edward's most stalwart supporter was probably William, Lord Hastings, a man of whom it was said by a Paston correspondent in 1472, 'what my said Lord Chamberlain might do with the King and with all the lords of England I trust is not unknown to you, or any other man alive'. Hastings hit it off well with both Clarence and Richard too. Prior to Tutbury Castle being reclaimed for the Crown, Clarence had made Hastings his Master of the Game (head gamekeeper) and Steward of High Peak. Throughout his career Hastings avoided getting on the wrong side of anybody, even men opposed to Edward, and yet he retained the king's affection: a measure it would seem of the lord's likeability and openness. Tudor historian Thomas More described Hastings as 'honourable', 'gentle' and 'well beloved'. He was also influential. Charles the Bold, who Hastings may have befriended while in exile, used him to gain influence with Edward and even granted Hastings an annuity. Later, in 1475, King Louis of France would do much the same. The only antipathy borne towards Hastings, so far as we know, was from Elizabeth and the other Woodvilles, in particular by men like the queen's son Thomas Grey and her brother Anthony Woodville, the latter titled Earl Rivers since 1469.

Less close to the king than Hastings, or Grey for that matter, Anthony was a complex man who was perhaps difficult to like. He was described by historian Elizabeth Jenkins as 'supercilious and sly'. Her source was probably Thomas More, who portrayed Anthony as unscrupulous, overbearing and power hungry. Mancini's contemporary portrait of the lord, on the other hand, was of 'a kind, serious and just man, one tested by every vicissitude of life'. De Commines also rated Woodville, viewing him as 'a very gentle knight'. More recently Professor Ross has identified in him a strange mix of 'melancholy and asceticism', reflected presumably in the knight's penchant for wearing a hair shirt 'beneath the silken clothes of the courtier'.[6] After Tewkesbury, rather than roll up his sleeves and help the reinstated king rebuild his administration, Anthony made plans to go on crusade instead. He might otherwise have become an important player in Edward's government. Key positions like the constableship of England and the captaincy of Calais, which might otherwise have been entrusted to the king's brother-in-law, went instead to Richard of Gloucester and Lord Hastings respectively. Anthony had proved a 'safe pair of hands' on more than one occasion, but the fluctuating fortunes of civil war, in particular his brief exile and the brutal deaths of his father and brother, persuaded him to fight in God's service against the heathen Turk rather than against his fellow Christians. As it turned out Anthony never got to go on crusade. Possibly Elizabeth persuaded him to remain at her side after the death of their mother, Jacquetta. The dowager duchess died on 30 May 1472. By this time plum posts in government had been filled. Instead Anthony was made the Prince of Wales's guardian, a post to which he was ideally suited, especially since it was one which might only be commended to someone the king and queen absolutely trusted. When, aged three, Prince Edward gained his own household at Ludlow Castle, Anthony Woodville accompanied him there.

Jacquetta of Luxembourg's burial place remains unknown. Married as a teenager to a middle-aged duke, widowed before the age of twenty, she had then married for love, contriving somehow to ennoble her new husband and elevate her children to the highest rungs of the nobility – no mean feat! In all she bore fourteen children – seven girls and seven boys – only two of whom died young. Much of what is known about her life relates to accusations made against her by her daughter's enemies of alleged witchcraft in particular. Discounting this the impression is of a formidable woman able to thrive in an often divided court.

Another of Edward's key men was John, Lord Howard. As well as a soldier, Howard was also one of England's great shipowners, with a dozen or so vessels in his mercantile fleet. One, a 'carvel', the *Edward*, was jointly financed with the king, costing almost £200 to build. His ships doubled as traders and convoy escorts. Even before Edward's succession to the throne, Howard had been a seafarer. In 1464 the king had appointed him to the post of deputy admiral, responsible for the East Anglian seaboard. By 1470 he was commanding a fleet in the Channel with the title Deputy Lieutenant of Calais, a post that was reconfirmed the following year after Tewkesbury. One of Howard's many tasks was to liaise with the kingdom's heavily taxed mercantile community and keep them onside. Edward never really had a fleet of ships he could call his own – he relied instead on chartering vessels from men like Howard to provide convoy escorts in the Channel. Not until the reign of Henry VII would an English king boast warships to match those earlier built by Henry V, whose flagship, the *Grace Dieu*, a 'carrack', may have rivalled the *Victory* in size and was twice the size of the *Mary Rose*. Struck by lightning, it had burnt at its moorings in 1439.[7]

Enemies of Edward's were still at large. Escaping the debacle at Barnet, John de Vere, his two brothers and Viscount Beaumont had fled to Scotland, later to re-emerge in France where they were warmly received at the court of Louis XI. Another potential enemy, Archbishop George Neville, a man with good reason to fear for his life, had earlier been pardoned by Edward. He regained his liberty in the summer of 1471, but was soon reoffending. What the archbishop hoped to achieve by his intrigues is not obvious, but circumstantially there is reason to believe he plotted with the likes of the exiled de Veres and Beaumont, among others.

With Neville's connivance these men and their supporters were soon again causing trouble for Edward, mounting attacks on Calais and attempting landings along the coast of Essex, where patchy Lancastrian support still existed. Maybe Edward had been awaiting his opportunity to square accounts with the archbishop and land bigger fish too. True or not, the Archbishop was brought back within the 'flint bosom' of the Tower overnight on 25/6 April 1472. A few days later he was shipped off to prison overseas in Calais. Edward then seized his cousin's material possessions, which included goods worth £20,000. A jewelled mitre belonging to the archbishop was converted into a crown for the king to wear. According to the moralising John Warkworth, 'such goods as were gathered with sin were lost with sorrow'.

With Edward of Lancaster's death the direct line of the House of Lancaster was now all but extinct. Only Henry Tudor and Henry Holland could, at a push, claim some legitimacy as Henry VI's heirs. After escaping from Wales upon hearing news of Queen Margaret of Anjou's capture and the death of the prince and king, Jasper and the fourteen-year-old Henry had fled to France. Possibly they had been encouraged to do so by Henry's mother, Margaret Beaufort, who must have feared her son might meet the same fate as Edward of Lancaster and Henry VI. Assailed by bad weather, they had been forced to beach their ships on the coast of Brittany. Duke Francis II had then detained them in what has been described as 'a kind of honourable confinement'. Their stay in Brittany was destined to last for thirteen long, impoverished years. When pressed by Edward to have the fugitives repatriated to England the duke demurred, but promised he would not allow them to escape his duchy to foment rebellion elsewhere. Edward persisted and at one point came close to gaining the duke's agreement for Henry to be repatriated. This, however, came to nought when his quarry feigned illness and successfully sought the sanctuary of the church at St Malo, avoiding Edward's boats waiting to ship him back to England.

In the autumn of 1473 John de Vere led a more serious assault than those made earlier against the coast of Essex, capturing St Michael's Mount in Cornwall on 30 September – a fortress described at the time as 'a strong place and a mighty'. Edward despatched forces to besiege him and managed to force his surrender in mid-February 1474. Viscount Beaumont and de Vere's two brothers were captured with him, as well as several hundred common soldiers. Under an earlier Edwardian administration the ringleaders would have lost their lives to the headsman's axe, and the fact that Edward instead assigned them to prison, joining Archbishop Neville at Calais, argues a strong case for the king wishing to put past bloodshed behind him.

The other dynastic contender, Henry Holland, Duke of Exeter, who had been left for dead on the battlefield of Barnet, later sought sanctuary in London, but in a repeat of what occurred at Tewkesbury had been forcibly removed and imprisoned in the Tower. Like de Vere, Exeter also escaped execution, possibly because his health was so frail and also because he was Edward's brother-in-law, not yet divorced from Edward's sister Anne. Edward had her feelings to consider. Anne divorced Holland in 1474, around the time their only child, a daughter – another Anne, married to Edward's step-son Thomas Grey – died. Holland accompanied Edward to France in 1475. The king probably did not trust him not to stir up trouble in England in his absence. Somehow Holland drowned on the way back. Edward's work? Anne of York died in 1476. By this time Archbishop George Neville had also passed away – he died a broken man, mourned by few.

Rather than civil strife, it was the resumption of Edward's warlike stance against Louis XI's France which was to dominate foreign affairs during the early part of the king's second reign. His stated intent to restart the Hundred Years War and win back the crown of France may have underpinned a desire to avenge himself on the French king for so openly siding with Warwick. Challenging England's ancient enemy was a way of uniting the English nobility in common cause in the wake of civil war. Edward made it known to Parliament that by seeking war abroad he might better safeguard against 'commotions' at home; additionally, war-booty would help underpin the country's finances. In making the case for war Edward was harking back to the glory days of Henry V and Edward III, to times when successful English foreign policy had been founded on confronting the French. Dismissing concerns that money voted for war in France might be wasted, as had happened before in 1463 and 1468, Parliament voted funds to be made available from taxation to secure the necessary weapons and soldiery. The *Croyland Chronicle* referenced also Edward's personal fund-raising efforts, saying, 'Everyone was to give [the king] just what he pleased, or rather what he did not please.' Edward feared complete reliance on taxation. He was well aware that this had been a factor in bringing down the old Lancastrian regime. Instead he looked to indirect methods of raising money by enforcing customs and feudal dues, investing in trading ventures and seeking benevolences. He also relied on the personal touch. Hall's Chronicle tells of Edward patronising a rich widow who promised the sum of £20. When kissed and fondled by the king she doubled her contribution.

How serious Edward really was about dethroning Louis XI remains open to debate. The days when an English army, even with allies, could confront the French and hope for an easy victory were well past their apogee. What is more, there was not really an appetite in England for any immediate foreign adventure. Edward's earlier promise to support his Burgundian brother-in-law's offensive of 1472 had gone largely unfulfilled: archers and ships promised to Duke Charles by Edward either failed to arrive or arrived in insufficient numbers to make a difference. Milanese reports angrily spoke of the English as 'wicked islanders who are born with tails'.[8] By the turn of the year 1474/5, however, the large number of English troops mustering on the downs near Canterbury and the hundreds of flat-bottomed boats gathering in and around Sandwich, 500 of which were provided by Charles the Bold, appeared evidence of renewed intent.

In 1415 Henry V had requisitioned 1,500 merchant ships, many also foreign owned, to transport his army to Normandy. Edward would have needed even more than this sixty years later; he boasted an artillery train stronger than the Duke of Burgundy's. Many of his guns were already at Calais. The most prestigious of these was the *Great Edward of Calais*, an enormous iron bombard which had been cast in 1474. The Milanese ambassador claimed, 'Every day [Edward] inspects all his artillery [and] notwithstanding that he has a very large number of bombards, he has fresh ones made every day.' Early in 1475 the king ordered that by the end of May his commanders should be ready at Portes Downe (Portsdown Hill), beside Portchester in Hampshire, 'in their best and most defensible array'.[9] The king's promise to invade France 'to take his old and due inheritance' would at last be honoured, or so it seemed.

To guard against any Scottish incursion Edward successfully expedited the betrothal of his four-year-old daughter Cecily to the one-year-old Prince James of Scots, later to become James IV of Scotland. The treaty terms this encompassed represented a major policy departure for the Scots. Distrustful of Edward's long-term intent, they demanded Cecily's dowry of 20,000 marks be paid in advance, by instalments.

Charles the Bold pressed Edward to invade Normandy or Gascony, rather than go via Calais. It was a suggestion the king must have for a time taken on board if the original muster venue on Portsdown Hill is to be explained. An undated letter from Charles to Edward argued that landing the English army at Calais would prove too constricting and would place the English forces too far north to cooperate militarily with Francis II of Brittany, their joint, albeit unenthusiastic ally. Calais was also 150 miles from Paris, with the marshy tracts of Picardy interposing. The duke, it seems, feared a large English army landing close to Burgundian territory and then marching through his lands before attacking Louis. Charles was at war in Europe on several fronts and therefore had good reason to be cautious. For Edward, invading hostile Normandy or Gascony would have meant immediately throwing the English army into combat after struggling to secure a beachhead, something the English king was not, on consideration, prepared to do. Charles's objections were laid aside and landings in the Pas de Calais eventually agreed upon. These took place unopposed at the beginning of June. Louis XI's fleet might have intervened, but it appears the French king was loath to be the first to open hostilities and provoke a conflict that would already be embittered by losses at sea.

Edward was at Canterbury on 4 June. His first contingent of troops (Geoffrey Gate's eight men-at-arms and sixty archers) had disembarked at Boulogne three days earlier.[10] Edward did not follow until a month later. He set his seal on his will in case of his death on campaign and his personal debts were cleared and provisions made for his wife and children. Covering all contingencies, work on his tomb at St George's Chapel at Windsor was ordered to be completed. In Edward's absence his four-year-old son, Edward, Prince of Wales, was proclaimed 'keeper of the realm'. A number of peers, prelates and officials were placed in control of running affairs of state under the leadership of Archbishop Thomas Bourchier. Elizabeth gained temporary charge over her son and his household while Anthony Woodville took a break from guardianship and accompanied Edward to Calais at the head of forty-two men-at-arms and 200 archers.

Edward was welcomed two days after his arrival at Calais by his sister Margaret, but had to wait a further week before Charles of Burgundy arrived at the head of a small bodyguard of men-at-arms.

The king had anticipated the arrival of a strong Burgundian army to support him and did not disguise his disappointment when it failed to materialise. A promised Breton force also went missing. Pouring salt on the wound, the Burgundian duke, in privy session with Edward, is said to have had the gall to express surprise that the English army had not yet set out to confront the French. When Charles later reviewed the English troops he did so in more politic manner, with much back-slapping, but later felt emboldened enough to remark that the English army seemed strong enough to overrun all of France, and Italy too, right up to the gates of Rome, without the need of any support from the Burgundians or Bretons. We can imagine Edward counting to ten.

Louis XI had by this time placed his forces on high alert and reinforced and re-victualed Dieppe, stripping the surrounding countryside 'so that the English [might] find nothing'. Towns along the border with Burgundy incapable of withstanding a siege were razed to the ground. All over Europe commentators were predicting a war 'of hideous proportions'. Directing operations from Neuchatel-en-Bray, situated midway between Dieppe and Beauvais, the French king positioned himself to prevent any sudden thrust on the part of the English into Normandy. He need not have worried; Charles's plan was now for the English to invade the province of Champagne instead. The duke's forces, still recovering after a setback at the hands of the Holy Roman Emperor, with whom Charles was also at war, were now prepared to march into the already much-fought-over province of Lorraine, further to the east. The objective of the allied armies would be to occupy Rheims to the north-east of Paris. Rheims was the traditional crowning-place of French kings. Once both allied pincers had closed on the city and Louis's army had been defeated or driven off, Edward would be enthroned as King of France.

Edward baulked at first when pressed to settle on this plan. Ranged against him that summer was a much larger enemy force comprising the French national army of 4,000 'lances', approximately 24,000 men, as well as a roughly similar-sized feudal levy. On 15 July Louis openly declared himself to be drawing out all his garrisons into the field, ready to fight. Not only did he have a marked advantage in numbers over the English, he was well dug-in behind a major river system: the Somme, the de-facto border between France and Burgundy.[11] He also had hefty reserves to call on and was able to respond quickly to an attack against any given bridging point. The French forces were not likely to repeat the mistakes of Crecy, Poitiers or Agincourt when English armies were attacked by the French nobility head-on and on any pretext. A successful southward move by the English forces across the Somme would be in the face of a scorched-earth withdrawal on the part of the French. Louis would wait until such time as he could to mount an overwhelming flank attack or threaten Edward's rear before fighting in the open. Overriding such considerations, Charles expressed scorn and surprise at the English king's caution. The more gung-ho Richard of Gloucester also favoured a determined advance, an early display of courage over prudence that would one day get him killed. Edward, Clarence, Hastings, Howard, Northumberland, Lord Stanley, Chancellor Rotherham and Sir Anthony Woodville, however, all considered pushing unsupported across the Somme to be far too risky. Anthony pointedly suggested that the Burgundians should themselves 'move into France', adding that 'his Majesty [Edward] will cross over and is ready, otherwise he will not do so at all'.[12] High-handedness on Charles the Bold's part clearly rankled with Edward and his commanders.

By 20 July Edward's forces were marching south-east through Burgundian lands in the direction of the duke's stronghold at Peronne, on the north bank of the Somme. As a morale booster, for two nights Edward encamped his army on the battlefield of Agincourt. Sixty years on the great battle had gained a semi-mythical status among the English. To be present on this celebrated field of battle on this important anniversary must have seemed a fitting curtain-raiser for even greater laurels to come. Richard of Gloucester must have earnestly hoped for a repeat encounter. It was he who led the largest contingent of men-at-arms and archers in the king's army. Richard may have had much in common with Charles the Bold: he too sought glory in battle. One observer noted of the Burgundian duke that 'all his pleasure, his every thought is in his men-at-arms, to make them look good and move in good order'.¹³ Although fancying himself another Caesar, Charles lost most of the battles he fought.

By the mid-1470s the make-up of armies and military tactics employed on the Continent was beginning to anticipate future modes of warfare. A Burgundian military blueprint of July 1471 specified each man-at-arms should have under his command a mounted page, a swordsman or javelin man (*coustillier*), three mounted archers, a crossbowman, a hand-gunner and a pikeman: nine men in all, a grouping known then as a 'lance' – the equivalent of a modern-day squad. Equivalent in size to a small nineteenth-century army corps, the main Burgundian tactical unit, the 'ordinance', comprised approximately 100 of these sub-units. The ordinance's optimal complement was set at between 8,400 and 9,000 effectives. Charles the Bold's drill book of 1473 detailed how the pikemen should march in front of their archers and that they should hold their pikes lowered to the level of a horse's back when ordered to kneel, 'so that the archers can fire over the pikemen as if over a wall'.¹⁴ The similarity to 'pike and shot' tactics of the later sixteenth and seventeenth centuries and to later bayonet tactics of the eighteenth and nineteenth is apparent. Yet when Edward mustered his army for service on the Continent in 1475 he relied predominantly on tried-and-trusted bowmen, with 10,173 mounted archers and just 1,278 men-at-arms on his payroll. Lord Howard's retinue provides a good example of this comparative weighting. Howard brought with him 200 archers and twenty men-at-arms. Although a retrograde model in comparison to either a Burgundian or a French equivalent army of the time, numerically the army of 1475 was the largest English force to cross the Channel in the fifteenth century, around 2,000 fighting men more than Henry V had with him in 1415. Edward's forces probably numbered around 20,000 all told, including supernumeraries.

The intermittent battles of the Wars of the Roses to one side, England had enjoyed a relatively long and sustained period of peace dating back to the early 1450s. Other than in the North of England after Towton, faction fighting in England did not have any indelible impact on the country's daily life or infrastructure; belligerents largely avoided unnecessary damage to towns, cities, castles and fortifications. Neither did the conflict result in a large, professional standing army or a substantial fleet being established, although, as already discussed, Edward did have at all times an impressive train of artillery, including heavy siege guns, and he could charter warships if the money was available. Because of an Englishman's legal duty to bear and practice the use of arms (most commonly the longbow) there remained right throughout the period a large pool of archers in the land, but well-trained and accoutred men-at-arms came at something of a premium.[15]

The Somme was reached in the first week of August. Louis's main army lay forty miles to the south. For security reasons Charles denied Edward's army access to the urban facilities at Peronne and the duke departed soon after to rejoin his commanders at Namur. Having the gates of the first allied fortified town they came to slammed in their faces did little to endear Charles to the English. A large fortified camp was successfully erected by Edward as a bridgehead on the south bank of the Somme, but an advance on the fortress of St Quentin – where the commander, the Constable of St Pol, a notorious intriguer, had been bribed by the Burgundians to change sides – was met with a hail of shot. Edward must by this time have been fast losing patience with his so-called allies. After borrowing heavily to finance the campaign he had so far achieved nothing that might warrant the expense incurred and was now being fired upon by supposed friends.

At around the same time as the duke's departure the English captured their first French prisoner. As was customary, the Frenchman was feted, then freed. Allegedly the Lords Howard and Stanley gave him a gold coin and asked him to recommend them to the French king. This small act of chivalry, if the story is to be believed, marked a sea-change in the campaign. At his headquarters, the Chateau de Compiegne to the north-east of Paris, Louis correctly interpreted the English lord's action as an opportunity to parley. He had 5,000 men at Dieppe (900 'lances'), plus an equivalent sized force at Amiens, as well as even more troops facing the Somme, occupying a line Beauvais-Creil-Compiegne-Noyon, all adequately supplied from Paris. His somewhat over-extended right wing stretched eastward to Rheims, bolstered by allied forces led by Rene II, Duke of Lorraine, and the Lord of Craon. He could therefore be optimistic of holding the English at bay militarily, but, not really wanting war with England, the possibility of achieving a negotiated peace was too good to ignore. Moreover, knowing Charles the Bold and Francis II of Brittany as well as he did, Louis correctly discounted the likelihood of the English being reinforced any time soon. With the approach of autumn the probability was that Edward would defer offensive operations until the following spring. Even so Louis preferred avoiding a clash of arms, even a deferred one, with a man he knew to have won every battle he had fought.

Louis sent an envoy to Edward saying he knew his cousin to be following a course set out by the English Parliament and the dukes of Burgundy and Brittany for their own ends. 'Should the King of England be able to heed his own best interests, he [Louis] would make such attractive offers that he [Edward] and his realm would be well satisfied with the result.'[16] In the circumstances he found himself in, this must have been music to Edward's ears and he was quick to respond. Once a number of preliminary demands (for instance, the crown of France to be relinquished in favour of Edward) had been rejected, the English king quickly settled on a large cash sum of 75,000 marks (£15,000) payable to him in cash in two lump sums, a truce of seven years during which period Edward would be paid a subsidy or pension of 50,000 marks (£10,000) annually, a free trade agreement between English and French merchants with no discriminatory tolls or rigged exchange rates and for Louis's son to be betrothed to Edward's eldest daughter, Elizabeth, for which Louis would pay the dowry. Also part of the deal was for a ransom to be paid by the French king for the release of Margaret of Anjou, as well as her renouncing her claims to any English territorial landholdings. The ransom was set at 50,000 marks. A secret codicil binding the two kings from giving succour to the other's enemies was also proposed.

Margaret of Anjou had been held under loose house arrest at Wallingford Castle since the late autumn of 1471, in the custody of her old friend Alice Chaucer, Dowager Duchess of Suffolk. Her placement there had been insisted upon by Queen Elizabeth, who can be commended for such empathy and kindness shown to a former enemy. Margaret eventually returned to France at the beginning of 1476 and Louis provided her with an annuity in return for all her hereditary rights. She lived out her days in Anjou, the countryside of her childhood, and died in August 1482, aged fifty-three. Lady Katherine Vaux, who had been with her in hiding near Tewkesbury in 1471, was at her bedside when she died, so she did not travel back to France friendless.

A number of Edward's key men also stood to benefit from Louis's largesse: Hastings was promised 2,000 marks a year, Lord Howard and Sir Thomas Montgomery 1,200 marks each and lesser amounts were pledged to others. In marked contrast to the way English soldiers had been treated by the Duke of Burgundy, several hundred wagon-loads of wine and food were sent into the English camp and the gates of Amiens were opened to Edward's troops, so that they might frequent the hostelries and brothels within. In retrospect it may have seemed to impartial observers that the late Earl of Warwick had been right all along to press for better relations with France.

Eyewitness De Commines described, somewhat critically, the moment the English army came into view outside the gates of Amiens:

> The King of England advanced within half a league of Amiens, and the King of France being upon one of the gates [of the town] saw his army marching at a great distance. To speak impartially, his [Edward's] troops seemed but raw and unused to action in the field, for they were in very ill order, and observed no manner of discipline. Our king [Louis] sent the King of England three hundred cart-loads of the best wines in France as a present; and I think the carts made as great an appearance as the whole English army.

Louis was taking a calculated gamble by acting in such an accommodating manner. At one point there were alleged to have been close to 9,000 drunken English soldiers in and around Amiens – this apparently much to Edward's anger and shame. There was also always the chance that Charles the Bold would engineer a reversal of what had been informally agreed, and this was something he attempted to do upon learning of the Anglo-French accord. Edward, however, held his ground. Short of cash, left unsupported by his supposed allies (so far neither Charles nor the Duke of Brittany had sent him any troops) and it being close to the end of the campaigning season, the English king claimed he had little choice other than to formalise a truce. It was also the case that Edward had not forgotten the guarded nature of the welcome, or lack of it, that he had received from his brother-in-law when he had landed penniless and unannounced on Burgundian soil in 1470. Bonds of brotherhood were different in medieval times than today; it was believed then that a man married to another's sister became in God's eyes his full brother. Edward had expected better of the duke.

Charles sent a delegation to deter Edward from formally signing anything, but it arrived too late to prevent Edward and Louis meeting face to face mid-stream on a specially prepared pontoon bridge, beside the town of Picquigny, on a wet day at the end of August. Edward half knelt at Louis's feet in the rain before swearing on a reliquary containing a fragment of the True Cross to uphold the terms of the treaty. De Commines considered Edward resplendent, dressed in a gold-lined gown and a black-velvet, jewel-laden cap. Backing Edward up, the whole English army in full battle array looked on from the north bank of the Somme. De Commines described how the English king was 'very nobly attended'. In his train were the Duke of Clarence; Henry Percy, Earl of Northumberland; Lord Hastings; Chancellor Rotherham; and other peers of the realm, 'among whom there were not above three or four dressed in cloth of gold like himself'. De Commines particularly noted Edward's physical appearance, remarking that the king was 'a little inclining to corpulence', adding that when he had last seen him, five years earlier, he had 'thought him much handsomer', and that 'to the best of my remembrance, my eyes had never [then] beheld a more handsome person'.

Interestingly, Clarence was at Edward's side at Picquigny, but not the hawkish Richard, who opposed the peace proceedings and who sulkily remained on the north bank with his men. Another man who may have opposed the king was Henry Stafford, Duke of Buckingham. The duke had provided four knights, forty men-at-arms and 400 archers for the campaign, but unaccountably returned to England prior to the truce being signed. He had presumably done something untoward and had as a result fallen from favour. Later he would be barred from court in England. Stafford's biographer, C. S. L. Lewis, has suggested the duke may have become a dangerously unstable individual, prone perhaps to acts of violence. This would explain why Edward discharged him and later sidelined him from any important role in government.

After everyone else departed, Lord Howard, one of the main

architects of the Picquigny deal, remained behind with Louis as a hostage. Possibly with Howard in mind, de Commines commented that, whereas the French relied on cunning, the English 'proceeded with more ingenuousness and straightforwardness'. He added that 'care should be taken not to affront them, for it was dangerous to meddle with them'.[17]

Being a diplomat, de Commines no doubt saw the wisdom of the deal that had been struck between the two countries, but some others saw things differently. Thousands of English soldiers subsequently took the opportunity to enlist in the Burgundian army, but in the main this was for financial gain rather than as an act of protest. Some soldiers, upon returning to England, fell 'to theft and rapine', in part because they had been denied the opportunity to ravage France. Others rioted or openly criticized the king for concluding the peace, angered that Edward and his nobles had enriched themselves at the expense of the state, which had put up much of the money for the campaign. At one point the situation became sufficiently serious for Edward to get personally involved to root out miscreants. The *Croyland Chronicle* reported that the king was compelled 'to make a survey of the kingdom; and no more, not even his own domestic, did he spare, but instantly had him hanged, if he was found to be guilty of theft or murder'. The chronicler further asserted that 'if this prudent prince had not manfully put an end to this commencement of mischief, the number of people complaining of the unfair management of the resources of the kingdom ... would have increased to such a degree that no one could have said whose head, among the king's advisors, was in safety'.

Duke Charles, of course, never forgave Edward for so quickly coming to terms with Louis, but, accepting the inevitable, a similar Franco-Burgundian accord was struck on 13 September 1475. Edward argued that he had gained the best deal possible for England and for his absent allies. He had seen enough of warfare to realise the terrible risks involved and had not been prepared to fruitlessly expend Englishmen's lives, especially without solid Burgundian and Breton support. He was not driven by the same quest for 'martial glory' as his brother Richard, Duke Charles or, for that matter, earlier English kings like Richard I or Henry V. By temperament, in his thirties at least, Edward was said to be a man more inclined to seek 'quiet pleasures'.[18] He saw avoiding war as something to celebrate rather than to make excuses for. A misericord carving on his personal stall at St George's Chapel demonstrates the truth of this. Although partially hidden, therefore not a propaganda device, Edward chose this motif of the meeting at the bridge at Picquigny so that he might be reminded at prayer of what he considered one of his most important achievements, on a par with any of his more famous martial victories. Contemporaries also saw the outcome as an accomplishment rather than a failure, stressing after Edward's death how the French had been forced to pay Edward tribute without the English king having to raise his sword in battle.

When Edward embarked for England Charles is alleged to have expressed relief that he had gone, remarking to a courtier that the English would no doubt soon go back to slaughtering each other. Though he did not know it, his own days were numbered. He was killed by the downward strike of a Swiss halberd at the Battle of Nancy just fifteen months later, on 5 January 1477. The duke's mutilated body was not discovered until several days after the battle. The defeat in effect erased the state of Burgundy as an autonomous political entity.[19] That Charles had not been offered quarter is unsurprising: less than a year before at Granson, beside Lake Neuchatel, he had hung or drowned the defenders of the town after storming it. The infuriated Swiss viewed him as a war criminal.

It was not long after returning to England that problems again broke out with respect to Clarence. They began, publicly at least, when Clarence brazenly took the law into his own hands by executing two commoners – Ankarette Twynho and John Thursby – after a mock trial. It was alledged that the pair were convicted by a 'packed [rigged]' jury of killing, or attempting to kill, Clarence's duchess, Isobel, by giving her 'a venomous drink of ale mixed with poison'. The whole affair remains thoroughly obscure. Little can be surmised other than that the duke rode roughshod over the laws of the land in having the accused dragged across three counties to face a mock trial. Isobel had in fact probably died from the complications of childbirth. In Clarence's defence it should be noted that poisoning was something much feared in medieval times. With medicine in its infancy, what might today seem an obvious cause of death was not necessarily so then.

After this Edward had angered his brother by blocking Clarence's resurrected plans to marry into the Burgundian royal family. It was a union that had been championed by Edward's sister Margaret of York. Marriage to Margaret's step-daughter, Mary of Burgundy, described as 'the greatest heiress of her time', was not a prize Edward was willing to bestow on his volatile and unpredictable brother, especially since Mary had inherited from her father, Charles the Bold, a distant claim to the English throne. Not only might Clarence's marriage to Mary of Burgundy compromise the English succession, but any resultant Anglo-Burgundian rapprochement might cost Edward his prized French subsidy.

Soon after this, in the late spring of 1477, three of Clarence's retainers were indicted by the king's court on charges of necromancy. Named Burdett, Stacy and Blake, the men were alleged to have attempted to conjure the deaths of the king and the Prince of Wales. Unwisely, Clarence arranged for a declaration of Burdett's innocence to be read out in public. There were also risings in Cambridgeshire and Huntingdonshire at around the same time, probably incited by Clarence or his supporters. Only Blake gained a reprieve; Burdett and Stacy were hanged. Once again, the affair is difficult to make sense of at a distance of over five hundred years, but the suspicion must be that the charges made against the men were a cover for more serious crimes, including plotting against the state. The bottom line was that Clarence had become a major embarrassment and even something of a threat to Edward.

Perhaps the last relatively happy time spent by the king with his brother had been during the summer of 1476 at Fotheringhay Castle, when Edward, Clarence and Richard had been together with the queen, Lord Hastings, Henry Percy, Lord Stanley and upwards of 1,500 other guests, including ambassadors from France, Denmark and Portugal. The occasion was to attend the lavish reburial of their father and brother's remains, which had earlier been hurriedly and unceremoniously incarcerated by the Lancastrians after the Battle of Wakefield.

Stirring the pot, Louis XI routinely alerted Edward to Clarence's continued plotting abroad – intrigues which may have involved the Tudors and their supporters.[20] The duke's eventual arrest on the treasonable charge of speaking against the king – probably replaying the claim that Edward was illegitimate and that the king's marriage to Elizabeth had been illegal – may have been a cover for more wide-ranging, unpublicised treasons. Edward publicly denounced his brother on charges of misconduct and contempt. According to the *Croyland Chronicle*, at Clarence's trial 'not a single person uttered a word against the duke except the king [and] not one individual made answer to the king but the duke'. Either the trial was heavily stage-managed, in effect a show trial, or none dared interpose between the king and his brother. Edward could have avoided a trial altogether by leaving Clarence to languish in the Tower, but that would not have prevented others from later plotting his freedom and therefore posing a threat to the succession. Probably for this reason, Edward allowed the process of law to unravel. Once Clarence had been convicted and sentenced to death, Edward did not publicly order his brother's execution, but nor did he do anything to prevent it. The Speaker of the House of Commons is said to have come to the House of Lords to request the implementation of the sentence sometime after the trial was over. Either because Edward wished the execution to be carried out quietly, or because Clarence or Dowager Duchess Cecily had successfully pleaded against a traitor's death, the condemned man may have been allowed to choose his own manner of execution. If so, he chose drowning. Tradition has it that his death was carried out by immersion in a butt of sweet Malmsey, an imported Greek wine. More probably, however, the duke was simply done away with in the same manner as Henry VI, strangled or battered to death in his cell.

It is possible that Edward may have been cajoled into convicting his brother against his will and Elizabeth has since been scapegoated for insisting on her brother-in-law's death. Some have called Clarence's execution 'judicial fratricide'.[21] If Elizabeth did have a hand in Clarence's death, she had good cause: the duke had connived in the killing of her father and brother in 1469 and in her mind still posed a direct threat to her family. Contemporaries certainly saw the hand of the queen at work, claiming her to have been fearful that Clarence might one day prevent the smooth succession of her son Edward. Circumstantially, the trial was arranged with considerable Woodville participation. Moreover, Edward is said to have later regretted his brother's killing and paid for an elaborate funeral in London, as well as a chantry chapel at Tewkesbury Abbey, where monks could pray for his brother's soul. On more than one occasion, when solicited to pardon an offender, he is alleged to have chastised himself, saying, 'O unfortunate brother, for whose life not one creature would make intercession.' Such stories are, of course, anecdotal. It could equally have been true that – cajoled into it or not – Edward felt relief after his brother's death and slept more soundly from then on in the knowledge that an outstanding piece of family business had finally been settled.

Because of the many loose ends surrounding Clarence's demise, the duke's character, trial and death has attracted much anecdotal analysis and speculation, much of it stoked by Shakespeare.

In his play *Richard III*, the bard imagined Edward to have been alarmed by a prophecy which claimed the king would be succeeded by someone whose name began with 'G', mistaking George of Clarence for Richard of Gloucester. In the play, the former becomes the target for elimination, when it should really be the latter, and it is Richard, rather than Edward or Elizabeth, who Shakespeare blames for engineering 'false, fleeting, perjur'd' Clarence's death. Circumstantially, Richard gained more from his brother's fall than anyone else: he recovered the chamberlainship of England for himself and the earldom of Salisbury for his infant son, another Edward. (At odds with such assertions, however, Richard is said to have been overcome with grief on hearing of his brother's secretive death and swore to avenge him.)

Professor Lander has gone so far as to claim Clarence to have been insane, but it is an accusation that jars with the *Croyland Chronicle's* description of the duke as 'an idol of the multitude' and also of other contemporary accounts describing the duke as a great giver of alms and a friend of the Church. Clarence was Margaret of York's favourite brother. Would she have continued to favour him and press for his marriage into the Burgundian royal family if he had become a dangerous lunatic? More plausibly, Professor Michael Hicks has viewed the duke as merely ambitious to a fault and that, although a charmer, he posed a growing dynastic threat to Edward and Elizabeth and therefore had to be removed.

As mentioned earlier, James III of Scotland had secured closer ties with Edward's England in 1474 through the proxy marriage of his one-year-old son to Edward's four-year-old daughter, Cecily. Edward engineered the alliance to forestall attacks on England by the Scots while he was absent in France. He had agreed to pay Cecily's sizeable dowry in instalments, beginning at 2,000 marks per annum. For reasons which remain obscure, relations between Edward and James suddenly broke down in 1481. A year before Edward had complained about Scottish intransigence and had been rewarded with a full-scale raid into the East March toward Scotland by forces under the command of the Earl of Angus. Reprisal raids against the Scots were carried out by Richard of Gloucester and Henry Percy by land and by Lord Howard at sea, who raided into the Firth of Forth, capturing and destroying Scottish shipping.

A cause of the friction may have been Edward's feting of Alexander, Duke of Albany, James III's rebellious brother. Albany was the second son of James II, King of Scots and Mary of Gueldres, Margaret of Anjou's one-time benefactor, who had died in 1463. The prince was well known to Edward. In 1464, at the age of just ten, Albany had been captured by the English in the North Sea and had remained at the English king's side for a year or more before being repatriated. His experience of English court life did nothing to endear him to his captors; ten years later, aged twenty, he was leading an army on the borders to confront the threat of an English invasion. The same year he fell out with his brother, the Scottish king, when the latter plumped to ally himself with Edward. Being a border magnate, Albany may have been pressurised by his followers into a continuance of border raiding despite the truce. Edward's complaints in 1480 to the Scottish king spoke of intermittent truce breaking and murderous behaviour, and an indictment for treason raised against Albany by James III's government in October 1479 specified the 'treasonable hurting, violation and breaking of the truce and peace'. By this time Albany had fled to France to avoid capture.

Quite why Edward should have involved himself with a man like Albany remains unclear – perhaps Louis XI pressed him to do so for reasons of his own – but on 11 June 1482 the Treaty of Fotheringhay was signed, whereby Edward promised military support in return for Albany's agreement to hand back Berwick and submit to Edward as his overlord should the duke usurp the Scottish throne. Richard was placed in command of the English army detailed to support him. Edward initially planned to join the expedition but unaccountably failed to do so. Presumably other pressing business prevented him from travelling north. Meanwhile, James III concentrated a Scottish force to oppose the invasion at Lauder, twenty-seven miles south-east of Edinburgh, on the western edge of the Lammermuir Hills, but before he could lead them into action he was seized by a group of disaffected Scottish magnates – allies of Albany's, namely the lords of Buchan, Atholl and Darnley – and incarcerated in Edinburgh Castle. The Scottish army dispersed. Unopposed, Richard and his Scottish charge struck north-east from Carlisle and occupied the Scottish capital, burning Dumfries on the way. With James III under lock and key, Albany now no longer needed Richard's army to back him and the English fell back to the borders. Before heading back to England, Richard had gained the promise of the Scottish council that the dowry advanced by Edward for Cecily's now-annulled proxy marriage would be repaid. In this respect at least the campaign was a success and not the write-off claimed by a number of contemporaries, including the Croyland Chronicler, who saw the whole affair as an unnecessary and expensive diversion for the English. The other good news for Edward was that James III's temporary difficulties resulted in the immediate surrender of Berwick Castle to Lord Stanley's forces.[22] Edward rewarded Richard for his efforts north of the border with the grant of Cumberland (modern Cumbria), as well as palatinate authority over any territories Richard could seize from the Scots along the borders of the West March (the dales abutting Strathclyde). Additionally, Richard gained control of Carlisle Castle, the key to control over the region. Like his late father, York, and late cousin, Warwick, the king's brother had now himself become an overmighty subject, constrained only by loyalty to Edward, a man whose once robust health was now failing.

10

FATEFUL OUTCOMES

The six years between Clarence's execution and Edward's own death, if not entirely devoid of incident, were, with the exception of the skirmishes on the Scottish borders, peaceful ones. Edward was able to amass revenues sufficient to expunge the national debt and also to maintain an extravagant court. In large part this was paid for by Louis XI's generous French subsidy – a regular income which helped make the Crown largely self-sufficient until at least 1482, the year of Richard's foray into Scotland. Two years earlier, on a brief return home to her native land, the widowed Margaret of York had been able to resurrect and kick-start the earlier Anglo-Burgundian alliance. A manuscript illumination representing her negotiating with Edward is still extant. By this time her stepdaughter, the twenty-three-year-old Mary of Burgundy – once tentatively earmarked for Clarence – was married to Archduke Maximillian of Austria. This event, which had occurred on 18 August 1477 in Ghent, ushered in over 250 years of Hapsburg dominance in the Netherlands.

Margaret and her stepdaughter Mary were close and shared many interests; their portraits appear jointly in several contemporary illuminations and paintings.¹ Clarence to one side, several other offers of bridegrooms for Mary had been rejected by Margaret. One had been the four-year-old Dauphin of France, a proposed union which caused such local outrage in the Netherlands that two influential government ministers, discovered engaging in secret correspondence with the French, were immediately executed. Another was to the relatively ignoble Anthony Woodville, a candidate pressed hard for by Queen Elizabeth to expand the Woodville family's dynastic reach into Europe. Although a Woodville suitor for Mary was rejected by Margaret, the dowager duchess worked tirelessly from then on to foster an alliance between Hapsburg Burgundy and Yorkist England. At a time of mounting political tensions on the Continent, this placed Edward, still allied with France, in an awkward position diplomatically. He may have been aware that Louis was suffering from bouts of recurrent seizures and might die at any time, and this gave Edward cause for concern. De Commines wrote that Louis looked 'more like a dead than a living man; so thin [that] no one would have believed it'. Louis had also become more irascible with age. According to de Commines, he liked to pass his time 'making and ruining men'. Little wonder, therefore, that the French king's response to the warming of relations between England and Burgundy was to temporarily withhold Edward's subsidy and to diplomatically sow discord between the English and the Scots. A result was the short border war of 1481, already described. Edward responded by going out of his way to re-establish friendly terms with Louis, openly betraying his concern at losing his French funding. Even so, he was forced by his council to also seek renewed friendship with Burgundy, since doing so attracted improved terms of trade with the Low Countries.

Emperor Maximillian, the de facto ruler of Burgundy, pushed Edward for military support against the Holy Roman Empire's enemies at the beginning of 1482. Edward prevaricated, claiming, with some justification, that he was now too heavily committed north of the border to sign up for a war on the Continent. The pope had also pressed Edward to support the crusade against the Turks, but Edward used the same excuse as he had with the emperor to avoid doing so. Lacking Edward's backing and pressed to do so by his wife, Mary, in the end Maximillian opened covert negotiations with Louis, something that the French king had probably been angling for all along. A few days later Mary was dead. She died on 27 March 1482, aged twenty-five, after her horse fell on her. The crisis this brought on did much to draw concessions from Maximillian, and at the Treaty of Arras on 23 December 1482 he and Louis signed an accord whereby Louis's son, the Dauphin, would marry Maximillian's infant daughter, another Margaret, bringing to France a dower of the county of Artois as well as other Burgundian territories. Louis could now afford to cut Edward loose. He had finally achieved his territorial ends and no longer needed English passive support. In one fell swoop, described by historian James Gairdner as 'a bold violation' on Louis's part, Edward lost his French subsidy and the husband (the Dauphin) promised to his eldest daughter, Elizabeth.

Had Edward lost his grip on governance? Had a luxurious and allegedly profligate lifestyle dulled his resolve and blunted his capacity to rule in his late thirties? Contemporaries certainly noted his growing corpulence and lethargy, but remarked too on his continued mental vigour. Dominic Mancini accused Edward of being 'most immoderate' with respect to food and drink, claiming the king was in the habit of vomiting Roman-style 'for the delight of gorging his stomach once more'. It was also Mancini who reported Edward to have been 'licentious in the extreme' when it came to women, and it is true that sexual tensions at court were doubtless a distraction for the king and became the cause of much unnecessary friction.

A case in point was rivalry between Edward's close friend, William, Lord Hastings, and the king's stepson Thomas Grey. This allegedly came about when both men vied for the attentions of the same woman at court – a sexually charged place where young men and women in close confines had little else to do but to flirt with each other.[2] One riotous episode in particular, Edward's sharing of a royal mistress with his friend Hastings (perhaps the same woman Grey was taken with), is said to have greatly upset the queen and other members of her family. Not all historians take the view that Edward's court was any more dissolute than others. Edward's biographer Rosemary Horrox is a case in point; she has suggested that accounts of the king's sexual excesses have been exaggerated, saying that the accepted view of Edward as 'an insatiable predator' may derive from slurs made by members of Richard III's entourage when asserting Richard's own claim to the throne, the justification of which also involved undermining the legality of Edward's marriage to Elizabeth Woodville and therefore the legitimacy of their two sons. Richard, according to Rosemary Horrox, presented Edward's womanising as 'a political grievance', whereas normally such behaviour by a king in medieval times was considered above criticism.[3] Royal marriages were almost always arranged and the queen almost continuously pregnant. The queen's primary objective was to bear children and not necessarily to engage in a close and sexually fulfilling relationship with her husband in the way we would expect today. Queens and noblemen's wives bestowed legitimacy to offspring, so there were proscriptions against a queen taking lovers. A king taking mistresses, on the other hand, was expected, even encouraged. Elizabeth bore Edward ten children in their nineteen years of marriage: three sons, two of whom – Edward and Richard – survived into boyhood; and seven daughters, six of whom – Elizabeth, Mary, Cecily, Anne, Catherine and Bridget – outlived infancy. So it cannot be said that Edward failed to regularly attend on the queen. Nonetheless, he also sired at least two illegitimate children by other women: Arthur (mentioned earlier) and a daughter, Grace, who attended at the death of Elizabeth in 1492.

Edward's death was not sudden, but the illness he suffered was short-lived and his failing health took the government and his family by surprise. The *Croyland Chronicle* stated that Edward died 'neither worn out by old age, nor yet seized with any known kind of malady'. According to Mancini, Edward caught a chill boating on the river. Other chroniclers claimed apoplexy or stroke brought on by too much good living. French observers believed the king's health to have failed as a direct consequence of the mortification he had felt on being betrayed by Louis, a man who would outlive Edward by just a few months. Possibly the anger, stress and anxiety brought on by the news of the Treaty of Arras did have an adverse effect and caused the king a deal of worry.

Among his last acts of state was to call Parliament to vote money to rearm. War appeared to threaten. The wording on the act spoke of securing 'the hasty and necessary defence of the kingdom'. Edward may have feared imminent attack from the French. Worryingly, the French army was more to be feared than before. Since 1475 Louis had incorporated Burgundian levies into its ranks and the cadres had been further strengthened by the addition of 6,000 Swiss mercenary pikemen and halberdiers.[4] Moreover, the Scottish Duke of Albany, who was still in open rebellion against his brother, had set up a court in opposition to James III at Dunbar, having been bolstered by Edward's renewed promise to back him, but in mid-March, less than a month before Edward's death, James III cleverly arranged full remission of Albany's treasons in return for his brother renouncing his allegiance to Edward. Imminent war with the Scots now also loomed. (As it turned out, Edward's death on 9 April upset the apple cart: James III was able to reassert himself without making any concessions and the Duke of Albany fled to England.)[5]

Claims that Richard of Gloucester had a hand in his brother's death can be ignored. Some writers would have it that Richard was a serial killer, blaming him for the deaths of Henry VI, Clarence, Edward and even his own wife, Anne Neville, as if the alleged murders of the princes in the Tower was not enough. No matter how thuggishly ambitious Edward's brother would prove to be, the poisoning of his elder brother cannot be held against him. Obesity, mid-life stressors and intractable neighbours are enough in themselves to explain the onset of hypertension that appears to have been the king's undoing. Edward remained conscious for ten days or so before dying, leaving time, at least, for him to make last amendments to his will and place his affairs in order. He passed away at Westminster, aged almost forty-one. He had reigned for twenty-two years with just one short break and was the first English king to die solvent since Henry II in 1189. His body was laid in state at St Stephen's Chapel until 16 April, before interment at Windsor. The indomitable Lord Howard led the cortege, holding aloft Edward's great banner. An overnight stop was made at Sion Nunnery on the north bank of the Thames at Isleworth. Next day the coffin was carried into the Chapel of St George at Windsor and overnight 'a great watch', or vigil, was kept. The king's body was entombed in a vault he had ordered built for himself, but which already contained two of his dead children – George and Mary. Funeral costs were met through the sale of some of the king's jewels. As has been pointed out by historian Mary Clive, the chapel now 'hardly acknowledges the existence of its founder'. In one of a number of such incidents during the English Civil War, Parliamentarian soldiers completely destroyed Edward's tomb and changes made to the chapel since have further diminished the sense that the remains of one of England's most notable kings lie nearby.[6]

Among the last amendments Edward made to his will had been to name his brother Richard of Gloucester as his eldest son's formal protector, in effect supplanting Anthony Woodville as the prince's guardian. The dying king also wished Prince Edward to be crowned with immediate effect, although the decision for an early date has since been laid on the Woodvilles, who, it is claimed, may have wished to act through the new king without delay. Edward probably died comforted in the knowledge that he had an intelligent, healthy teenage son to succeed him and a loyal brother to oversee what should have been a relatively short minority, but even before the uncrowned Edward V had left Ludlow to travel to Westminster for his coronation the kingdom had become wracked by division. Robert Fabyan wrote, 'Grudge and unkindness began to take place between the king's [Edward IV's] and the queen's [Elizabeth Woodville's] allies' – in other words between men once loyal to Edward, like Richard of Gloucester and Lord Hastings, and the queen and her extended family. The immediate cause of this was disagreement as to how any formal regency should be administered. The *Croyland Chronicler*, an involved contemporary, reported all were keen to see the new king crowned without delay, but thought it a mistake, given the dead king's wishes, to allow the Woodvilles unfettered governance of him. Without Richard being consulted, the Woodville clique at court set the coronation date for 4 May. Thomas Grey, the dead king's stepson, is reputed to have said, 'We are so important that even without the king's uncle [Richard] we can make and enforce these decisions [ourselves].' The decisions he referred to may also have included the overturning of Edward's wishes with respect to Richard's protectorate and the voting of money for Sir Edward Woodville to take command of the fleet with men loyal to the Woodvilles. Edward's desire to forge greater unity within the kingdom and provide safeguards for his son was rapidly being overtaken by events.

Rather than pander to prevarication, Richard acted with decision: at the end of April he and his new-found ally, Henry Stafford (a man who had been sidelined from government by Edward), took possession of Prince Edward at Stony Stratford. Anthony Woodville and other members of the prince's entourage were disarmed and then imprisoned. From London, Hastings had earlier prevailed in limiting the size of the king's bodyguard to 2,000 men – a considerable force nonetheless. Hastings publicly claimed that he would be fearful for his life should Anthony Woodville amass a larger force than this and seize the regency. It appears Hastings alerted Richard to the danger that this might happen and this may have set in train much of what then occurred; Woodville enmity toward Hastings was behind this. The lord's casual access to Edward's 'privy pleasures' and his controlling the access of others cannot have sat well with the queen and her rich and powerful relatives, although there may have been other causes for the divisions that we do not know about.

Having gained possession of the prince and imprisoned Anthony Woodville, Richard's assumption of the protectorship was now assured, so far without any blood having been spilt. At first his governance ran smoothly. Not until 10 June (two months after Edward IV's death) did he openly declare his concern that the queen's faction at court sought to destroy him and Henry Stafford. The pair claimed that the 'old royal blood of the realm', namely theirs, was threatened by the new, corrupting blood of the Woodvilles. Richard wrote to his supporters at York requesting military support, stating that the dowager queen 'daily doth intend to murder and utterly destroy us'. The opposite, by now, was true. Richard had decided to seize the kingship for himself and planned to use the earlier alleged invalidity of his brother's marriage as a pretext to make his dead brother's children bastards. When these plans were divulged to Hastings, the lord demurred. He remained King Edward's man and would not move in such a way against the dead king's son. It was an outcome that must have come as a surprise to Richard, who counted Hastings as a close supporter.

Richard had misread the signals, but was not to be deterred. Distrusted now by both factions, Hastings' fall became inevitable. Without recourse to trial, Richard had him executed at the Tower on 13 June.[7] His estates in the North Midlands were immediately appropriated and made over to the already super-rich Henry Stafford, who was by this time Richard's viceroy in Wales and the Marches, a role he may have coveted for some time.

Fearing further bloodshed, Elizabeth placed herself and her family into sanctuary at the Abbot of Westminster's house.[8] Although, as before, described as in 'great penury', the queen would have been more comfortable at the abbot's house than at the Westminster Sanctuary. She was joined by her brother Lionel, Bishop of Salisbury, and her son Thomas Grey. Prince Edward had by now been consigned to the Tower, awaiting, so it was said, his coronation. Elizabeth kept her other son, Prince Richard, at her side and it was only through the intercession of Church leaders like the abbot and Cardinal Thomas Bourchier – both men no doubt acting in good faith – that Richard of Gloucester was able to prise him from her, on the pretext that the younger prince needed to be present at his brother's coronation.

Once the young Duke of York was in his uncle's custody, secure in the Tower, Richard of Gloucester's coup was all but complete. Prince Edward's coronation was put on hold, then later cancelled. All the royal children, girls included, were formally declared illegitimate in a sermon preached at St Paul's Cross by the theologian Ralph Shaw.[9] To help legitimise Shaw's claims, stories that Jacquetta of Luxembourg had used magical powers to enchant Edward IV into an illegal marriage were revived. Richard's formal declaration of kingship followed a few days after Shaw's sermon, on 26 June. Anthony Woodville was already dead by then, having been executed on Richard's orders the day before at Pontefract. Elizabeth's son Richard Grey and Prince Edward's chamberlain, Sir Thomas Vaughan, died with him. The closeness of Anthony Woodville to the young Edward and his strong regional ties with the Welsh – a principality Richard had good reason to fear – had made the death of the prince's guardian a prerequisite.

Soon Richard had gathered together almost all that strands of power under his control. Edward's sons, languishing in the Tower, disappeared forever from public view. The Tower was damp and insanitary, so it is possible they died from neglect or disease rather than directly at their uncle's hands. It is more probable, however, that Richard had them murdered in the late summer of 1463. Young Edward was well aware of the danger he was in and may have anticipated his death. According to his physician, he prepared himself spiritually by daily confession and penance.[10]

Possibly the murders were carried out by Richard on the urging of Henry Stafford, who also harboured designs on the throne.[11] A few months later Stafford was dead too, executed after a failed rising in the West Country. Relying on Welsh levies who had little love for him and even less desire to fight, he predictably botched things when asserting himself.[12] In an attempt to avoid further insurrections, an alarmed Parliament quickly rubber-stamped Richard's legitimacy to rule. Less than two years later Richard would also be killed, betrayed by men he had hoped to count on and butchered when floundering in the mud at Bosworth Field. Yorkist diehard Lord Howard fell there too. In Richard's place would step Catherine of Valois's grandson, Henry Tudor, 'the last imp' of Henry VI's bloodline, supported by his ever-durable uncle, Jasper, and by the warlike and incorrigible John de Vere, Earl of Oxford. Henry Tudor seized the crown just as his namesake had once prophesised. As Henry VII, his marriage soon after to Edward's eldest daughter, Elizabeth of York, would symbolically seal three decades of dynastic dispute and usher in England's most-celebrated royal family. Through them we might best weigh Edward IV's legacy.

CHRONOLOGY

28 April 1442	Birth of Edward at Rouen
9 April 1445	Margaret of Anjou arrives in England
23 February 1447	Death of Humphrey, Duke of Gloucester
9 December 1447	Richard, Duke of York, made Lieutenant of Ireland
Spring of 1449	Loss of Normandy to the French
2 May 1450	William de la Pole murdered
21 May – 12 July 1450	Cade's rebellion
February–March 1452	York's armed stand-off with Henry VI at Dartford
17 July 1453	Battle of Castillon; death of Lord Talbot
24 August 1453	Percys and Nevilles clash on Heworth Moor
13 October 1453	Birth of Edward of Lancaster
31 October 1454	Battle of Stamford Bridge; the Nevilles and Percys openly clash
22 May 1455	First St Albans
25 March 1458	The 'Love Day' at St Paul's
23 September 1459	Battle of Blore Heath
12/13 October 1459	Ludford Bridge; the leading Yorkists flee abroad
2 July 1460	Yorkist earls arrive at London from Calais
10 July 1460	Battle of Northampton
10 October 1460	York made Lord Protector of England
30 December 1460	Battle of Wakefield; death of Richard, Duke of York
3 February 1461	Battle of Mortimer's Cross

17 February 1461	Second St Albans
29 March 1461	Battle of Towton
28 June 1461	Edward's coronation
22 July 1461	Accession of Louis XI in France
25 April 1464	Battle of Hedgeley Moor
1 May 1464	Traditional date of Edward's marriage to Elizabeth Woodville
15 May 1464	Battle of Hexham
25 May 1465	Elizabeth Woodville crowned queen
11 February 1466	Birth of Elizabeth of York
11 July 1469	Marriage of George, Duke of Clarence, to Isobel Neville at Calais
26 July 1469	Battle of Edgecote
12 March 1470	Battle of Empingham
30 July 1470	Betrothal of Edward of Lancaster to Anne Neville
3 October 1470	Edward lands at Texel in Burgundy; Henry VI crowned for a second time
2 November 1470	Birth of Prince Edward of York at Westminster Sanctuary
15 February 1471	Richard Neville, Earl of Warwick, declares war on Burgundy at the behest of Louis XI of France
12 March 1471	Edward lands at Ravenspur in Yorkshire
14 April 1471	Battle of Barnet
4 May 1471	Battle of Tewkesbury; death of Richard Neville, Earl of Warwick and Edward of Lancaster
21 May 1471	Henry VI murdered
29 August 1475	Treaty of Picquigny
5 January 1477	Battle of Nancy; death of Charles the Bold
18 February 1478	George, Duke of Clarence, executed
23 December 1482	Treaty of Arras
9 April 1483	Death of Edward IV
13 June 1483	Execution of Lord Hastings
25 June 1483	Execution of Anthony Woodville and others
26 June 1483	Richard III's kingship declared
2 November 1483	Henry Stafford, Duke of Buckingham, executed
22 August 1485	Battle of Bosworth; death of Richard III
30 October 1485	Henry VII's coronation
18 January 1486	Henry VII and Elizabeth of York marry, unifying the houses of Lancaster and York

NOTES

Prologue

1. Charles Ross, *Edward IV* (Methuen, 1983), page 126.
2. They were respectively: Richard of Gloucester; George of Clarence; Lord Rivers; Lord Hastings; Richard Neville, Earl of Warwick; John Neville, Marquis Montagu; and Henry Holland, Duke of Exeter.
3. In 1300 the population of London has been assessed at around 80,000 souls, but the plague of 1348/9 claimed up to a third of these. It took almost two centuries for numbers to recover.
4. This was the Breton nobleman Jean du Quelennec. The context was Henry Tudor's aborted repatriation from Brittany to England in 1473. Quelennec argued that Henry would be 'torn in pieces by bloody butchers', namely, Edward and his two brothers.

1 Bitter Rivalries

1. Described by historian Anne Curry as 'obsessive and cruel', Henry may have engineered Cambridge's downfall as a contingency against the possibility of rebellion while out of the country. Anne Curry, *Agincourt – A New History* (Stroud, The History Press, 2010), page 53.
2. By 1459 Calais was all that remained of England's once-vast French-territorial holdings. It was a fortress and trading post for English exports to Burgundy: wool, leather goods, tin. It was also an unofficial base for privateers from Devon and Cornwall operating against French and other foreign shipping. From as early as the 1330s nationally raised armies received wages, the old feudal method of raising troops having fallen out of use.
3. *Rolls of Parliament*, 'Wars of the English in France', series 22, volume 2, part 2, page 598.

4. Helen E. Maurer, *Margaret of Anjou* (Woodbridge, The Boydell Press, 2003), page 18.
5. *Rolls of Parliament*, 'Wars of the English in France', series 22, volume 2, part 2, page 619 onwards. The list of losses appears catastrophic, but the Hundred Years War had seen similar collapses before encompassing whole regions. Garrisons rarely held out if there was no chance of being relieved.
6. Ibid., page 474. The Isle of Wight was described as in 'jeopardy and peril' at this time.
7. William de la Pole, Earl of Suffolk, may have been captured by commonplace pirates lying in wait for him in the hope of winning a hefty ransom.
8. J. R. Lander, *The Wars of the Roses* (Stroud, Alan Sutton, 1990), pages 39–42.
9. In the words of Professor Michael Hicks, author of *The Wars of the Roses* (Yale University Press, 2010), page 69, it 'let a genie out of the lamp that was not entirely returned for another thirty years'.
10. Edmund Beaufort's paternal grandfather was John of Gaunt, Duke of Lancaster.
11. R. A. Griffiths, *The Reign of King Henry VI* (Stroud, Sutton Publishing, 1998), page 688. Griffiths states that Edward's father presented himself as 'the champion of justice and the smiter of the corrupt in the tradition of the parliamentary commons and Cade's rebels'.
12. William of Worcester (1415 to about 1482) was the supposed author of *Annales rerum Anglicarum*, a history of England under Henry VI, published in 1728 for the Rolls series.
13. Catherine's liaison with Owen Tudor has been seen by some historians as merely one of convenience: it was supposedly suggested that she named him as the father of her son to prevent Edmund, Duke of Somerset – said to be the real father – from suffering censure. If true, the future King Henry VII had Beaufort blood from both his father and his mother and no Tudor blood at all. Because of Catherine's behaviour, a statute was passed requiring Parliament to tighten restrictions on the remarriage of future dowager queens.
14. The historian Helen Castor has described Henry VI in this way. She also considers him to have been generous and artless. It seems apparent, however, that the young king could on occasion raise his game and assert himself. *Joan of Arc* (Faber & Faber, 2014), page 219.
15. In the words of Helen E. Maurer, 'Margaret's proposal constituted an effort to protect her son's interests by maintaining or re-creating a real royal centre that stood above private enmities and could command the loyalty of all.' *Margaret of Anjou*, page 101.
16. Henry Holland's father, John, 1st Duke of Exeter (1395–1447), was the second son of another John Holland (Richard II's half-brother) and Elizabeth of Lancaster (Henry IV's sister). He was executed and attainted in 1400 for plotting against Henry IV.
17. Charles H. Ashdown, *Battles and Battlefields of St Albans* (no date), page 3.

18. If the Battle of Shrewsbury, Jack Cade's rebellion, Heworth Moor, Stamford Bridge and other earlier flare-ups are discounted, First St Albans was the initial confrontation of the Wars of the Roses. Some historians, however, view the fighting after Richard II's usurpation as a first phase and the recurrence in the 1450s as a second phase.

2 Captive Throne

1. Carole Rawcliffe, *Humphrey Stafford, first Duke of Buckingham* (Oxford Dictionary of National Biography, ODNB).
2. John Watts, *Richard of York, third Duke of York* (ODNB).
3. *Rolls of Parliament*, 'Wars of the English in France', series 22, volume 2, part 2, page 511.
4. The Paston Letters are a collection of letters and papers; in the main they are the correspondence of members of the Paston family of Norfolk between the years 1422 and 1509.
5. Implausibly, the queen is said to have watched the proceedings from the steeple of Mucklestone Church, behind the Yorkist lines.
6. Richard Brooks, *Cassell's Battlefields of Britain & Ireland* (Weidenfeld and Nicolson, 2005), page 238.
7. Ibid., page 237. Brooks places the Yorkist army south of the River Teme on rising ground, much of which is still open land. A good view of the position can be gained from the battlements of Ludlow Castle.
8. The 'Parliament of Devils' was so named because the Yorkists later claimed the MPs were indiscriminately packed in, many unelected: therefore their vote was unlawful.
9. E. F. Jacob, *The Fifteenth Century 1399-1485* (Oxford University Press, 1961), page 518.
10. The traditional Lancastrian position is located close beside the River Nene on the south bank, south-east of Northampton, but is now thought to have been a kilometre or so further south. See Brooks, page 239. In theory, by operating on 'interior' lines, the king's forces, positioned at Northampton, could respond to a threat materialising from any direction. Throughout the Wars of the Roses commanders routinely fell back on this tactic, but rarely successfully.
11. 'The ordnance of the king's guns availed not, for that day was so great rain, that the guns lay deep in water, and so were quenched and might not be shot'. Quoted in Lander, page 76.
12. Ibid., page 75.
13. Historian R. Ian Jack has speculated that Grey's action shows him to have been shrewd and unscrupulous. The baron 'sensed the turning of the tide and threw in his lot with the Yorkists in an inspired gamble' – see *A Quincentenary: The Battle of Northampton, 1460* (Northampton Past and Present, volume 3, 1960), pages 21-25. Following normal military precedent, Grey's men would probably have been located on the extreme right of the Lancastrian line.
14. John Watts, *John, Viscount Beaumont* (ODNB).

15. Lisa Hilton, *Elizabeth: Renaissance Prince* (Weidenfeld and Nicolson, 2014).
16. 'The lords would fain had her unto London, for they knew well that all the workings that were done grew by her, for she was wittier than the king'. Quoted in Lander, page 81.

3 Sun of York

1. After Henry V's death, Humphrey of Gloucester, fearing another Mortimer takeover bid, had ensured Edmund Mortimer's virtual exile across the Irish Sea.
2. Tudor historian Edward Hall, writing at around the same time as Leland, dramatically embellished the event, reducing Edmund's age from seventeen to twelve and having the young earl accompanied by his unarmed tutor (as if at his schooling) when Clifford struck.
3. John Watts, *Richard of York, third Duke of York* (ODNB).
4. As pointed out by Professor Michael Hicks, after Wakefield 'every victorious side systematically despatched any opposing leaders who fell into their hands [with a few notable exceptions], thus making the results more decisive'. *The Wars of the Roses*, (Yale University Press, 2010), page 160.
5. A. J. Pollard, *William Neville, Earl of Kent* (ODNB).
6. Margaret Beaufort was the daughter of John Beaufort, Duke of Somerset, and Margaret Beauchamp.
7. Later, Tudor propagandists claimed Edmund to have been the bastard son of York's enemy, Edmund Beaufort, Duke of Somerset, killed at St Albans.
8. Care needs to be taken with respect to military terminology when considering numbers. The term man-at-arms might encompass a unit of at least three men and four horses, comprising the fighting man, a lighter armed varlet and one or more mounted archers. Similarly, an individual gallowglass warrior would have been accompanied into battle by two or more 'horse boys' – spear-carriers who themselves fought with javelins, clubs and knives.
9. *A Short English Chronicle* claimed the parhelion phenomena occurred on 'the Monday before the day of battle, on the day of Feast of the Purification of Our Blessed Lady, at about ten o' clock before noon'.
10. Michael Drayton, *The Miseries of Queen Margaret of Anjou.*
11. Ashdown, pages 14 and 15. Ashdown identifies Warwick's main mistakes as not manning St Albans with sufficient troops and allowing his three divisions on the common to get too far apart from each other.
12. Major towns and cities, like Canterbury, paid professional soldiers to man their walls and guard the city gates. Canterbury's city fathers are known to have paid seven shillings for the carriage of a great gun from Blackheath to guard the approaches to the town and five shillings and seven pence for four armed men to guard it.
13. The Chronicle of Robert Fabyan.

14. Prospero di Camulio's statement is quoted in George Goodwin, *Fatal Colours, Towton 1461* (Phoenix, 2012), pages 162–3.
15. 'There is no virtue like necessity' is a quote from William Shakespeare's *Richard II* referencing Henry of Bolingbroke's usurping the throne.
16. On a somewhat less positive note, the men who helped raise Edward to kingship were, in the words of historian Mary Clive, 'neither his natural subordinates nor his natural companions'. *This Glorious Sun of York* (MacMillan, 1973), page 55.

4 Consolidation

1. The near-contemporary Hearne Fragment reported that when the Yorkists arrived at Ferrybridge 'there was a great skirmish ... thereupon [they] advanced themselves to Towton ... awaiting the residue of their company'. The advanced party were described in the fragment as 'fore-prickers', meaning (loosely) outriders.
2. The locale of the battlefield is stated in the subsequent Act of Attainder.
3. Brooks, page 250. The ranks of soldiery may have extended up to thirteen ranks, depending on absolute numbers, allowing for one pace (approximately three feet) per file. Brooks estimates there to have been around 40,000 combatants at both Second St Albans and Towton. Unlike St Albans, Towton was a head-on clash until its later stages. References to a Lancastrian ambush being sprung from Castle Hill Wood, flanking the Yorkist left wing, occur only in later accounts and can be discounted.
4. The chronicle quoting 9,000 dead is the writer of the Neville Chronicle. In the words of historian John Gillingham, author of *The Wars of the Roses* (Baton Rouge, Louisiana State University Press, 1981), page 135, 'Whatever the real total ... Towton was generally regarded as a disaster, a cause for lamentation.' That Towton was the biggest and bloodiest battle of the Wars of the Roses may be true, but so far archaeological evidence has failed to back up such claims. The so-called 'death pit' at Towton contained fewer than forty individuals.
5. Bishop George Neville's letter and the letter to Portinari are quoted in Lander, pages 92–3.
6. The practice of the blackening of severed heads with tar preserved the facial features and highlighted the rictus of horror, frozen in time at the point of death.
7. Lander, page 97.
8. Keith Dockray (ed.), *Three Chronicles of the Reign of Edward* (Gloucester, Alan Sutton, 1988), page 32. The description is of a pageant held in Edward's honour at Bristol, contained in a manuscript found at Lambeth Palace.
9. Lander, page 95.
10. Ben Wilson, *Empire of the Deep: The Rise and Fall of the British Navy* (Phoenix, 2014), page 68.
11. Ross, *Edward IV*, page 44.
12. Ibid., page 60.

13. Instead of measles, Edward's biographer James Gairdner claimed Edward to have been struck down 'by an illness brought on by youthful debauchery'.
14. John Warkworth was Master of St Peter's College, Cambridge, from 1473 to 1498.
15. Gillingham, page 146.
16. There was even a tournament held in Henry Beaufort's honour which further established him within the king's inner circle. Beaufort is said to have feigned reluctance to joust until pressed to do so by Edward, then, according to Gregory's Chronicle, 'he ran full justly and merrily'.
17. Lord Fauconberg was buried at Guisborough Priory, in the former county of Cleveland.
18. Battlefield historian Dorothy Charlesworth locates the battlefield site at or near Swallowship Hill, south-east of Hexham, a mile or so north-east of the Ordnance Survey Map designation – see *The Battle of Hexham 1464* (Archaeologia Aeliana 30, 1952), pages 57–68. William of Worcester is supposed to have written a full account of the campaign, but the relevant page covering the battle is missing from the manuscript.
19. C. M. Fraser, *Robert, first Baron Ogle* (ODNB).
20. Sir Ralph Grey was the grandson of Sir Thomas Grey, beheaded at Southampton in 1415 with the Earl of Cambridge, Edward's grandfather.

5 The Woodville Connection

1. The biographer in question is Professor James Gairdner. His conclusions were based on critical comments made by observers at the time, like Philip de Commines.
2. Jacob, page 547. The Professor wrote that 'in a sense, the whole campaign of 1462–4 displays the energy of the king against the sources of riot and treason.'
3. Ross, *Edward IV*, page 87.
4. Elizabeth has been described this way by Elizabeth Jenkins, author of *The Princes in the Tower,* (Hamish Hamilton, 1978). They are comments based on an illuminated portrait of the queen in the British Museum.
5. David Baldwin, *Elizabeth Woodville, Mother of the Princes in the Tower* (Stroud, The History Press, 2002), page 11. Baldwin has suggested that 'the idea of a young, handsome king marrying for love on Mayday may have been borrowed from romantic tradition [that] ... Edward, who was constantly attended by courtiers and had virtually no privacy, would have found it difficult to meet his bride secretly over a period of almost five months'.
6. Hicks, page 173. The king's debt comprised the national debt inherited from past monarchs, the outstanding wages of the Calais Garrison (£37,000), Edward's father's personal debts and those incurred in London to finance the Yorkist takeover in 1471.
7. Ross, *Edward IV*, pages 84–5. John of Gaunt, Duke of Lancaster, was the great-grandfather of (among others) Charles the Bold, Henry VI and Henry Holland, Duke of Exeter.

8. Dockray, page 35.
9. Edward IV was descended from the second and fourth sons of Edward III, namely Lionel of Antwerp, father of Philippa, Countess of Ulster, and Edmund of Langley, father of Richard of Cambridge.
10. Michael J. Bennett, *Thomas Stanley, first Earl of Derby* (ODNB).
11. C. S. L. Davies, *Henry Stafford, second Duke of Buckingham* (ODNB).
12. Amy Licence, *Elizabeth of York, Forgotten Tudor Queen* (Stroud, Amberley, 2014), page 31.
13. Ibid., page 38.

6 Infighting

1. Edward's main sources of income in 1469 were from Crown lands in England, the principality of Wales, the duchies of Lancaster, Cornwall and York, the earldoms of Chester and March and the Lordship of Ireland.
2. Ross, *Edward IV*, page 112.
3. George and Isobel were second cousins, which meant a papal dispensation was required for the marriage to legally proceed.
4. Michael Hicks, *Anne Neville: Queen to Richard III* (Stroud, The History Press, 2007), page 70.
5. Hicks, *The Wars of the Roses*, page 193. He states that England rapidly became ungovernable when Edward was briefly incarcerated by Warwick in 1469.
6. Ross, *Edward IV*, page 126.
7. Henry Summerson., *Robin of Redesdale* (ODNB).
8. The fighting is said by Edward Hall to have taken place 'on a fair plain near to a town called Hedgecote, three miles from Banbury, wherein there be three hills, not in equal distance, nor yet in equal quantity, but lying a manner although not fully triangle'.
9. Pembroke's army was claimed to be 14,000 strong, Devon's contingent an additional 7,000; they are said to have been opposed by 20,000 rebels led by Redesdale. The *Croyland Chronicle* claimed 4,000 slain; the Milanese envoy claimed 7,000. These figures are all likely to be exaggerations. The opposing armies were probably relatively small and the casualties much less severe.
10. In truth there was little likelihood that such a marriage would ever take place, the king was gambling that he might withdraw his daughter's hand when the time was right.

7 Ravenspur

1. *Three Chronicles of the Reign of Edward IV: Chronicle of the Rebellion in Lincolnshire*, (Gloucester, Alan Sutton, 1988), page 109.
2. Ibid., pages 111–12.
3. David Santiuste, *Edward IV and the Wars of the Roses* (Barnsley, Pen &

Sword Military, 2010), page 169, note 50. Santiuste has highlighted the discovery that a local field at Empingham is named Losecoat, from the old English *hlose cot*, meaning 'pigsty cottage'.

4. Professor Michael Hicks considers Warwick and Clarence's flight to have been less precipitate than is generally assumed. See *Anne Neville: Queen to Richard III* (Stroud, The History Press, 2007), page 75.
5. Richard's biographer David Baldwin, author of *Richard III* (Stroud, Amberley, 2013), page 51, suggests that because Edward's youngest brother arrived in Flanders later than the king there is every possibility he remained behind in England, 'acting as a focus for those who wanted to join his brother in exile before escaping himself'.
6. Gruthuyse was created Earl of Winchester in September 1472. It was he who inspired in Edward a love of lavishly bound and illustrated manuscripts, an aspect of Edward's tastes and habits not covered in the narrative.
7. Michael K. Jones says that Margaret and Charles quickly settled into a domestic routine which kept them largely apart – see *Margaret, Duchess of Burgundy* (ODNB).
8. Raphael Holinshed, *Chronicle of England, Scotland and Ireland* (J. Johnson, 1807).
9. Wilson, page 66.
10. According to Lord Stanley's biographer Michael K. Jones, Stanley might have ended up on the wrong side at the coming battles but managed to hold aloof in the North West. See *Thomas, Lord Stanley* (ODNB). *The Arrivall* mentions Sir William Parr and Sir James Harrington as 'two good knights' arriving at Nottingham with 600 men. Warkworth's Chronicle only mentions Sir William Stanley with 300 men and Sir William Norris and 'diverse other men and tenants of Lord Hastings'.
11. Joseph A. Nigota, *The Vernon family* (ODNB). Vernon avoided the Battles of Barnet and Tewkesbury and gained Edward's pardon in 1472.
12. A. J. Pollard, *Richard Neville, Earl of Warwick,* (ODNB).
13. Professor Michael Hicks says that the Readeption brought Clarence financial loss and a degree of resentment; moreover, Edward's defeat and exile forced the king to adopt 'a more conciliatory stance': see *The Wars of the Roses*, page 202.
14. Gerhard von Wesel's Newsletter.

8 Battles for the Throne

1. Gerhard von Wesel's Newsletter.
2. Ibid.
3. Warwick's supposed preference of remaining on horseback was by no means untypical of medieval generals. Leaving tactical leadership to subordinates mirrored Edward III's stance at Crecy in 1346 and that of the Black Prince at Poitiers in 1356. Henry V only fought in the front rank of the English army at Agincourt in 1415 because the small number of men at his disposal ruled out the luxury of a reserve. The French

king, Jean II, remained with the reserve division at Poitiers and only got involved in the fighting once his leading 'battle' had been defeated and those flanking it had fled. He acted, or so it would appear, much like Warwick did at Barnet. See Christopher Rothero, *The Armies of Agincourt* (Osprey, 1981), page 20.

4. Gerhard von Wesel's Newsletter.
5. P. W. Hammond, *The Battles of Barnet and Tewkesbury* (Gloucester, Alan Sutton, 1990), page 81.
6. Some secondary accounts claim the Lancastrian right flank to have been buttressed by the ruined walls of Holm Castle, a former stronghold of the Clare earls of Gloucester which at one time commanded access to the tidal crossing at Lower Lode. The dating of Holm Castle's ruination is uncertain. It was claimed by Edward Hall in the sixteenth century that there had been parts of the castle standing in recent memory, but that 'now [only] some ruins of the bottoms of walls appear'. For further details see Lt Colonel J. D. Blythe, *The Battle of Tewkesbury* (Transactions of the Bristol and Gloucestershire Archaeological Society, 1961), pages 99–120. The broken-down remnants of walls may have served as cover for the Lancastrian defenders. Hammond, however, disputes there were any ruins still evident in the fifteenth century, claiming instead that the Lancastrians occupied an unfortified position further to the south.
7. William Seymour, *Battles in Britain and their Political Background: Volume 1* (Book Club Associates, 1975), page 157. Seymour has argued that Edmund Beaufort might have commanded Warwick's centre, with Montagu and Oxford teaming up on the right flank; however, based on von Wesel's account of him and Courtenay riding west from London, this seems unlikely. Beaufort is not mentioned in any contemporary or near-contemporary account as being at Barnet on the morning of the battle.
8. An extract from John Drinkwater's poem 'At Grafton'.
9. Warkworth claimed Edward tricked the priests in the abbey church into handing over Edmund Beaufort and the other men who had sought refuge, promising he would pardon them. The author of the *Arrivall* stated more prosaically that the fugitives were discovered 'in the abbey, and other places of the town'. See also Dockray, page 65.
10. Steven G. Ellis, *Henry Percy, fourth Earl of Northumberland* (ODNB).
11. See Henry of Howden's account of the death of Henry II for a similar instance of this. Howden believed Henry's son, Richard I, to be responsible for his father's death.
12. John Boyle, *Portrait of Canterbury* (Robert Hale, 1980), pages 93–5.
13. Ross, *Edward IV*, page 183.

9 The King's Brothers

1. Michael Hicks, *George, Duke of Clarence* (ODNB).
2. Amy Licence, *Anne Neville: Richard III's Tragic Queen* (Stroud, Amberley, 2013).

3. According to the *Croyland Chronicle* she had been disguised by Clarence as a serving maid; however, for a number of reasons, not least that Anne would have been too grand to have carried off such a charade, this claim has been challenged by modern historians.
4. Baldwin, *Richard III*, page 72.
5. The Paston Papers.
6. Jenkins, page 80 and Ross, *Edward IV*, page 98.
7. Carracks were 'full-rigged' bulk carriers/warships with two or sometimes three masts, described as 'orrible, grete and stoute'. They had square mainsails and triangular fore and aft lateen sails, making them highly manoeuvrable, able to sail in all winds, which was ideal when they were armed as warships.
8. Richard Vaughan, *Charles the Bold* (Woodbridge, The Boydell Press, 2002), page 83.
9. Ibid., page 348. Portchester was the same disembarkation point Henry V had used in 1415.
10. Ibid. The date of the order was 1 February 1475.
11. The overall number of soldiers guarding the Somme crossings and routes south has been assessed at around 50,000 fighting men: see Paul Murray Kendall, *Louis XI* (Cardinal, 1974), page 341.
12. Vaughan, page 349.
13. From a despatch dated 11 July 1475 from the Milanese ambassador to the Burgundian court, quoted in Vaughan, page 197.
14. Vaughan, pages 206–7
15. Gillingham, pages 40–2.
16. Kendall, page 343.
17. Anne Crawford, *John Howard, first Duke of Norfolk,* (ODNB).
18. Santiuste, page 145.
19. The Battle of Nancy was the final, decisive battle of the Burgundian Wars, fought on 5 January 1477. Duke Charles was defeated and killed by the forces of Rene II, Duke of Lorraine, and the army of the Swiss Confederacy.
20. Both Louis and Edward had problem brothers. In 1468 Edward formed an alliance with the dukes of Burgundy and Brittany, at the time in league with the French king's rebellious brother, the Duke de Berri. In some respects the careers of the Duke de Berri and George of Clarence paralleled each other. Louis remarked on this to Edward when they met in 1475.
21. Clarence's trial and execution has been described this way by Chris Skidmore, *Bosworth: the Birth of the Tudors* (Phoenix, 2014), page 107.
22. First reports from Scotland spoke of the capture of Edinburgh. Celebratory bonfires were lit in Calais and were probably relit when news of the recovery of Berwick emerged. However, the *Croyland Chronicle* saw the recovery of Berwick as more of a loss than a gain, saying, 'The safe-keeping of Berwick each year swallows up 10,000 marks.'

10 Fateful Outcomes

1. Michael Jones, *Margaret, Duchess of Burgundy,* (ODNB).
2. Lisa Hilton, *Elizabeth: Renaissance Prince.*
3. Rosemary Horrox, *Edward IV,* (ODNB).
4. Brian Todd Carey, *Warfare in the Medieval World* (Barnsley, Pen & Sword, 2006), page 201.
5. Albany returned to Scotland once again, but without the aid of Richard III, who favoured a renewed alliance with James III. Albany was defeated by his brother at the Battle of Lochmaben on 22 July 1484. Exiled, he died in Paris toward the end of 1485. James III survived the attentions of his rebels until 1488. He was killed at the Battle of Sauchieburn, near Stirling, on 2 June that year.
6. Mary Clive, *This Sun of York: A Biography of Edward IV* (Cardinal, 1975), pages 253–4.
7. Hastings' corpse was buried, in accordance with his wishes, near where Edward IV had been interred at St George's Chapel, Windsor, and a chantry was later founded for him there in 1503.
8. Any property under the Abbot of London's control was considered as constituting 'sanctuary'.
9. Shaw's death the following year was reputed to have been due to the humiliation he had felt at the cold reception his sermon received. Most Londoners were loath to see the late king attacked in such a way.
10. The bones of two boys discovered in the Tower in the seventeenth century were later reinterred at Westminster Abbey. Up until now they have remained out of reach of modern forensics.
11. French historians de Commines and Molinet confirmed the belief current in Europe at the time that Henry Stafford, Duke of Buckingham, was responsible for having the princes murdered.
12. H. Ellis (ed.), *Polydore Vergil's English History* (1844).

INDEX